ROMANCE,
She Wrote

ROMANCE, She Wrote

A HERMENEUTICAL ESSAY ON SONG *of* SONGS

André LaCocque

Wipf & Stock
PUBLISHERS
Eugene, Oregon

Wipf and Stock Publishers
199 W 8th Ave, Suite 3
Eugene, OR 97401

Romance, She Wrote
A Hermeneutical Essay on Songs of Songs
By LaCocque, André
Copyright©1998 by LaCocque, André
ISBN 13: 978-1-59752-496-4
ISBN 10: 1-59752-496-4
Publication date 1/1/2006
Previously published by Trinity Press International, 1998

To Claire, my wife,
to Elisabeth, my daughter,
to Rebecca, Natalie, and Anne,
my granddaughters

[T]he making of the Scriptures was already a hermeneutical process in which earlier biblical materials were rewritten in order to make them intelligible and applicable to later situations.

—GERALD L. BURNS, "Midrash and Allegory:
The Beginnings of Scriptural Interpretation"

҆҅҆

[T]he prophets look forward to a peaceable kingdom at the End of Days. The Song of Songs locates that kingdom in human love, in the habitable present, and for the space of our attention, allows us to enter it.

—CHANA BLOCH, *The Song of Songs*

҆҅҆

Et c'est bien souvent par le moyen de transgressions de l'ordre établi, à coup d'exceptions exemplaires, que l'amour poursuit son oeuvre de conversion au niveau même du sens de la justice.

—PAUL RICOEUR, "Théonomie et/ou autonomie"

CONTENTS

ॐ ॐ ॐ ॐ ॐ ॐ ॐ ॐ ॐ ॐ ॐ ॐ ॐ ॐ

PREFACE

The present book is a hermeneutical essay on Song of Songs (or Canticle), and it aspires to lay the foundations for a modern commentary. It was born out of my growing fascination with this short poetic book of the Bible, its aesthetic beauty, its theme, the deftness of its author, and, last but certainly not least, the conflicting hermeneutics at work in ancient and modern readings of the poem. I start with a (joyful) confession: the more I entered into it myself, the more I became enthralled, and it is my dearest hope for the present book that some of my readers will share my enthusiasm.

Such pleasurable reception is not guaranteed, however. We learn that, already before the beginning of the Common Era, there were strong objections to considering Canticle as a sacred document; I shall return to this point in the course of this essay. But, one is also not at a loss to find even more recent regrets about its presence in the canon, so, for instance, Seb. Castellion (1544); W. Whiston (1723); J. G. Semler (1771); Ed. Reuss (1879).

On the other hand, one suspects that the Song's admission into the Canon has not always been granted on the right ground. It may be that the title "The Song of Songs, which is Solomon's" (1.1, NRSV), was an early attempt at "clearing" the poem for its inclusion among the sacred texts, even through classifying it as wisdom literature (not a mistake in itself, but a tendentious slant). As we shall see, to make Solomon the author of Canticle is something of a blunder. It is probably why this attribution has not been retained by all traditionalists. Michael Fox (*The Song of Songs*, p. 250f.) calls attention to the fact that none of the ancient Tannaim (of the Mishnah) invokes Solomonic authorship to justify canonization. Furthermore, still on the issue of the sacred or profane nature of Canticle, the very rich Midrashic interpretations, in general having recourse to "allegoresis" to "tame" a content that some diehard conservatists found objectionable in its plain meaning, are not a sufficient reason for accepting Canticle as a "spiritual book." Midrash cannot be cause for canonization, but, on the contrary, only a text already considered inspired will be explained by Midrash.

It is still proposed by some contemporary critics that there used to be pagan religious usages in the background of the Song of Songs. . . . But why then were they not obliterated by unequivocal Yahwistic expressions? This argument pointed out by Rowley (*The Servant of the Lord,* p. 223) is still valid.

Fox agrees with Aage Bentzen who thinks that the Song was canonized thanks to an incidental connection made between Canticle and religious festivals, "whence its later association with Passover." Such an association would indeed call forth appropriate Midrashic reinterpretations. . . . But it is hard to believe that a highly controversial acceptance of a document into the canon would be due to an "incidental connection"! The argument does not fare any better than the opinion according to which the book of Daniel was also included because the "custom officers" of sorts — the canonizing authority — looked at the beginning and at the end of the book and saw to their satisfaction that it was written in Hebrew!

The issue of canonization is a difficult one. The problem of authorial intention is even more so. True, one should be better inspired than Fr. Schleiermacher, who thought that the meaning of a text was synonymous with its author's intent in writing it. But, as far as Canticle is concerned, more than as regards many another example, the interpretation should at least respect and honor the author's orientation that he or she gave to the poem. Now, the distance between the plain sense of the text, on the one hand, and the allegorical reading of it, on the other hand, is so considerable that a grave hermeneutical problem arises. One could formulate the issue in terms of a yawning gap between the allegorical traditional interpreters of the Song, and its modern "naturalist" commentators. The contemporary rededication to the plain meaning of the document is, to be sure, refreshing by its healthy honesty, but it raises more strongly than ever before the question of the Song's legitimate place in the Hebrew Scripture. If Canticle is a love-song between a woman and a man; if it is a poem devoid of any reference to God, to Israel, to the *Heilsgeschichte,* to the cult; if, as someone said, Canticle is the "most unbiblical book of the Bible," can there still be a bridge of sorts between the modern "naturalist" understanding and the traditional spiritualizing interpretation?

More than any other task in a book that is replete with stumbling blocks, this one has proved the most enriching to me here. It is in my opinion the greatest hermeneutical challenge facing a Bible scholar, especially if, as I contend here, the author of the Song was a female poet who intended to "cock a snook at all Puritans," as says Francis Landy (*Paradoxes,* p. 17). For then, what the original author of Canticle wrote with a subversive and liberating intent, became forcibly reintegrated into a "bourgeois" mentality by later readings of the text. To the Eros of the poem was artificially substituted a disembodied Agape. Because of this, the rebellious spirit of the work was tamed to fit a dualistic worldview, whereby the male character is no longer a man and the female character is no longer a woman; they are asexual personae. Such an edulcoration of a vigorous and daring piece is unbearable.

On the other hand, is it not too much of a loss when one leaves behind "allegoresis"? After all, a romance between a man and a woman can be charming, but also less edifying than an allegory of the relationship between God and Israel, or between Christ and the Church. Not so, for the Song is about the highest "virtue" in Israel's understanding of reality, namely *love.* The whole motif of the book is a rediscovery of plain human love, the uninhibited erotic relations between genders. Were we in a strictly "religious" sphere, to deal with such a topic would simply be taboo, even blasphemous. But not in Israel, where the greatest commandment of loving God is inseparable from its corollary of loving the other. Here, one cannot love God but through loving one's "neighbor," as he or she is "like myself."[1] This perhaps is not considered "religious" by the many dualistic sets of beliefs in the world, but it is eminently theological according to biblical revelation. As Landy writes, "[Can-

---

1. On earthly love giving impulse to the love of God in the Bible, cf. Hosea 1–3; Isaiah 62.5; Jeremiah 2.2; 2 Corinthians 11.2; Ephesians 5.31–33; Revelation 21.2; Matthew 9.15; John 3.29. See Rashi on Exodus 38.8. *Yoma* 54a: "The love that God bestows upon you is similar to the one of a man for his wife."

ticle] points to something essential in holiness . . . all creatures' perfect relationship" (ibid., p. 17).

So much so that, for her discourse, the poet has chosen a decidedly "biblical" vehicle. I do not forget the above-mentioned correct statement of one critic, that Song of Songs is the most unbiblical book of the Bible. But, paradoxically, Canticle is an expansive anthology of *biblical traditions!* It will be my task in this book to signal the many borrowings by the poet of texts that, remarkably, come mainly from the prophetic corpus. Furthermore, it will be important to plumb the dynamism of *intertextuality* established by the Canticle's rereading of sacred traditions in a new spirit and with a new orientation.

೬ஒ

In this essay, I use the masculine personal pronoun when I speak of God. This might surprise some, but I believe that my usage here conforms to the intent of the Song's author. My thesis is that the poet identifies herself with the Shulammite and celebrates her relationship with a lover. True, she proclaims her independence, her total freedom, "my vineyard, my very own, is for myself" (8.12), but she finds her autonomy within her relationship with a man, not in a "splendid isolation." Hence, although the shepherd is no allegorical substitute for God, the God that she meets through her lover is undoubtedly a "he." (Conversely, if the roles in the Song had been reversed, the use of the feminine personal pronoun for God would have been appropriate in this book.)[2] At any rate, God, in this case and perhaps in all cases, is not a role-model, seductively mirroring the self, but the dialogical vis-à-vis, the "I" of a relationship in which the human partner is always the "thou." In more general terms, it is remarkable that, in a society that is often described as patriarchal, the self-describing metaphors for "Israel" in prophetic and rabbinic literature are female figures such as bride, fiancée, daughter, and the like. . . .

೬ஒ

All scriptural quotations in the book are my translation, unless noted otherwise. All references are to the English Bible (following the LXX

---

2. So, for instance, *CantR* 103.1 (on Cant 8.1) sees God as the "sister" and Israel as the "brother"!

version) with the other versification (following the Hebrew Masoretic Text) noted in brackets immediately following. For example,
Cant 7.1 in Hebrew ("Return, return, O Shulammite!" NRSV) is
6.13 in the LXX, hence the reference to that text in this essay is
Cant 6.13 [7.1].

🙵🙶

The Song of Songs was an "authentic," that is, a "worldly"
love lyric; precisely for this reason, not in spite of it, it was a
genuinely "spiritual" song of the love of God for man. Man
loves because God loves and as God loves. (F. Rosenzweig, *The
Star of Redemption*, p. 199)

ABBREVIATIONS

ᗜᙀᗜ ᗜᙀᗜ ᗜᙀᗜ ᗜᙀᗜ ᗜᙀᗜ ᗜᙀᗜ ᗜᙀᗜ ᗜᙀᗜ ᗜᙀᗜ ᗜᙀᗜ ᗜᙀᗜ ᗜᙀᗜ ᗜᙀᗜ ᗜᙀᗜ

AB	Anchor Bible
AgadShir	*Aggada* on the Song of Songs
AJSL	*American Journal of Semitic Languages and Literature*
AKM	Abhandlungen für die Kunde des Morgenlandes
ANET	*Ancient Near Eastern Texts Relating to the Old Testament,* edited by J. B. Pritchard
AOAT	Alter Orient und Altes Testament
AOT	*Altorientalische Texte zum Alten Testament* by H. Gressmann
Aq	Aquila
Aqht	Ug. "The Legend of Danel and Aqht" (D)
Aram.	Aramaic
ARN	*Aboth de-Rabbi Nathan*
ATD	Das Alte Testament Deutsch
BBB	Bonner biblische Beiträge
BBET	Beiträge zur biblischen Exegese und Theologie
BH³	*Biblia Hebraica Stuttgartensia* (3d ed.)
BKAT	Biblischer Kommentar zum Alten Testament
BT	*The Bible Translator*
BTB	*Biblical Theology Bulletin*
BZ	*Biblische Zeitschrift*
Cant	Canticle, Song of Songs
CantR	*Canticle Rabba*
CantTg	*Targum of Song of Songs*
CBC	Cambridge Bible Commentary
CBQ	*Catholic Biblical Quarterly*
CD	The *Damascus Document* (of the Cairo Geniza)
DBV	*Dictionnaire de la Bible,* edited by P. Vigouroux
ET	English translation
ETL	*Ephemerides theologicae lovanienses*
Et. Bib.	Etudes bibliques
ExpTim	*Expository Times*
fem.	feminine
frg(s).	fragment(s)
GenR	*Genesis Rabba*
HAR	Hebrew Annual Review

HAT	Handbuch zum Alten Testament
Heb.	Hebrew
Hexapl.	Hexaplar
HKAT	Handkommentar zum Alten Testament
IB	*Interpreter's Bible*
IDB	*Interpreter's Dictionary of the Bible*
IDBSup	Supplementary volume to *IDB*
Int	*Interpretation*
IOSOT	International Organization for the Study of the Old Testament
J	Yahwist (literary source)
JA	*Jewish Antiquities*
JAAR	*Journal of the American Academy of Religion*
j. Berak	*Jerusalem Talmud*, tract. *Berakot*
JBL	*Journal of Biblical Literature*
JCS	*Journal of Cuneiform Studies*
j. Erub	*Jerusalem Talmud*, tract. *Erubin*
JES	*Journal of Ecumenical Studies*
JPS	Jewish Publication Society
JSOT	*Journal for the Study of the Old Testament*
JSOTSup	Journal for the Study of the Old Testament–Supplement Series
KAT	Kommentar zum Alten Testament
KB	*Lexicon in Veteris Testamenti libros* by L. Koehler and W. Baumgartner
Ketub	*Ketuboth*, tract.
KHCAT	Kurzer Hand-Commentar zum Alten Testament
KJV	King James Version
LCBI	Literary Currents in Biblical Interpretation
LD	Lectio divina
LXX	Septuagint
Mek Exod	*Mekhilta* (Exodus)
MIOF	*Mitteilungen des Instituts für Orientforschung*
mKet	*Mishna Ketuboth*
mMoed Qat	*Mishna Moed Qatan*
mSanh	*Mishna Sanhedrin*
mShabb	*Mishna Shabbath*
MSS	manuscripts
MT	Masoretic Text
mTa'an	*Mishna Ta'anith*
mYad	*Mishna Yadayim*
mYoma	*Mishna Yoma*
NF	Neue Folge
NRSV	New Revised Standard Version
NT	New Testament
OBT	Overtures to Biblical Theology
OT	Old Testament
OTL	Old Testament Library
P	Priestly (literary source)

P.A.	*Pirke Aboth*
PEQ	*Palestine Exploration Quarterly*
Pesh	Peshitta
PL	J. P. Migne, *Patrologia latina*
1QGenApoc	(Qumran) Genesis Apocryphon
1QH	(Qumran) Hodayot (Hymns)
11QTemple	(Qumran) Temple Scroll
4QCant	(Qumran) frg. on Song of Songs
4QShirShabb	(Qumran) Shir Shabbath (Songs of Sabbath Sacrifice)
RB	*Revue biblique*
RechBib	Recherches bibliques
RHPR	*Revue d'histoire et de philosophie religieuses*
RTF	Robert/Tournay/Feuillet (coauthors of *Le Cantique des Cantiques*)
Sanh	*Sanhedrin*, tract. (Babylonian Talmud)
SBLDS	SBL Dissertation Series
Shabb	*Shabbath*, tract. (Babylonian Talmud)
SR	*Studies in Religion*
s.v.	sub verbo
Sym	Symmachus
Syro-Hexapl.	Syro-Hexaplar
Ta'an	*Ta'anith*, tract. (Babylonian Talmud)
Tan de b El	*Tanna de Bey-Eliahu*
Tg	Targum
Th	Theodotion
The Song	*Das Hohelied*; ET *The Song of Songs* by O. Keel
TOB	*Traduction Oecuménique de la Bible*
Tos Sanh	*Tosephta Sanhedrin*
TQ	*Theologische Quartalschrift*
T. Reu.	*Testament of Reuben*
TRu	*Theologische Rundschau*
Ug.	Ugarit/Ras Shamra
Vg	Vulgate
VLat	Vetus Latina
Vss	Versions
VT	*Vetus Testamentum*
VTSup	Vetus Testamentum Supplements
WSol	Wisdom of Solomon
ZAW	*Zeitschrift für die alttestamentliche Wissenschaft*
ZBK	Zürcher Bibelkommentare
ZDMG	*Zeitschrift der deutschen morgenländischen Gesellschaft*
ZDMGSup	*Zeitschrift der deutschen morgenländischen Gesellschaft — Supplement Series*
ZTK	*Zeitschrift für Theologie und Kirche*

Introduction

METHODOLOGICAL PRESUPPOSITIONS

A Hermeneutical Problem

If we are to believe the Song of Songs' superscription, the author of the poem is none other than the great King Solomon! But already on that score, there is a problem. And it is only the first in a long list of difficulties that the student of the Canticle must face. Not least among them is the fact that the biblical book is a sui generis work. It is not really a piece of wisdom writing, in spite of its editorial attribution to Solomon. Neither is it a hymn, a psalm, a poetic narrative (it has no plot), an oracle. Categorizations that work for other parts of Scripture are inoperative here. So much so that, incapable of reaching a consensus, ancient as well as modern scholars have proposed an impressive array of hypotheses about the nature of this literary piece — its authorship, its date, its provenance, its *Sitz im Leben,* its purpose, its language, its message, the meaning of its metaphors, and more. No theory, however, seems to fit without at some point forcing the text into a Procrustean bed.

It must be conceded that it makes all the difference whether the Canticle is read as aphoristic and apologetic of an established worldview or as a poetic pamphlet denouncing that worldview as wrong and deceptive. Another stark opposition is between considering the poem as a remnant of court and banquet ditties (cf. 2 Sam 19.36; Ezra 2.65; Qoh 2.8) or as an original satirical piece; between being a sample of an otherwise lost erotic literary production — and therefore a marginal booklet smuggled into the biblical compendium on the basis of a profound misunderstanding — or a "Swiftian" poetic banter subverting the very core of contemporary social-religious propriety.

In large part on account of the uncertainty regarding its literary genre, the Song of Songs has been diversely interpreted. In fact, each of its components has been submitted to a veritable violence, either at the level of its textual tradition (through textual alterations) or at the level of its natural meaning (through forced allegorization). There is no more regrettable example of a biblical text being tormented by its critics than this one. Every single verse of the Canticle has been one way or another hypothetically or tentatively altered by traditional reuse or by textual reshaping. If those "corrections" were to be brought together in a modern edition, the Song as transmitted and canonized would all but completely disappear under a new, artificially reconstructed text.

In spite of all this, one cannot but marvel that very few readers of the Canticle would fail to notice its descriptively naturalistic character, so remarkable for its playing upon all the human senses. It has been my repeated experience with a great variety of students of the Song of Songs that the history of violence made to the text has proved incapable of thwarting their immediate and honest response to the "poem-as-it-is." Its poetic power and its force of persuasion are so irresistible that no cover-up has been able to put a conventional fig leaf on the controversial parts of the love song.

But then the reader may be disconcerted by the intervention of yet another scholarly criticism, grounded this time on aesthetical canons, which declares that some of the poem's hyperbolic descriptions of the physical aspect of the beloved — a genre that is often called by its Arabic name, *wasf* — are "grotesque"![1] This new onslaught is itself the outcome of another type of misunderstanding. In the development that follows, under the heading "Metaphor and Intertextuality," I shall discuss the use of metaphors in the Canticle and show their impressionistic nature. That, for example, the Shulammite's neck be like the tower of David (Cant 4.4) or that her nose be likened to towering Lebanon (7.4 [7.5]) says only about these parts

---

1. But the *wasf*s in question were sung by nineteenth-century Syrian peasants! More on this below.

of her anatomy that they are as awe inspiring as the tower of David (in Jerusalem? cf. Neh 3.25–26) or as majestic as Mount Hermon. There is nothing "grotesque" in these similes.

In short, the history of interpretation of the Canticle is one of multifarious attempts at avoidance. "Spiritual" readers of the poem have felt a deep-seated repugnance before its erotic nature. In order to tame the wild, so to speak, they have repeatedly used a panoply of artificial devices. The MT has been at times altered; the metaphors have been allegorized; similes have been called "grotesque"; the date of composition has "traveled" along the whole gamut of biblical chronology, thus avoiding the linguistically obvious Hellenistic provenance; the authorial purpose has been reduced to nothing and the poem itself to an exercise in futility; even the person of the author has not escaped disowning.

As to the "naturalist" commentators, they sometimes indulge in embarrassingly "steamy" interpretations. Suffice it to refer to Paul Haupt's reading of Cant 5.4. Furthermore, it happens more than once that another kind of embarrassment obtains, for it is clear that the commentator does not know how to make sense of over twenty centuries of traditional allegoresis as regards Canticle. The reader is thus put before opting exclusively for an allegorical/spiritual, or for a scientific/mundane interpretation.

In other words, the issue with which any reader of the Song must come to grips is definitely hermeneutical. This issue is more acute here than in any other literary piece that I know of, whether biblical or secular. To fit a preconceived understanding of the poem as an allegory, some have gone so far as to alter the gender of pronouns in the text, reading the feminine for the masculine, and conversely (see p. 168 below). Anywhere else, such unwarranted intervention would be condemned as eisegesis. An oft reiterated argument is that the Song has been retained within the canon of Scriptures thanks only to its allegorical interpretation within the synagogue and later within the church.[2] Hence, to the violence done to the text is added the veiled threat that, in case of resistance on the part of the reader, we will lose the poem altogether.

---

2. In 1962, I wrote an article advocating that very thesis ("L'insertion du Cantique des Cantiques"). Since then, enlightened by the work of contemporary scholars, my views have radically changed.

Nowadays, one finds a healthy return to more sobriety and discretion. A 1979 declaration by Roland Murphy acknowledged a new consensus. In an article significantly titled "The Unity of the Song of Songs," he states the following, "Scholars [in our times] seem to be in agreement that the Song of Songs deals with love." He then continues by referring to the question of whether we are dealing with "human love (the moderns), or divine love (the ancients, Jews and Christians), or both."[3] To this question, the response of most recent commentators goes definitely in the direction of human love.[4]

But, if we follow the stream of modern consensus, another formidable issue arises for the reader who is unwilling to consider more than two thousand years of mystical interpretation of the Canticle as null and void. To just dismiss the traditional reading as sheer distortion of the text should make us most uncomfortable. For it is one thing to say that the allegorical reading of the Song does not do full justice to the document; it is quite another to shun more than twenty centuries of collective cultivation of the poem. To take such a position would betray arrogance; furthermore, it would be based on a deep misunderstanding of the nature of *text*, confusing the question of meaning with that of authorial intent, in the manner of Schleiermacher. True, the original intention of the author is indeed a most important aspect of the text, so important that our interpretation dare not go against it, whenever known. But once a text is composed and published, it becomes the property, so to speak, of its audience or readership and, as a painting, remains open to interpretations ad infinitum. As my colleague Dow Edgerton writes (about text in general),

> Owners are not necessarily authors, although they may be. A community of authoritative interpretation can be the owner. Even the idea of "meaning" itself can be the owner of a text, as when we say interpretation must be true to the "meaning of the text." The idea of a meaning which stands behind a text,

---

3. Murphy, "The Unity of the Song of Songs," p. 436.

4. So Pope, Fox, Murphy; in French, Lys; in German, Keel (see his *Das Hohelied*, now in English translation *The Song of Songs*; I shall refer to the latter under the abbreviation *The Song* in the course of this study). As Clines says, "What has reading the Song done to its ancient readers? . . . The main thing is that it has persuaded them that it is not about the one thing that it is self-evidently about: human sexual love" ("Why Is There a Song of Songs," p. 16).

to which one may appeal for a judgment, is part of this same economy.[5]

Reflecting upon this issue, Paul Ricoeur discusses the different allegorical approaches to the Song and decisively distinguishes between ancient liturgical and modern exegetical works.[6] As far as the former are concerned, Ricoeur insists, there is a legitimate reutilization of the Canticle's language within a different "setting in word" (*Sitz im Wort*). For instance, in the old liturgy for baptism put forward by Cyril of Jerusalem and Ambrosius, quotations from the Song of Songs, such as "Who is this one who comes up whitened [*sic*] from the desert?" or "Let him kiss me with the kisses of his mouth," designate respectively the baptized catechumen and Christ — but without Cyril or Ambrosius claiming that this liturgical use constitutes an exegesis! This Ricoeurian distinction is most important. Liturgy is not exegesis, although it must be conceded that reusing the Song in such a manner assumes that allegory does not constitute a distortion of the text but rather espouses its *Tendenz*.[7] That contention of traditional liturgists cannot remain unchallenged.

Beside liturgy, a few modern works still adopt allegory as an exegetical method for reading the Canticle. Among the best exemplars of the allegorizing school, a trio of outstanding French scholars has written a major commentary on the *Cantique,* with the overt purpose of salvaging that approach. Using a hermeneutical method they call "anthological" because it relies heavily upon scriptural parallels, André Robert in conjunction with André Feuillet and Raymond Tournay explore the Canticle's allusions to other biblical texts and deem the Song eschatological.[8] In fact, according to these scholars, the sacred author has disguised as an erotic poem a genuinely mystical message on the theme of the mutual quest of God and his people. This literary mask, they continue, is easy to remove once it is realized that a great number of biblical texts have been here reemployed. Such borrowing from a diversity of sources was all the more natural and hermeneutically sound, as a common denom-

---

5. Edgerton, *The Passion of Interpretation*, p. 34.
6. See LaCocque and Ricoeur, *Thinking Biblically.*
7. The same might be true of the Midrash, of course.
8. Robert, Tournay, and Feuillet, *Le Cantique des Cantiques.* So does, e.g., Krinetzki, *Das Hohe Lied.* (Robert, Tournay, and Feuillet hereafter cited in notes as RTF.)

inator unites "lender" and "borrower," namely, the eschatological encounter between God and Israel. On that basis, they conclude it is perfectly legitimate for the Christian church to pursue that line drawn by the texts themselves between promise and fulfillment and to read the Canticle in terms of Christ's relation to the church.

My opinion on this heroic exegetical operation of salvation is mixed. Put in a nutshell, I think that it mobilizes a formidable scholarship to establish the validity of an erroneous thesis. I discern a striking, although unintended, irony in their statement dismissing alternative readings of the Canticle as arbitrary, "As one can see, these writers are all prisoners of their own general understanding of the Song [*sic*]" (p. 229). It is of course easier to see in the others' eye the speck.

Thesis

Clearly, we need some kind of warrant in order not to indulge in eisegesis but to stick, as much as we can, to the objective and plain sense, which Robert, Tournay, and Feuillet call "naturalist."[9] Concomitantly, our reading of the Canticle must take most seriously the erstwhile interpretation of a text that has so deeply influenced the lives of synagogue and church alike. In so doing, we are aware that the allegorical interpretation demands too many textual distortions and far too much arbitrariness of explanation in its support. Conversely, the plain reading that is taken in isolation flippantly bypasses levels of meanings that Judaism and Christianity have acknowledged as legitimate.

In what follows, while squarely endorsing the naturalistic approach, I shall insist on the fact that the reading of any poem is necessarily *intertextual*. Doing so, I shall argue that this stance is a bridge to the traditional Midrashic and allegorical interpretation. I will assay to show that, for the Bible reader, the interpretation of the Song of Songs is the hermeneutical challenge par excellence. The

---

9. In the words of Ricoeur, the plain sense is "original, intentional, and immanent to the text itself" (personal communication with author).

exercise is unique because the allegorical exegesis of the text is not just at some distance from the original intent of the work but takes us to its extreme opposite.

The poem under consideration, I will show, is fundamentally a critique of the mores of conformist societies and of the dualism between body and soul prevalent in sophisticated as well as in popular mentalities. The allegorical reading, by contrast, forces it into the mold of an apologue of the status quo. No "taming" of a troublesome text could have gone further afield. The result is not just a softening accommodation of the text but its total reversal.

Such a stance of accommodation is not exclusively the work of ancient editors. Even today, in the aftermath of the sound scholarly reaction I have mentioned, the best of specialists sometimes revives a dimension of reassurance allegedly present in the Song and strongly emphasized by the allegorical school. It is taken for granted, for instance, that the Canticle celebrates conjugal love — in spite of the fact that no mention of marriage between the lovers can be found in the poem.[10] The atavism of sorts displayed by commentators is exemplified in the following statement by Brevard Childs,

> The Song is wisdom's reflection on the joyful and mysterious nature of love between a man and a woman within the institution of marriage. The frequent assertion that the Song is a celebration of human love *per se* fails utterly to reckon with the canonical context... Nowhere is human love in itself celebrated in wisdom literature, nor in the whole Old Testament for that matter. Wisdom, not love, is divine, yet love between a man and his wife is an inextinguishable force within human experience, "strong as death," which the sage seeks to understand (cf. Prov 5.15 ff).[11]

---

10. As says Trible, "Never is this woman called a wife, nor is she required to bear children. In fact, to the issues of marriage and procreation the Song does not speak. Love for the sake of love is its message" (*God and the Rhetoric of Sexuality,* p. 162).

11. Childs, *Introduction to the Old Testament,* p. 575. I also take exception to Frymer-Kensky's statement, "The Bible...never really incorporates sexuality into its vision of humanity or its relationship with the divine." She also writes (in oblivion of Song of Songs), "To the Bible, the sexual and divine realms have nothing to do with each other"; she then refers to Exod 19.15; 1 Sam 21.4–5: "in order to approach God one has to leave the sexual realm" (*In the Wake of the Goddesses,* pp. 187, 189).

Childs's statement is highly interesting in what it reveals about hidden agendas in modern, as well as in ancient, readings.[12] First of all, he is forced to maintain the fiction that the Song is a wisdom piece. In fact, its ethos is anything but wisdomlike. Whereas wisdom exhorts its disciples to be deliberate and to keep their balance in all circumstances, the lovers in the Song display their impetuous and passionate feelings, without regard for what society — not to mention sages — considers as propriety and poise.[13] Second, if the Song's subject is indeed the love between a woman and a man, to add as Childs does "within the institution of marriage" does not stand examination. Marriage is alluded to in Cant 3.6 only, where we find an epithalamium for Solomon's wedding — possibly in the context of a dream (cf. 3.1)![14] Here it serves no other purpose than to provide contrast. For, on the contrary, the entire Song strums the chord of "free love," neither recognized nor institutionalized. Third, if indeed Childs is statistically and objectively correct to say that human love is never celebrated for its own sake in the rest of the Bible, two conclusions — not one — are possible. Either the Canticle is following suit with the "whole Old Testament" or is taking exception to it. We should not exclude the possibility of the Song creating a precedent. Barring oneself from new avenues may foreclose access to the message of the text.[15]

Another element in Childs's assertion is that a reading of the Song of Songs as a love song "fails utterly to reckon with the canonical context." We are thus sent back to the process of canonization to which Rabbi Aqiba contributed so forcefully in his protest against the singing of the Song in "banquet places."[16] The fact that such a

---

12. As regards ancient readings along the same line, see my excursus on Origen (p. 11).

13. Salvaneschi speaks of "norma anticlassica di dismisura" (*Cantico dei cantici*, p. 115).

14. The whole poem, for that matter, is "hovering between reality and dream" (Landy, "The Song of Songs," p. 316). Even Krinetzki admits that Song of Songs is not a wedding ritual and that some of the poems "had nothing to do with wedding" (*Das Hohe Lied*, p. 37).

15. Landy also takes exception with Childs's stance. "In so doing," Landy writes, "he misses the mischievous antithesis between the sensual love song and the rest of the Bible...[and] its perennial shock to bourgeois complacence" (*Paradoxes of Paradise*, pp. 31–32). Clines envisages also that "it might have been a maverick text by an eccentric author" ("Why Is There a Song of Songs," p. 4).

16. *Tos Sanh* 12.10; the same opinion but anonymously stated is found in *Sanh* 101a. Rabbi Aqiba said, "The whole world's worth is not up to the one of the day when the Canticle was given to Israel" (*mYad* 3.5). He also was quoted as saying, "If Torah had not

protest was felt necessary should alert us at least to the possibility that another understanding was entertained by others before (and after) Aqiba's intervention. Indeed, much was at stake; Aqiba and his disciples were fighting against a "profane" interpretation. They were advocating a deeper reading of the poem, which would entitle it to belong with full rights to the canon of Scriptures. In that context, there is a saying in the marginal Talmudic treatise *ARN 1.5* that, though difficult to understand, seems to imply that the Books of "Proverbs, Song of Songs, and Qoheleth were put aside [as apocryphal?] because they were *mešalim* [(mere) proverbs? parables?]." They remained in this sort of quarantine until "the men of the Great Synagogue came and *pir^ešu* [interpreted?] them." From this ambiguously phrased statement, we are probably justified in thinking that there existed, prior to the intervention of the "men of Hezekiah," different interpretations of these "Solomonic" documents.

The Talmudic testimony, therefore, by no means provides a proof of an original allegorical interpretation of the Song. Besides, as regards Rabbi Aqiba's reading of the Song of Songs, a clear distinction must be made between Midrash, on the one hand, and exegetical allegory or *allegoresis,* on the other.[17] Only the latter is here under fire on the double ground of its exclusivity claim and of its socioreligious agenda. First, it claims to be the plain sense of the text and deems all other interpretations unacceptable, unintended by the author of the Canticle. Second, what is at stake with allegoresis is the preservation of a reactionary view of the world, the veritable antipode of the poem's socioreligious ideal.

Midrashic and Kabbalistic reading corresponds to another kind of claim, the claim of revealing what medieval exegetes were to call the *sod,* the secret theosophical meaning of the text, not its $p^e\check{s}at$ (plain sense). These approaches do not attempt to throw a veil of modesty over literal expressions they deem offensive, and the approach

---

been given, the Canticle would have been enough as a guide for the world" (*AgadShir,* ed. Schechter, 1896, p. 5).

17. *Allegoresis* is the term used by Boyarin to characterize the "allegorical reading of the Philonic-Origenal type" (*Intertextuality and the Reading of Midrash,* p. 108). See also this declaration of Bruns, "[A]llegory is . . . the interpretation of a text or corpus that has been resituated within an alien conceptual framework. Allegory presupposes a cultural situation in which the literal interpretation of a text would be as incomprehensible as a literal translation of it" ("Midrash and Allegory," p. 637).

does not correspond to an apologue. For instance, in a hymn by Isaac Luria (sixteenth century) for the Friday evening meal, it is said that, "Her [the Sabbath's] husband embraces her in her foundation [sex], gives her fulfillment, squeezes his strength."[18] Kabbalistic mysticism does not balk at specific descriptions of the hierogamy within God of male and female powers, calling the latter "Shekhinah" and distinguishing her, by contrast with rabbinic Judaism, from God of whom she is a sort of *paredra* (companion). Thus, the Song of Songs is understood as referring to an inner divine dialogue between God and his Shekhinah. In that sense, we are beyond allegory and reaching to "a mystical symbol expressing something that transcends all images."[19] This truly entails eroticism, not only in words but in action. Already in the Talmudic period, "disciples of sages" performed marital intercourse on Friday night (cf. *Ketub* 62b) at a time when Sabbath-the-bride is introduced.

The difference between the Midrashic and the allegorical is clear. The former acknowledges that there are several levels of understanding of the sacred text, any given level *not* being in conflict with another level but complementing it. By contrast, as stated above, exegetical allegory claims that its reading is the only one possible.[20] In other words, while allegoresis is not helpful because it distorts the text that it alleges to explain, the discovery of a mystical meaning grounded in the plain sense of the text simply acknowledges the plurivocity of meaning of the Canticle.

Rabbi Aqiba's passionate defense of the Song of Songs was made in the name of its *sod* meaning, in which he saw the profoundest mystery revealed to humanity or the Holy of Holies of all Scriptures. Now, if a text, so to speak, "hides and reveals" such a *sod*, all other levels of understanding of that text, including the $p^e\check{s}at$ (plain), may not and cannot be used in a profane way, for the different levels correspond to each other. In other words, in the plain meaning the secret

---

18. See Scholem, *On the Kabbalah and Its Symbolism*, p. 143.

19. Scholem, *Major Trends in Jewish Mysticism*, p. 139.

20. Hence, in what follows, the references to the allegorical school of interpretation are to be understood as applying to an exegetical method, not to the mystical reading of the Song of Songs. Let us note in passing another allegorical reading of the Song that seems to show how anything becomes possible according to that method: Stadelman (*Love and Politics*) sees in the Canticle a covert political pamphlet expressing (in a language purposely cryptic for Persians in ca. 500 B.C.E.) Judean hopes for the restoration of the Davidic dynasty.

meaning is to be found, while the secret/mystical meaning opens up a hidden sense of the text nested at the surface level of the text.[21]

To anticipate one of the conclusions of this essay, let it be said from the outset that there is indeed a bridge between the naturalist reading of the Canticle and its mystical reading: both readings are dealing with different levels of understanding. No bridge, however, exists between the naturalist approach and allegorical exegesis because they compete for the same bank of the river.

Excursus: Origen's Reading of Song of Songs

Christian allegoresis starts with the old Alexandrian school and particularly with Origen (born in 185). In the prologue to his *Commentary on Song of Songs* (written ca. 245), Origen advances the idea that Solomon wrote the Canticle as an epithalamium "in the form of a play, which he recited in the character of a bride who was being married and burned with a heavenly love for her bridegroom, who is the Word of God . . . She is the soul made after His image or the Church."[22] Whoever reads the Song of Songs in a naturalistic way, he continues, will be "badly injured," thinking that here the question is of "the outer and fleshly man." He adds that "passion [is] something certainly shameful . . . especially among those who do not know how to elevate themselves from the flesh to the Spirit."

Origen, interestingly enough, sees a parallel between the Song and Greek books on love, "some of them even written in a dialogue style." More perceptively still, he reflects on the title Song of Songs, which he compares with the Holy of Holies of Exod 30.29! Along the same line, he speculates that it is called the most beautiful song because it used to be "sung of old by prophets or by the angels."

Another interesting idea of Origen's is that the Song of Songs was written by Solomon after he did Proverbs and Qoheleth. In Origen's

---

21. Furthermore, says Landy, Aqiba's condemnation of trilling the Song in taverns "may well not imply a rejection of its literal meaning, but the vulgarization of its essential mysticism" (*Paradoxes of Paradise*, p. 14). Or, as Banon writes, "Il faut, par une dialectique descendante, lester le *pshat* des découvertes des autres niveaux et lire enfin le texte dans sa littéralité" (*La lecture infinie*, p. 206).

22. For a handy translation in English of the text under consideration, excerpts of which are quoted in what precedes, we refer the reader to Greer, *Origen*, pp. 217–44.

view, Proverbs deals with morals, Qoheleth with the natural, and the Canticle with contemplation, "urging upon the soul the love of the heavenly and the divine under the figure of the bride and the bridegroom." Let us recall that Origen was well informed about contemporary Jewish intellectual activity. E. E. Urbach states that the rabbinic exegesis of the Song of Songs deeply influenced Origen's approach.[23]

Plain Sense, Allegory, and Midrash

As I indicated earlier, the problem I want to tackle in this study is hermeneutical. My opting for the naturalist reading of the Song of Songs is nothing novel in the field of scholarship. But less customary is the exploration of the problem as to what there is within the $p^e\check{s}at$ of the text that "hides and reveals" its *sod?* The problem, differently formulated, is whether there is in the Song of Songs a surplus of meaning that allows it to be read mystically. This issue looks all the more paradoxical as the Canticle is areligious in its expression and, therefore, would hardly seem conducive to a mystical and theosophical understanding, let alone to Rabbi Aqiba's consideration of it as the Holy of Holies of Scriptures! Its patent praise of the erotic seems refractory to an ethical or theological interpretation. But furthermore, the areligiosity of the Song of Songs does not remain on neutral ground, for, as I show in the body of this study, the author of the Canticle produced not just a secular love song but, more embarrassingly, a defiant, irreverent, subversive discourse, which at times constitutes a satirical pastiche of prophetic metaphors and similes.

Thus, whereas with any other biblical text the passage from one level of understanding to the next poses each time a grave hermeneutical problem, as regards the Canticle the issue is much aggravated at both ends, so to speak. For, as we saw above, the vexing problem of its literary *Gattung* renders the question of its interpretation difficult at the extreme, and the stakes as defined by Rabbi Aqiba among others are the highest possible! In other words, the text under consideration may be nontheological and areligious, but the traditional

---

23. See Urbach, "The Homiletical Interpretations."

and consecrated usage of it by the communities of faith is fundamentally religious and theological. In fact, no other biblical book is
more "unbiblical" (Carol Meyers), and no other interpretive reading is more sacred (Rabbi Aqiba). That combination of opposites is
unique. It constitutes the challenge par excellence to the hermeneut.
The question of legitimacy arises from the outset. Was it legitimate
to include the Song into the canon?[24] Is it legitimate to interpret the
Canticle Midrashically? even allegorically? And if legitimate, does it
bar the road to a critical-historical reading?

Text conveys more than one meaning. Text is plurivocal, innerly
dialogical. To reduce the Song's meaning to the allegorical is unwarranted. To read it as exclusively naturalistic is another aspect of the
same mistake. However, the hermeneut raises, at the minimum, the
problem of the relationship between one reading and the other and,
at the maximum, whether one of the two is at all legitimate. The
difficulty is compounded by the presence of still another traditional
approach to the Canticle, namely the Midrashic. We have already
distinguished between the mystical and the allegorical. Rabbi Aqiba's
reading does not shun the plain meaning of the text, as does allegory
(Origen, for instance). But at this point, we must proceed further and
stress with Daniel Boyarin that "[t]he direction of Origen's reading
is from the concrete to the abstract, while the direction of midrash is
from abstract to concrete."[25] For Origen, there is correspondence between the visible and the invisible; "the divine wisdom . . . carries us
over from earthly things to heavenly." The church father continues,

> [I]t undoubtedly follows that the visible hart and roe mentioned
> in the Song of Songs are related to some patterns of incorporeal
> realities, in accordance with the character borne by their bodily
> nature . . . We ought to be able to furnish a fitting interpretation
> . . . by reference to those harts that are unseen and hidden.[26]

In the Midrash, on the contrary, the interpretation is not allegorical, that is, relating signifier to signified, for it relates signifier to

---

24. Cf. *mYad* 3.5: "For all the Scriptures are holy [said Rabbi Aqiba], but the Song of
Songs is holiest of all."

25. Boyarin, *Intertextuality and the Reading of Midrash*, p. 108.

26. In the ET by Lawson, *Origen, The Song of Songs*, bk. 3, sec. 12, p. 223, quoted
by Boyarin, *Intertextuality and the Reading of Midrash*, p. 109.

signifier (the passage of the Red Sea; the events of Sinai, for ex-ample).[27] The signifiers are in cross-reference with one another; there is no discarding of signifier as if it were the shell around the signified.

Allegory and Midrash belong to opposite anthropologies and cos-mologies. In Israel's anthropology and cosmology, the truth supreme is not the ideal or the intelligible but belongs to "emotion and sentiment rather than proposition and argument," as says Jacob Neusner.[28] Emotion and sentiment are epitomized in love; it is the Holy of Holies of biblical kerygma. Having clarified the incom-patibleness of allegory and Midrash, we now turn to the issue of whether the Midrashic and the historical-critical readings of the Can-ticle can coexist. I find an astute statement by Neusner most helpful. Regarding the Midrash *Song of Songs Rabba,* he writes,

> The Song of Songs is not read whole and complete, or even in large units. It is read phrase by phrase, or, at most, verse by verse. So the historical or original intent of the poet/author is set aside, and his work is dismantled and recomposed in its smallest parts. In that way, the received poem is taken out of its original context, which is treated as inconsequential.[29]

Such a Midrashic reading is not just possible; it is illuminating. Suf-fice it to read *CantR* and to let oneself be guided by Neusner or Boyarin,[30] for instance. The Song of Songs treated as a Midrash of Exodus — the crossing of the Red Sea and/or the events of Sinai — is pure delight. That also on that score the Canticle is part of the canon was self-evident to Rabbi Aqiba, "for the entire age is not so worthy as the day on which the Song of Songs was given to Israel" (*mYad* 3.5). To him, the Song was not just part of the canon, but its center, its tower of control.

The rationale for such a consideration of the Canticle-as-Midrash-of-Exodus provides by ricochet the solution to our other problem

---

27. See Boyarin, *Intertextuality and the Reading of Midrash,* p. 115. It is true, adds Bo-yarin, that such a Midrashic reading was later replaced by allegoresis, and already during the Midrashic age by someone like Philo.

28. Neusner, *Israel's Love Affair with God,* p. 122.

29. Ibid., p. 16.

30. Boyarin, *Intertextuality and the Reading of Midrash.*

about the legitimacy to have concomitantly a critical-historical reading of the Canticle. For what actually stirs Rabbi Aqiba's enthusiasm
is that "for our sages, the starting point of all love is love of God
for Israel, love of Israel for God, and from there, their work com-
mences."[31] Note that "the starting point of all love" is a love not
exclusive but inclusive of all other manifestations of love. God-Israel
mutual love invites us in return to reflect upon the love between
the Canticle's human lovers. In doing so, we will not take the Song
apart and deal with discrete decontextualized bits and pieces, as the
Midrashic explanation proceeds to do. Indeed, keeping in mind that
the foundation of all love is the mutual love of God and people, we
shall turn our attention to its reflected image in the love of the Song's
protagonists as we find it shining in the poem as a whole.

The task of the modern hermeneut will not be easy, precisely to
the extent that the Midrashic kerygma is carried by a vehicle so
refractory to any theological or religious interpretation. It was not
groundless when some rabbis, as reported in the Mishnah, were
unsure about the status of a book so thoroughly devoid of religious language and concluded, "[A]s to the Song of Songs, there
is dispute" (mYad 3.5). In the course of this inquiry, I will show
that absence is but camouflaged and subversive presence. The poet
protests; she writes a manifesto purportedly devoid of religious jargon. We dare not forget it when the Midrash and the allegorical
interpretation transform it into an apologue.

Thus we find ourselves on a tight rope, caught between opposites. Earlier, we identified them as secular versus sacred. Now their
specificity appears to us more sharply; they are subversion versus
apologia. Is there any bridge between the two? What happens to
the subversive when it is turned into apologetic? Subversion is itself subverted. Subversion is gagged and muted. This is what results
from the Song read allegorically; it is not only defanged but rendered
toothless. In what follows, allegory and allegoresis are considered as
a snare for the readers, for they are exploring a language that constantly conveys a surplus of meaning and that says more, but not
other, than itself (the etymological meaning of the word *allegory*).

---

31. Neusner, *Israel's Love Affair with God,* p. 16.

Eros and Society

The need for a "hermeneutics of suspicion" (Ricoeur) is made even stronger by virtue of the fact that Eros was — justifiably, it must be conceded — regarded with distrust by rabbis and bishops alike. After all, biblical culture takes for granted that "women's sexuality poses a dangerous threat to the social order," as Renita Weems says.[32] See adds,

> In fact, sex in Israel was completely confined by law to marriage; any deviations, according to the law codes, bore fatal consequences for women and severe penalties for men...considerable care was taken especially in Hebrew law to define when, with whom, and under what circumstances sex was permissible and when the boundaries of intimate relations might be undermined (see Leviticus 18).[33]

Add to this that during the Hellenistic era, the time when the Song was composed, Greek influence with its view of Eros as human weakness was strong on Jewish mentality. In the early years of that period, the first misogynistic statements are already found in Hebrew literature (cf. Qoh 7.28; Ben Sira, later, keeps this motif unflagging [Sir 9.2–9; 25.23–26; 41.21; 42.9–14]; so does *T. Reu.* 5; 6.30). In fact, in the words of Tikva Frymer-Kensky, "[T]he lack of emphasis on eros in biblical thought creates a vacuum." Further, she writes, "Biblical monotheism's lack of a clear and compelling vision on sex and gender was tantamount to an unfinished revolution."[34] To which can be added that, when at last such a revolution was brought to its fulfillment in the Song, the latter's breakthrough was deflected toward a nonsexual interpretation!

---

32. Weems, *Battered Love*, p. 119. It is perhaps not superfluous to explicate here that I am using the word *Eros* in a sense that is exactly contrary to the Platonic. It is no yearning of the soul to be freed from the chains of the body! In classic Greek tragedy, Eros is shunned as detrimental to family and state. Only in the Hellenistic period is Eros looked at more sympathetically by Hellenistic authors, but still as a weakness, as woman incarnating wiles and snares for man. The absence in the Bible of (Platonic) Eros elicits this Frymer-Kensky commentary, "[The] ignoring of eros is part of the Bible's homogenization of gender" (*In the Wake of the Goddesses*, p. 141). In Cant there *is* Eros, but again not as a tool to ensnare the male. The equality of male and female is perfect.

33. R. Weems, *Battered Love*, pp. 4–5.

34. Frymer-Kensky, *In the Wake of the Goddesses*, pp. 188, 202.

Such misgivings look puritanical today, but who can blame Jewish and Christian institutions alike for displaying an extreme prudence in handling the sexual aspect of human existence?[35] Sex has always played havoc in societies. One of the surest signs of individual as well as sociocultural maturity is the balance between sexual liberty and control. On that score, be it said in passing, Israel in biblical times appears remarkably well adjusted. If, as I claim here, the Canticle must be understood as a protest against the prevailing mentalities of the late second temple period — which doubtlessly took advantage of the contemporary process of Hellenization — such protest arose to counter the distorted worldview of some at the time. That by the way is why the subverting message may well constitute a *return* to erstwhile sanity, and the questioning of the established order may be a chastening of the institution in a manner that recalls prophetic remonstrance. (The Song taking exception to some prophetic metaphors is another matter, as we shall see.)

In addition to what precedes, I must stress that it is out of the question for us to recognize in the Song a sweeping attitude of condemnation of the establishment in the second temple period. True, some of the priests, especially in the higher clergy, did not set examples of morality or of tolerance, but priests of that period were deeply divided. Evidently, what could appear as subversive to some was judged differently by others. Although viewed as controversial on the model of other pieces of literature, in particular those written either by or about females,[36] the Canticle was evidently not deemed offensive by everyone: it was so treasured by some bantering minds that they transmitted it to later generations.

I shall return to this point below (see p. 20) and will now broach another aspect of the problem. Even if the Song is protesting an economically slanted concept of gender relations aggravated by a sclerotic puritanism at the service of ritual purity in the community

---

35. This effort of mine to understand does not detract from a severe judgment upon a history of interpretation of the Song that "is one of massive repression of sexuality, of denial of the book's ostensible subject matter, a testimony to male fear of female sexuality. Sexuality has been thought an unsuitable, unworthy, undignified subject for a work of this rank, for a work in this context... and its challenge to patriarchal norms of female submission" (Clines, "Why Is There a Song of Songs," p. 19).

36. See my *The Feminine Unconventional*, pp. 12–14. Note that some of the Hellenistic Neopythagorean works were attributed to women. It is the only Greek prose literary body to be attributed to women in the pre-Christian era.

of the restoration, one could object that such a circumstance did not necessarily obtain in the time of Origen, for instance. What then did the Alexandrian father, some four centuries later, find so intolerable in the Canticle that he prompted a nonerotic understanding? A partial answer to this question is simply in his persistent concern for the welfare of the community. It is indeed in the light of such pragmatism that we can better understand Origen's rejecting any celebration of carnal love, however beautifully it chose to sing its "many splendored thing," because he regarded it with skepticism and suspected it of amorality.[37]

Preserving the plain meaning of the Song while making sure not thereby to open the door to sexual laxness or worse presupposes two conditions that certainly did not obtain in Origen's time: a relaxed atmosphere conducive to objective research, on the one hand, and a scientifically sophisticated audience sensitive to tensions and conflictive arguments within the texts, on the other hand. Practically speaking, the church fathers were not interested in raising, as we do today, heuristic hypotheses about the person of the author, her motivation, her purpose, her deftness in reusing religious vocabulary and themes, her contempt in dealing with established societal mores, her subversiveness.[38]

Not being subject to the same constraints, we are at liberty to pose certain questions of principle before adopting or rejecting ancient hermeneutical presuppositions. Thus, if it indeed appears that the poem is a hymn to Eros, our problem is to discover *why* and *how* it celebrates Eros, not whether it is (in)felicitous to do so — a consequential problem dependent upon the resolution of the first question.

---

37. The same pragmatism is found among the rabbis; "since they addressed themselves to a wide audience — including simple folks and children — they could not readily formulate the problems in an abstract way, nor could they give involved theoretical answers" (Heinemann, "The Nature of the Aggadah," p. 49, quoted by Boyarin, *Intertextuality and the Reading of Midrash*, p. 3).

38. Also Landy, *Paradoxes of Paradise*, writes, "The Song is both polemically and integrally related to its society" (p. 18); and he adds, "In the Song...the lovers' world is created more or less in opposition to a repressive society" (p. 24). Goulder places the *Sitz im Leben* of the Song in the time of the anti-foreign-women measures taken by Nehemiah and Ezra, for the Shulammite, he thinks, comes from an Arabian tribe called Nadib (cf. Cant 7.2). "Solomon" has been chosen precisely because of the large number of foreign women in his harem. The striking term of endearment "my sister, my spouse" in chap. 5 must be understood as the naturalization of the foreigner (*The Song of Fourteen Songs*, p. 71).

We are also entitled to ask whether the Song of Songs might not have been composed by a female author celebrating the erotic attraction between a man and a woman. As I stressed above, the loves that are sung are independent of any marital bonds, and this represents an unusual stance, collective or personal, readily raising suspicion. Why so? Obviously the stance does so because the only control authorities and society have on gender relationships — a most basic and fundamental aspect of the res publica — is through their institutionalization. When they escape control, they become a factor of disorder, of heteronomy, of anarchy, and any judicial or literary approval of such unconventionality can be properly called, as I do here, subversive. It is all the more so when its defense of the abnormal is conducted in language that parodies prophetic discourse, as will be shown below.

We may suspect that those who would react negatively to the poet(ess)'s stance, or at least express reservations, were recruited especially among authorities. As Francis Landy writes about Cant 7.5 [7.6] ("a king is imprisoned in those tresses"),

> As prisoner of her hair, he is emblematic of the vulnerability of kings, and hence of the whole body politic, to sexuality, the ultimate power of women that is the object of repression... [T]he Beloved reverses the predominantly patriarchal theology of the Bible. Male political power is enthralled to her...The poem is unfailingly critical of a society that does not know the true value of love and that imposes shame on lovers... [Love] threatens social order: a king falls in love with a country girl and forsakes his kingdom.[39]

In fact, the kind of negative reaction stirred by the Canticle either in the upper or the lower echelons of society would be essentially the same, the difference being only a matter of degree and influence.[40] True, hard evidence about such condemnation, especially emanating from the populace, is not easy to muster from such a highly selected

---

39. Landy, "The Song of Songs," pp. 315–18.
40. As Murphy puts it, "There is, in any event, no compelling way of discriminating between what was 'popular' and what was deemed courtly or 'cultivated' in ancient Israel" (*The Song of Songs*, p. 5).

literature as the biblical. But as to the reactions of social authorities, documents such as Ezra, Nehemiah, and the books of the Chronicler are revealing. They do not set examples of broad-mindedness as regards divergent opinions or styles of life. This sort of impermeability to what we today would call "pluralism" is characteristic of the establishment throughout history and everywhere. This is almost a truism, for the establishment is naturally conservative. A celebration of Eros in an unfettered form readily tends to be considered as subversion.[41]

True, the Song of Songs must have been patronized; otherwise, it would not have survived. It is clear that not everyone in Israel raised virtuous objections; the poet was not the only one of her kind. It is a fact that the Canticle's subversiveness triumphed over its objectors, for it resisted time, became a classic and, eventually, one of the sacred books of Israel. The reason for such a promotion is due to the very object of the poem, that is, human love seen as an awe-inspiring wonder. Furthermore, the plurivocity of biblical texts was no doubt recognized in the ancient world; the Song of Songs has probably never been read at one level of understanding only. The presence of the Canticle at Qumran, a community of radical ascetics allowing little room for Eros, would prove that much!

This sectarian example shows the amazing extension of the scale of meaning of the Canticle, as indeed love is a subject susceptible to an infinite range of variations and hence of interpretations. But, again, the fundamental message of the sacred text — which coincides with its authorial agenda — is its plain and obvious sense, a sense that is so unexpected and unpalatable to some that it "subverts" the world instead of confirming it. On that score, the Canticle is not unique in the Bible. The example of the Book of Ruth comes to mind. To learn from that document about a Moabite ancestry of King David (and of the Messiah) was certainly not to the taste of everyone. Strikingly there is a theme that ties together Ruth with

---

41. "The very notion of a woman not under a man's control [as Ishtar the unencumbered] awakens the fear of danger to societal harmony," says Frymer-Kensky, *In the Wake of the Goddesses*, p. 68. To recall, Freud (*New Introductory Lectures on Psychoanalysis*) says that religion forbids thinking, specifically thinking of love. This prohibition is especially addressed to women. Freud calls both the church and army "conventional crowds," for they resist all modification of their structures (see *Five Lectures on Psychoanalysis*).

the Song of Songs and other such upsetting texts as Genesis 19 (Lot and his daughters) and Genesis 38 (Judah and Tamar). The theme is called "bed-trick" by Harold Fisch: "Lot is deceived into cohabiting with his daughters, Tamar disguises herself as a prostitute, and Ruth comes secretly to the threshing-floor."[42] To these, we can adduce the ambiguous attitude of the Shulammite, which sometimes brings others to regard her as a loose woman (see Cant 5.7). Particularly as concerns female liberation, the issue is not infrequently that of sexual mores.

Liberation is not the exclusive turf of women, of course. Sexual mores are also a choice ground on which men at times indicate their nonconformism. In the literary production of Milan Kundera, *The Unbearable Lightness of Being*, the hero finds that the only expression of liberty left to him is to be human in unbridled eroticism. The sexual realm has always been a predilection among malcontents with the regime, including a certain brand of early Christians, for example.

But at this point, another possible objection must be met. Instead of characterizing the Song of Songs as subversive, might we not read it as the remnant of an upper-class entertainment literature, cultivated at royal courts, for instance? With this question, we sharpen the horns of a dilemma. A first alternative is that such ditties did exist in Israel as in neighboring countries where the court life appears to us as much richer than in Samaria or Jerusalem. Ancient Near Eastern documents show the erotic literature firmly at home in Egypt and in Babylon, for instance. Suffice it to advert to Michael Fox's book on Egyptian parallels to the Canticle (*The Song of Songs and Ancient Egyptian Love Songs*) or to James B. Pritchard's *ANET*.[43] But this speculation would address only the early generic background of the Song of Songs, for its language attests to a much later date of composition: late second temple period, long after the demise of kingship in Israel. A second alternative short-circuits the preceding one: Israel's otherness is stressed in such a manner as to defuse any attempt to draw parallels with "pagan" life in foreign palaces. What

---

42. Fisch, "Ruth and the Structure," pp. 430–31.
43. *ANET*, pp. 383, 467–69. Incidentally, these ancient Near Eastern songs are originated by women and men alike.

was current and customary elsewhere, due to a religious and societal insistence on fertility/fecundity, was not acceptable in Yahwistic milieus.

The first hypothesis — that the genre of court-ditty existed in Israel — itself dovetails in two possibilities. One possibility is to see the Canticle coming from the Jerusalem court (its late diction being due to later redactors). Then the Canticle is a remnant of that repertoire, and its late avatar (as transmitted in the MT by successive editors) is but an imitation, a sort of pastiche. As such, it would be defiant and potentially subversive, for the Canticle would constitute a window open on "another" Israel, that is, another milieu, one more accustomed to "banquet tables," as says *Sanh* 101a, than to altar, and to "houses of merry" than to the temple ground. There is, indeed, nothing in the poem to disprove that it may have been composed to scorn "the altar." Another possibility is to envisage a different chronological origin for the Canticle, say after the demise of the Persian Empire, but the conclusion is not much different. Yes, there also existed Hellenistic courts that might be considered a comfortable contemporary setting for an erotic poem. But the fourth-century (by hypothesis) version of the Song of Songs, certainly written in Palestine, is too critical of city culture, too critical of the "polis," to be read as a witty madrigal for flirting aristocrats.

In the second alternative — insisting on Israel's difference — the Song of Songs is no escapee from a broader corpus of love songs that sank into oblivion, but a really discrete and exceptional piece, with no other model but foreign, especially Egyptian, lyric poetry and with no other congenial material to work with but the Israelite traditions, embodied particularly in prophetic oracles that used erotic metaphors to convey their messages. This second alternative is the favored one in this essay, and intertextuality will constitute the heuristic method of investigation into selected pericopes of the Canticle.

The tally between such pericopes and preexisting biblical traditions renders, I hope, unnecessary the recourse to extraneous material (Tamil, Egyptian, Canaanite — textual or iconographic) to "explain" the Song of Songs. There was no need for the poet to do so as she found a mine of erotic similes used by Israelite prophets. She did not want, however, to reuse their figurative material without alteration. For, as will be shown, the prophetic metaphors are not beyond criticism. They betray a definitely patriarchal view of the sexual, a view certainly shared by the prophetic audiences in general, for the populace also responds to erotic provocation with mixed reactions. There are, to be sure, those who espouse the revolutionary stance and find it liberating. In general, however, slow-evolving societies are not ready to question institutions and customs. Frymer-Kensky writes,

> It is not often enough noted that women have as great an inter-est in female chastity codes as men, and are often the greatest policers and enforcers of the code. The dishonor of one makes the other women feel more virtuous by contrast, and makes the men prize the virtue of virtuous women even more.[44]

The sexual is entirely a social affair, totally under the societal juris-diction and control, "who is with whom and when."[45] Those who with the officials feel threatened by the revolution are quick to call themselves the majority guardian of civic and moral virtues. They represent "the society," and they particularly frown at any deviation from received sexual mores.[46]

In short, civilization entails constraints on sexuality. Mythologists see this made abundantly clear in myth. In the Legend of Gilgamesh, the uncivilized Enkidu escapes such constraints before he accepts them as worthwhile. They are the price to pay to leave the wild and enter society. In the Song, it is striking how often the couple in love leave town for their lovemaking in the countryside; in other words, they leave society to (re)enter the wild, which symbolizes the absence of sexual constraints. Even the nonconventional and unen-cumbered woman in Sumerian mythology, the goddess Inanna/Ishtar, is concerned with parental approval of her relations with Dumuzi. She does not violate social conventions and remains a virgin until her wedding.[47]

---

44. Frymer-Kensky, *In the Wake of the Goddesses*, p. 263 n. 11.
45. Ibid., p. 197.
46. To note a modern example, society at large tends to look at the spreading of AIDS as the deserved chastisement of abominable sinners!
47. Cf. Frymer-Kensky, *In the Wake of the Goddesses*, p. 26.

Metaphor and Intertextuality

Two aspects of the Song's discourse need be highlighted: its meta-phoricity and its intertextuality.[48] To these points, we now turn. The Song of Songs is largely metaphorical. As Ricoeur recalls, the meta-phor is less a word than an assemblage of words (a sentence).[49] That is, "[m]etaphor is only meaningful in a statement."[50] Con-sequently, the same words ("tenor") used in different assemblage ("vehicle") produce another semantic field, hence another meaning. That is why, as a phenomenon, the Canticle's metaphors bring us very close to allegory, for here also the literal, nonfigurative in-terpretation is made impossible by its absurdity (remember that some critics call "grotesque" certain anatomic descriptions in the Canticle's *waṣfs*). Ricoeur calls the metaphor's inconsistency "se-mantic impertinence...the mutual unsuitability of the terms when interpreted literally."[51] In the Song, the images make the reader uncomfortable by "dislocation of expectations," thus diverting our attention from the parts of the human body described to the images themselves, which become "independent of their referents and mem-orable in themselves."[52] Robert Alter writes that what "contributes to the distinctive beauty of the Song of Songs is the flamboyant elab-oration of the metaphor in fine excess of its function as the vehicle for any human or erotic tenor."[53]

This is all the more remarkable when one realizes with Oth-mar Keel that in antiquity metaphors largely reflected the prevailing

---

48. As regards intertextuality in the Song of Songs, no one, I believe, went so far and so profoundly as did Salvaneschi (*Cantico dei cantici*). I discovered — late — her book, thanks to Landy. My approach is clearly close to hers. She also, as well as Heinevetter (*"Komm nun, mein Liebster"*), whom I shall also cite occasionally, reads Cant intertex-tually within Israel's tradition. My own conclusions are, however, for better or worse, much more far-reaching than theirs.

49. Ricoeur, *The Rule of Metaphor*.

50. Ricoeur, "Biblical Hermeneutics," p. 77.

51. Ibid., p. 78.

52. Fox, *Ancient Egyptian Love Songs*, p. 329.

53. Alter, *The Art of Biblical Poetry*, p. 196. He takes as an example Cant 7.1–8 with "the vertical description of the woman, ascending from feet to head (7.2–6)." The focus of the peculiar Canticle's parallelism, he says, is such that "the second or third verset concretizes or characterizes a metaphor introduced in the first verset in a way that shifts attention from the frame of reference of the referent to the frame of refer-ence of the metaphor.... Your curving thighs are like ornaments / the work of a master's hand.... Your sex a rounded bowl — / may it never lack mixed wine! Your belly a heap of wheat / hedged about with lilies...."

conventions.[54] He writes regarding lyric poetry, "Die Sehnsucht der Liebeslieder bewegt sich in stereotypen Vorstellungen."[55] Not so, however, in the Song of Songs, for here the metaphor purposely increases the distance between vehicle and referent. If a metaphor and its referent must necessarily share a common ground, there is also a "metaphoric distance" between them, as says Colin Martindale.[56] And Fox speaks of "the degree of unexpectedness or incongruity between the juxtaposed elements and the magnitude of dissonance or surprise it produces. Greater metaphoric distance produces psychological arousal, a necessary component of aesthetic pleasure."[57]

In the case of the Song of Songs, the use of metaphorical language generically deviates discourse from its former communicating thrust. Thus, even on the level of the vehicle, the message is altered and creatively made significant in a different way. In short, the situation obtained in the Canticle is complex. The equivalence term by term is in practice excluded, for the figures are out of the common; they disorient readers and force them to retrace the process of the author's thoughts. The allusion is never obvious; the parallels drawn with otherwise well-known elements are uncannily unexpected; the references are purposely unclear. The poet has chosen a vehicle fitting the complexity of the tenor. Her language veils as much as it reveals. In hindsight, it may be said that, in its own way, the allegorical school has paid tribute to the complexity of the Canticle, a complexity that is not to be found, however, in a dualistic contradiction between the materiality of the language and the intelligibility of the message, for the language is the message.

One striking characteristic of metaphors and similes in the Canticle is that they reverse the customary order of terms of comparison. In Ezekiel 16, for example, the prophet compares Jerusalem (meaning-receiver) with an abandoned female child at her birth (meaning-giver). Elsewhere, as in Hos 2.7–13, the prophet identifies the people of Israel (meaning-receiver) with a wayward woman

---

54. Keel, *Deine Blicke sind Tauben*, p. 13; cf. also Dalman, *Palästinischer Diwan*, p. 122.
55. Keel, *Deine Blicke sind Tauben*, p. 15; also see pp. 13–17.
56. Martindale, *Romantic Progression*, pp. 23–30, 119–29, in particular.
57. Fox, *Ancient Egyptian Love Songs*, p. 276.

(meaning-giver). By contrast, in the Song of Songs the receiver of meaning is the woman herself (or the man as she sees him), and the typical meaning-receiver becomes the giver of meaning: "Your neck is like the tower of David" (Cant 4.4); "His appearance is like Lebanon, choice as the cedars" (5.15 NRSV); "You are beautiful as Tirzah, my love, comely as Jerusalem" (6.4 NRSV).[58]

This reversal of the traditional metaphoric pattern is very important, for it underscores the distance taken by the poet from his or her prophetic models, a distance that becomes, at various points, a chasm, especially when the model is a prophetic oracle of doom. The Canticle has little room for evil and evildoers. The only traces of such are societal incomprehension (on the part of brothers, of watchers of the city) and "the little foxes" that damage the vineyard (2.15). But the lovers sport with such hurdles, and they definitely find no fault within themselves. They are ever and totally innocent of any offense. They need no prophet and no chaperon. Even what temporarily separates them — a misunderstanding, a failure in communication, a spurt of impatience — eventually becomes an ingredient in their love-play.[59] We find such an absence of inhibition nowhere else in Israel's literature, biblical or postbiblical.

Let us take again the example of Cant 4.4, "Your neck is like the tower of David." This, which elsewhere would be a "grotesque" simile, works here as a parable.[60] It is not self-contained but points in a certain direction indicated by its comparative dimension. As a *mašal*, the comparison leaps out of its literality. It mobilizes, in the service of erotic description, terms and images that are filled to the brim with traditional contents and that, therefore, previously appeared as definitely unavailable for any use but the religious. To find such terms and images in the most irreligious book of the Bible is so unexpected as to leave no doubt that an effect of surprise was intended from the start. They were created in the first place *for* that effect of jolt, in other words, for subverting worldview.

---

58. Another example is provided by Isa 40.9 where Zion is personified as a herald of good news. In the Canticle the same metaphor would be reversed, the shepherdess becoming Zion (cf. 6.4).

59. The same applies, of course, to the "terrifying" aspects of the beloved (see 6.4). They only increase the lover's awe and ravishment (6.10).

60. One is reminded of *ARN* 1.5 quoted above, which states that the Song of Songs is a *mašal*.

The worldview thus subverted was identified above with a societal insistence on propriety in sexual mores. Furthering that purpose, the Canticle's metaphors, qua linguistic vehicles, also reverse the trend toward linguistic metaphorization of the erotic undertaken by the prophets of Israel. Time and again in the various pericopes of the poem, we will see the decisive substitution of a new/old reference for one actually contained in former prophetic writings.[61] In other words, a second-order reference will supersede a former reference that, itself, was not of the first order, having already become second order in prophetic oracles through metaphorization.

On the stylistic plane, this inner transformation is already evident. However original its metaphors, the Song of Songs is from start to finish literarily allusive. But the texts and similes to which the poem adverts are here purposely disfigured; they are reused *defiantly*. They are demoralized, desacralized, decanonized. Here, irony is on the verge of banter.[62] For the purpose of praising Eros, the poet dares adopt a language that prophets and priests had traditionally used to describe metaphorically the intimate relations between God and his people. In short, it is a language at home in the religious realm by virtue of having been used figuratively. Now, however, the figures have other referents,[63] so that the more the readers are familiar with biblical metaphors, the more they are disconcerted.[64] Because, on the surface, the language has remained the same, the allegorizing school has no trouble in showing impressive commonalities with prophetic discourse. André Robert, in particular, calls attention to

---

61. Within that perspective, it is striking how frequently the older exegetical traditions did tally or contrast the Song of Songs with prophetic literature. For the Targum, for example, Cant "is composed of songs and praises, which the prophet Solomon, King of Israel, addressed, in the spirit of prophecy, to the Lord of the whole world" (*CantTg* 1.1). Above, we saw that Origen shares the same view. By contrast, Theodorus of Mopsuestia states that the Song of Songs does not harbor "prophetic words about the salvific goods of the Church." A modern commentator, Krinetzki, purports to "show how close are the prophetic and the Cant eschatological expectations" (*Das Hohe Lied*, p. 35).

62. Using a love song to express irony is not without parallel. Keel quotes an ancient Egyptian love song in which the impatient lover, addressing the closed door, promises extravagant sacrifices to the various parts of the bolt as if they were divinities (see *The Song*, pp. 191–92).

63. Alter, *The Art of Biblical Poetry*, 189: "...figurative language plays a more prominent role here than anywhere else in biblical poetry."

64. Ibid., p. 193: "[W]hat makes the Song of Songs unique among the poetic texts of the Bible is that, quite often, imagery is given such full and free play there that the lines of semantic subordination blur, and it becomes a little uncertain what is illustration and what is referent."

the incontrovertible fact that biblical prophecies also mention, as does the Canticle, kings, shepherds, herds, vineyards, gardens, Lebanon, spring flowers, nocturnal awakenings. He concludes that these terms and expressions have, in the Song as in the prophets, an eschatological meaning: both stances allude to God's restoration of his unfaithful people and the resumption, so to speak, of their honeymoon. Within this relationship, Israel and her land are both called "the Shulammite." Why is not clear, but the Shulammite can alternatively designate the people or its land in dialogue with God. Robert also claims that the numerous topographical terms in the Canticle become clear when interpreted as descriptive of Palestine during messianic times.

The truth in this is that the topographical names in the Song are rather connotative than denotative. They belong to the Canticle panoply of metaphors and evocations that are to be put on a par with other tropes such as the belle's nose towering like Lebanon (7.4 [7.5]) or "Solomon." That is why finding a clue for the dating of the Song in its reference to the city of Tirzah (6.4) is out of place. Indeed, it is no better grounded than to conclude from the expression "a Pyrrhic victory" that the text comes to us from the third century B.C.E.! It is because the Canticle is throughout permeated with the symbolic and the metaphorical that it has offered itself so liberally to symbolic and even allegorical interpretations.

Particularly impressive, say Robert, Tournay, and Feuillet, is the prophets' erotic language ever since Hosea, who described the covenant between God and Israel metaphorically as conjugal love. The Hosean simile is indeed striking, but one must also say that prophets generally took great pains in avoiding sensuous explicitness deemed to adhere too closely to Canaanite naturalistic symbolism. Consequently, prophets used to provide the key to unlock their metaphors, especially those in the sexual realm. Yet in the Song, one searches in vain for a decoding key.[65] True, some prophetic metaphors could be very pointed, even graphic (precisely something we do not find in

---

65. Arendt writes in her introduction to Benjamin's *Illuminations*, "[A] metaphor establishes a connection which is sensually perceived in its immediacy and requires no interpretation, while an allegory always proceeds from an abstract notion and then invents something palpable to represent it almost at will. The allegory must be explained before it can become meaningful, a solution must be found to the riddle it presents" (p. 13).

the Canticle). On that score, one might say that Israel's prophets (especially Ezekiel) went further into libidinous territory than would the Song of Songs, their later "recipient field" (Nelly Stienstra's expression).[66] But paradoxically prophetic boldness pales in comparison with the less audacious Canticle metaphors when it is realized that the prophetic figures qua vehicle refer to a tenor that is itself metaphoric (YHWH has children with his people, for instance, in Hosea 2). The difference is that, in the Song, the metaphors refer to a nonfigurative tenor. To exemplify this difference, let us imagine that Ezekiel's expression in 23.1–3, or in 16.25 ("you have parted your legs"), be borrowed verbatim in one of the shepherd's addresses to the Shulammite. It is evident that the bearing of the image would be totally altered in the process!

Such comparison between two kinds of discourse allows us to go one step further in the study of metaphor. Paul Ricoeur among others has taken us with authority into the poetic device of shifting from "ordinary language" to the symbolic reinterpretation of reality. Because, like art, the trope reorganizes reality, there is a "literal falsity [that is] an ingredient of metaphorical truth."[67] But now the question is, what is happening when the shift occurs from the particular reference of an already "metaphorized" language to another referential reality? Certainly, the quality of tension is transformed in the process. As far as the Canticle is concerned, by virtue of its abandonment of religious discourse, that is, a discourse understood only within an interpreting religious community, the outcome is highly unusual. Clearly, the very use by the Canticle of a nonreligious vehicle for its message is already at this stage critical both of the community's way of communication and of the community itself as interpreter. We witness a process of disorientation by way of a secular borrowing of forms of expression with which the community is familiar within the religious realm.

The poet reused a metaphorical language that she or he first found in Israel's traditions. In doing so, the poet took advantage of the margin of interpretation such language naturally leaves open. In fact, she or he poetically inserted the prophetic symbolism within another,

---

66. See Stienstra, *Yhwh Is the Husband* (see esp., as regards our study, chaps. 4–5).
67. Ricoeur, *The Rule of Metaphor,* pp. 86–87.

contiguous area of interpretation. Then a shift occurred, from certain possibilities of interpretation offered by the metaphor's earlier contexts to new possibilities afforded by the new context. Here more than ever the symbol (the word, for instance) has no other meaning but within its surroundings (what the sentence is to the word, as we saw above). The new vehicle transforms the symbol itself, or rather it taps the "surplus of meaning" of the symbol. For meaning is plural; there are congeries of meaning attached to the symbol, and their various nuances essentially depend upon a worldview that pivots on a seminal symbol that controls all others. In the Song of Songs, the controlling symbol is the erotic mutual quest of "he" and "she."

Inherent in that particular symbol is a tension whose resolution is contingent upon our specifying the literary genre of the Canticle. If the poem is regarded allegorically — as emitting, say, an eschatological message comparable with the prophetic — then the literary genre's association with the historical is stressed. Its inner tension is released precisely at a chronological moment, let us say when the couple eventually meet and the coitus is achieved. But if the Canticle is regarded as supratemporal, as elevating the prophetic discourse to the level of atemporality, then the symbol's tension is relieved existentially in the suprahistorical. The temporality specific to the new setting-in-life is one of "always and ever true in human life." It reaches its apex in a particular kind of experience, or rather in a *"limit-experience* which would correspond to the *limit-expression* of religious discourse."[68]

This Ricoeurian statement is important for understanding the very paradoxical situation afforded by the Song of Songs. In the analytic part that will follow, I will repeatedly show that the poem's language is parodying traditional (prophetic) literature. It does so through the secularization of the discourse to the point of becoming a quasi-blasphemous satire in a florid style. There is here no mention of God, of Israel, of temple, of sacrifices, of ritual, of laws, of land, and so on. Were it not for one single word (or part thereof) in 8.6, the Song could almost be non-Israelite! For, with the mention of Palestinian topographical or personal names such as Jerusalem, Tirzah, David, or Solomon, we remain at a surface level. They are

---

68. Ibid., p. 34; emphasis in the original.

conceivably replaceable without fundamentally altering the nature of the poem, *at least it may appear so.*[69] There are few, if any, characteristic features that identify the Canticle as a bona fide link in Israelite tradition;[70] only *interpretation* is able to draw a divine melody from that marvelous instrument susceptible of being played in different fashions. For, in point of fact, in this nonreligious language interpretation recognizes "a limit-expression of religious discourse" and even the theological fullness of a "limit-experience." Such possibility can only become certainty at the end of our research, when it will be realized that the Canticle "finds its final referent" in the fact that "ordinary experience [here, love] has recognized itself as *signified* in its breadth, its height, and its depth, by the 'said' (*le dit*) of the text."[71] In other words, if God's name is not found, it is because God is to be tasted, smelled, heard, seen, and touched in the Song.

The kind of literary phenomenon we are dealing with has been called "intertextuality," a textual dialogic relationship that also includes what Michael Fishbane calls "inner-biblical discourse."[72] Speaking specifically of Job, Fishbane shows that there is in that book a reuse of Psalm 8; Gen 11.6; and Prov 3.11–12. He writes, "The positive ambiguity of the words in Ps 8.5–7 is negatively employed in Job 7.17–18."[73] He then calls such reuse in Job "biting provocation," "sarcasm," or "diatribe" — all terms that apply, I believe, to the Song of Songs as well.[74]

---

69. For instance, the mention of Damascus, Lebanon, and Mt. Hermon does not make the poem Syrian in origin!

70. We shall return to this point in our concluding remarks at the end of this introduction.

71. Ricoeur, *The Rule of Metaphor,* p. 128; emphasis in the original.

72. Fishbane, "Inner-biblical Discourse," pp. 86–98. "Intertextuality" is susceptible of several understandings. The first considers the text as a mosaic of citations. The second sees the text as dialogical in nature. The third recognizes the presence of "a mosaic of signifying, dialogic, and culturally coded material" (Phillips, " 'What Is Written?' " 111–47; the quote is from p. 115). Points two and three are by far preferable to point one. In the same issue of Semeia, Aichele and Phillips write, "Meaning does not lie 'inside' texts but rather in the space 'between' texts. Meaning is not an unchanging ideal essence but rather variable, fluid, and contextual depending upon the systemic forces at work that bind texts to one another. On this view meaning can no longer be thought of as an objective relation between text and extratextual reality, but instead it arises from the subjective, or ideological, juxtaposing of text with text *on behalf of* specific readers in specific historical/material situations in order to produce new constellations of texts/readers/readings" (pp. 14–15; emphasis in the original).

73. Ibid., p. 89.

74. Ibid.

In his turn, Ricoeur says that the *work* of intertextuality consists in relating to another text that is thereby displaced and provided with an enlarged meaning.[75] The preexisting text finds itself surrounded, so to speak, by a new text that both informs it and is informed by it. The reader is invited to go back and forth, upstream and downstream, so to speak. The reader is also expected to be fully aware of the metaphoric process itself in passing from one term to the other. Such a shift is not neutral, for metaphor "transgresses the semantic and the cultural codes of a speaking community."[76] When it results from the tally of two (seemingly or not) conflicting texts, it certainly does shatter the cultural foundation of the community. The following conclusion of the French hermeneut is fully confirmed by the Song's reuse of prophetic discourse,

> Through configurating the most deeply rooted and compact human experience [in the Song, love] and through correcting traditional religious representations, limit-expressions pursue their itinerary beyond the narrative [here, the prophetic traditions].[77]

The supratemporality of the Song of Songs is emphasized by the typification of the characters. Lacking personal data about the personages in the Canticle, we generalize from the sole clue found in 6.13 as to the heroine's identity and call her *the Shulammite*. We would be at a loss to give a name to the male character. He is the "shepherd." Paradoxically, only the secondary figure of Solomon,

---

75. The only provision I would insert here is the multiplicity, at times, of the textual references for a single theme. Intertextuality can be multireferential. When this happens, the freedom displayed in the borrowing text may be so creative that the modern Western mind may feel somewhat abashed. What Second Isaiah, for example, does with the Exodus motif is eloquent in this regard. Isa 50.2 speaks of God drying up the sea, turning the ocean depth into a wilderness, so that "their fish rot for lack of water and die of thirst." There is in the Isaianic text a telescoping of Exod 7.18, 21 and 16.20, 24: the dying fish, the piling up of dead frogs, the stench in the land of Egypt, and the rotting manna left over for the next day. Along the same line, it is to be underscored that, in order for two texts to be in mutual correspondence, a root common to both need not be in the same form (or tense). Again an example from Second Isaiah will suffice: Isa 44.27 alludes to Exod 14.21, the common term is *leḥarabâ* in the latter and *ḥorabî* in the former.

76. Ricoeur, "La Bible et l'imagination," p. 355.

77. Ricoeur, "La Bible et l'imagination," p. 360. Elsewhere, Ricoeur adds, "What binds poetic discourse, then, is the need to bring to language modes of being that ordinary vision obscures or even represses.... [T]he poet's speech is freed from the ordinary vision of the world only because he makes himself free for the new being which he has to bring to language" (*Interpretation Theory*, p. 60).

evoked but absent from the stage, is firmly identified! But even in this case, the identification designates a type. It would be a mistake to take "Solomon" as a chronological indicator for the date of composition of the Song. "Solomon" belongs to the conventional style of the *wasf.*[78] Leo Krinetzki is right when he sees in that name a type, and so is Gillis Gerleman speaking of a "literarische Travestie."[79] In the Canticle its correspondent descriptive term is "prince's daughter" (Heb. 7.2), which brings up "Shulammît" to a corresponding level with "Sh^elomoh" (Heb. 7.1).

The Canticle puzzles the scholars as to its dating precisely because of its typification of characters and "plot." Apart from clues given by vocabulary and syntax, both indicating a late second temple period, the Canticle could as well be preexilic. The mainly geographical references are themselves disorienting ("the mounts of Bather," for instance) and contribute to the disappearance of the "plot" behind what we might call heraldic movements and scenes in the poem. Every detail is set at the service of the quest.[80] The author went as far as possible in the direction of transcending the syntagmatic sequence into a paradigmatic order, meant to supersede the existing order. That is why, far from being a gratuitous exercise in poetry, the Song is mediation to salvation. To call the Song of Songs "eschatological" makes sense only on that score. It indeed speaks of the ultimate triumph of Eros, in the future as in the present (a *sich-realizierende* eschatology, in the terms of Joachim Jeremias).

Song of Songs and Prophetic Literature

The Canticle borrowings from the prophets, from Hosea in particular, are numerous. When one remembers that the eighth-century prophet of Israel in the North is the probable creator of the metaphor of matrimony as a fitting description of the covenantal relation-

---

78. I use the term broadly, with a nontechnical meaning.

79. Krinetzki, *Das Hohe Lied*, p. 36; Gerleman, *Rut — Das Hohelied*, p. 61. The idea is strongly emphasized in the work of Heinevetter, *"Komm nun, mein Liebster."* He sees in the Canticle a third-century B.C.E. "Königstravestie" and, at times, a "Götter-travestie" meant to critique society and, especially, the city culture. The Canticle, he says, is "anarchic" (p. 178).

80. One thinks of A.-J. Greimas!

ship between God and his people, the Canticle dependence becomes perfectly understandable. Both Hosea and the Song share a common interest in gender relationships. A closer look at the *way* Hosea uses his metaphor(s), however, is revealing of a definitely patriarchal conception. To imagine the relations between God and Israel on the model of those between male and female doubtlessly was an ideological breakthrough — so much so that it was adopted by many later prophets in Israel. YHWH as a masculine god needed no *paredra*; his "wife" was his people. In one stroke, the prophet was thus emphasizing the oneness of God and the intimate relationship binding him with his people. Hosea was the first prophet to express with such power the love of God, stronger even than death (Hos 6.1–2).

But this is not the whole story. So much theological insight had some strings attached. The prophet's metaphorical expression insisted not only on the staunch fidelity of the male god; it also denounced the stubborn whoring of the female partner and also the degrading chastisement to which she would be submitted. At this point, the imagery becomes highly disparaging. With good conscience and total self-complacency, the husband strips his wife naked, exposes her pudenda for all to watch, beats her, humiliates her, exposes her to every outrage. From Judg 19.29 depicting the butchery of the Levite's concubine to Hosea's metaphors, there is not much progress towards gender equality! Modern commentators too lightly assert that for the prophets Hosea, Jeremiah, or Ezekiel, these were just metaphors. On the contrary, it is evident that the images reflect a real societal conception of man and woman, on the one hand, and inevitably perpetuate that conception, on the other, extending a sort of blanket justification in advance over women's alienation or worse.

Perceptively, Renita Weems calls attention to the fact that the prophets' audiences must have been overwhelmingly male:

> Only an audience that had never been raped or had never perceived rape or sexual abuse as a real threat could be expected to hear the kind of ribald descriptions of abused women, sexual humiliation, assault, gang rape, violation, and torture that the prophets described and not recoil in fear.[81]

---

81. Weems, *Battered Love*, p. 41. Note, however, the reservations of Frymer-Kensky, who calls attention to the fundamental distinction between the all-powerful God in Israel's

Among Weems's strong indictments against a certain language used metaphorically by prophets, I select yet this one:

> The point of the marriage metaphor...is to justify the violence and punishment the subordinate endures and to exonerate the dominant partner from any appearance of being unjust...[I]n the hands of Israel's poets and demagogues,...[women's] sexuality poses serious threats to society if it is not in the service of procreating legitimate heirs for their husbands.[82]

This is, I believe, one of the two keys that unlock the understanding of the Canticle's challenge to prophetic discourse. No woman with a sense of her gender dignity (and a deft calamus) could condone such rhetoric that prophets and sages took for granted and justified. The second key lies in another challenge. The prophets Hosea, Jeremiah, Ezekiel, and so many others saw their duty in calling the people to repentance; they were stern in their determination to force their contemporaries to face their guilt. Israel's prophets have powerfully contributed to promoting a sense of guilt, and no language better than the one denouncing promiscuity within marriage could capture the sense of shame more fully. The anti-Semitic assertion that guilt and shame are a "Jewish" teaching is not without substance, although fundamentally misconstrued.[83]

The poet's agenda was different. For her, the sense of guilt before God is perhaps theologically sound; so is the need for repentance. But the whole notion is ruined if one group among the people is genetically and sociologically designated as so much guiltier than the rest that the latter may feel exonerated in comparison. *Errare humanum est,* and sin is universal, but, according to a prevalent patriarchal interpretation, the initiative in evildoing is Eve's; the naive Adam is dragged into it by his cunning wife. So it was at the beginning of times; so is it till the end of times. The male is rather the victim than the author of evil.

This conceptual backdrop serves as a foil to the Canticle's composition. For here the contrast is striking. Not only is the author

---

understanding and the limited range of human husbands' rights toward their wives (*In the Wake of the Goddesses*, pp. 147–52).

82. Weems, *Battered Love*, pp. 19, 30.

83. This I see as one of the main rationales behind the Nazi annihilation of the Jews. (See my article "God after Auschwitz.")

most probably a female (see below pp. 39–53), as is also the main character of the composition, but so is the intended audience (not exclusively, of course, as the prophets' audiences were not either exclusively male). The female singer sings first for her sisters, the "daughters of Jerusalem." True, she is not necessarily heard or approved, but what she has to say is at their benefit; she is their eyes, their ears, their voice, their soul. The male lover is spoken to and of. In response to the prophetic point of view and its mistrust of female sexuality, the poet adopts a female standpoint and promotes an infinitely more compassionate and positive view of male sexuality. Thus, the Song of Songs is truly *pharmakon,* a healing text, an antidote to a marital metaphor that had "gone awry."[84] In this respect, Canticle 4 describing female nudity in ecstatic terms starkly contrasts with the uniformly negative prophetic evocations. Canticle 4 is the only place in Scripture where the naked woman is praised and admired without restriction. It is also the only place where the female is not "saved by becoming a mother" (1 Tim 2.15), but is glorified in her eroticism.

Above, I discussed the ostensible absence of Israelite elements in the Song of Songs. But I must stress that this absence is only a dummy window. The Canticle is actually and fully an Israelite composition because its discourse is essentially in a relation of intertextuality with the constitutive traditions of Israel. The subversive nature of the Canticle is from within, not from without. Its very rereading of Genesis, Hosea, Isaiah, Jeremiah, and Ezekiel sends the reader back to those traditional texts; it does not obliterate them. But neither does it merely correct their trajectories, for in most cases, it opposes the vision embodied in narrative and prophetic metaphors.

Again I must emphasize that what the Canticle takes exception to is, not the primacy of love in the rapport between God and people, but the patriarchal discourse conveying a certain conception of gender relationship. According to that discourse, the male god has been steadily wronged by the female Israel. In turn, between man and woman there is systemic inequality. The female's lengthy and cumbersome pregnancy and her birth pangs are *understood* to be a special chastisement that the wrathful masculine god metes out to

---

84. Cf. Weems, *Battered Love,* pp. 12–44.

the perverse woman where it hurts her most and where feminine sinfulness finds its origin: her sex. In other words, the man's sin is a choice, while the woman's sin is a condition.[85]

The patriarchal interpretation sees an inexorable consistency in Genesis 3, adding that sexual intercourse, from which woman suffers so much, is a curse to the second degree, as *her* desire for the male initiates a vicious circle in which she is trapped by her own fault. Hence the male is from beginning to end innocent. He not only bears no ill consequence from the sexual act; he does not even selfishly initiate it but is himself provoked into it by the woman's guile. In our day and age, Jean Giraudoux presents us with a candid Holophernes connived by a crooked Judith. In modern courts of justice, the defense asks the victim what kind of clothes she wore when she was raped, as if her miniskirt would in advance exonerate and even excuse any violation of her person. To all this, the poet's response is that "her" desire does not stand alone; the desire is also "his," and the sexual drive does not initiate an ontological or an ethical inequality between the genders. For love-eros is mutual; it puts the two partners on a perfectly equal footing: "My beloved is mine, and I am his . . . among the lotuses" (2.16). If there is guilt in creation, it is not here to be found. As long as there is mutual commitment between the genders, sex is good; it is very good. No shadow of shame is cast on it.

Intertextuality blazes a two-way street. In the case under consideration, it means that the Canticle and the provider-texts are in mutual reaction. Not only is the Canticle to be read while keeping in mind narrative and prophetic figurative discourse, but the narratives and oracles must in turn be reread in the new light shed by the Canticle. In such rereading, Genesis 3 or Hosea 2 are severely chastened by the Song of Songs. As we saw above, by reading them exclusively, we run the risk of consciously or unconsciously perpetuating a grave injustice embedded in their formulation. In their effort to liberate humans from their slavery (to hubris), they themselves need to be liberated. When we read that the prophet must go looking for Gomer because she is unruly, we must also make allowance for an "untameness" that is another name for a nonestablished, unconventional, subver-

---

85. This fundamental distinction is necessary for an understanding of the Jewish and Christian barrier erected between genders in terms of priesthood and mediation.

sive form of relationship on the part of one "Gomer," which may well be at times regarded as dangerously flirting with impropriety but is only expressing freedom in a totally faithful attachment to her one lover.

Intertextuality opens up, by ricochet, another interpretation of Genesis 3. "Your [fem.] desire will be onto him" must be understood as only one aspect of a mutual attraction, for "his desire is onto me [fem.]" as well. "Your desire will be onto him" of Genesis is no longer taken to emphasize an ontological weakness of woman. Only the female side of a mutual relationship is mentioned here because that side is highly paradoxical. In spite of the great sufferings incurred by the female after a "successful" intercourse with the male, "[her] desire [is still] onto him." In spite of a long cumbersome pregnancy, of the excruciating pain of childbirth, of the real danger of losing her life in the process, of the inexorable statistical reality of infantile decimation by maladies, her sexual drive allows for the perpetuation of the human species. The other (or male) side of the relation is not mentioned because it stirs no surprise. The male libido causes no wonder. About man, more than about the lewd woman of Prov 30.20, it can be said that he wipes his mouth and says, "I have done no wrong."

The same phenomenon of mutuality applies to the intertextual relationship between Song of Songs and Hosea (Jeremiah, Ezekiel). In light of the true nature of love as depicted by the Canticle, that is, a love that "bears all things, believes all things, hopes all things, endures all things" (1 Cor 13.7 NRSV), the prophetic portrayal of woman's debasement by her husband would become the evocation of an "impossible possibility." It would concern only a case at the outer limit of imagination, something that is conceivable as the ultimate effect of a cause that has escaped all control and must be punished by law, but nonrealistic within the framework of love/covenant. In the same way, the Deuteronomist may present the covenant with God as conditional, and the prophets may threaten Israel with total and definitive rejection (see Isaiah 1), even with total and definitive annihilation (see Amos). Again, in the same vein, the Israelite narrative may evoke an infanticide by a loving father ("your son, your only son, the one you love, Isaac"; Gen 22.2) anxious to please an all-demanding God, and the Israelite law may envisage that parents relinquish their authority over their unruly child to the community, which will put him to death (Deut 21.18–21).

These texts, and many others, picture the limits. They take the reader to extremes. They envisage situations that are so exceptional that, while they might potentially occur, actually they do not. They are demonstrations *ab absurdo*. Israel will never be rejected; she will never be annihilated; the covenant will never be cancelled for unfaithfulness; no parents will ever delegate the community to put their child to death; Gomer will never be stripped naked. Never ever will God lay his people bare for everyone around to see her shame. He is not the God who strips but the God who clothes (Gen 3.20). To have recourse to a "stripping of her clothes" and to an "uncovering of her genitals under the eyes of her lovers" (Ezek 23:26; Hos 2.10) is in the Canticle conception out of the question. For the woman's love for the man is exclusive, even though it takes sometimes unexpected forms, and the man's love for her is such that humiliating her would never come to his mind. Even when he looks for her everywhere without finding her, and she looks for him without finding him, they draw no suspicious conclusion, assured as they are, once for all, of their mutual and indefectible love.

Literalism/fundamentalism is defeated by the intertextuality inherent in the texts themselves. Texts shed an interpretative light upon one another. They must be read within the trajectory of their *Wirkungsgeschichte*. To consider the Song of Songs as the Holy of Holies within the sanctuary of biblical literature means that, with Canticle, the reader has reached the omega-point of textual itinerary. Love is the core of revelation; all the rest is commentary.[86]

The Enigma of Sexuality Seen by a Female Author

By now, we have gathered enough material to broach in a systematic fashion the issue of the author's identity. This endeavor will provide

---

86. So said Hillel, Jesus, Aqiba. Perhaps more surprisingly, so is it also stressed by Vishnu Sarman (*Hitopadesa* I,114), "What is the supreme virtue? Tenderness towards all beings"; and by Confucius (*Luen Yu* IV,15), "My doctrine consists in rectitude of the heart and love of the neighbor." In *The Analects of Confucius*: "Is there any word," asked Tzu Kung, "which could be adopted as a lifelong rule of conduct?" The Master replied, "Is not Sympathy the word? Do not do to others what you would not like yourself."

a crucial hermeneutical key to the understanding of the Canticle. As intimated above, it will be argued here that the author was a woman. I realize that nowadays such a thesis sounds suspiciously demagogic. My only defense against this unjust accusation is the evidence that I can muster in this essay. If my attempt is successful, however, it will not just satisfy a reader's natural curiosity but will be part and parcel with my general thesis that we are here dealing with a subversive, or at least contesting, piece of literature. For it is self-evident that the scandal occasioned by a hymn to Eros would be compounded by its female authorship. More than in the case of a male composer, the paean then takes on overtones of protestation.

In point of fact, there are two possible retorts to the customary male mistrust of alleged feminine amorous wiles and deceit. One consists in demonstrating that woman is capable of great achievements in other domains. The other is to defiantly claim a leading role in the erotic realm. The latter became the poet's option.

At this point, I shall, however, make a concession. In spite of the accumulation of material in what precedes and what follows in favor of a woman author, I recognize that conclusive evidence will ever be lacking. There is no extant colophon indicating the author's identity. Moreover, a male writer may author a fictional female character's discourse, and vice versa.[87] It is what actually occurs in the Canticle which is intergender dialogical. Male or female poet? The amount of evidence, I believe, works rather in favor of a female author.

The German critic Otto Eissfeldt writes the following about the attribution of the poem to Solomon, "[He] was thought of as the king who was the most famous because of his splendor and his reputation for love."[88] Such attribution to the son of David, as we saw above, not only is unwarranted by the poem but is simply misleading. Solomon never speaks here in the first person singular, but is

---

87. I cannot agree with Clines that the Canticle is written by a male author who imagines woman according to his own standards. Clines's understanding of the poem is, in my opinion, twisted. What would be for him a genuinely female voice is itself a fantasy disregarding the real social and aesthetic ancient world. That a "liberated" woman proclaims "I am beautiful!" is definitely no concession to male expectations. Feminine beauty is not a male creation (cf. Clines, "Why Is There a Song of Songs").

88. Eissfeldt, *The Old Testament: An Introduction*, p. 487.

spoken *about* or *to*,[89] and in less than a favorable manner.[90] But, if not Solomon, who?

A female author is hiding behind the Shulammite character of the poem.[91] Remarkable, for instance, is the fact that the majority of the discourses are set in her mouth and that, if the lover speaks often and lengthily as well, it happens several times that his utterances consist of citations from her speeches.[92] She has the first and the last word in the poem. She is the one who arouses him (8.5). Such a preponderance of a female is simply unique in the Bible, although, in the ancient Near East (including Israel), poetry was often composed by women. Samuel N. Kramer has shown that "the first [known] love song" was composed within the framework of the sacred marriage between the king and the fertility goddess in the person of a priestess (the *hieros gamos*).[93] In the liturgical poetry that accompanies the ritual, the goddess is called a spouse, a mother, a daughter. But more importantly, in this poetic genre it is mainly the woman who speaks. "In the fertility liturgies," writes Daniel Lys, "the role of women is preeminent."[94]

True, the sacred-marriage liturgy is not of Israel's concern, but in Israel as elsewhere in the ancient Near East, women were specialists in love songs and war songs — in particular the songs welcoming back warriors after battles. Shlomo Goitein mentions these as examples from the Old Testament: 1 Sam 18.6–7; Exod 15.20; Judg 4.9 (see also Ps 68.12; Isa 37.22; Jer 38.22).[95] The Canticle is a love song; it is also regarded traditionally as a piece of wisdom literature. Now, we know that women did belong to wisdom guilds. One such

---

89. In an exception to the rule, Solomon is addressed in the second person in 8.12, but as an archetype, not a person.

90. Goitein suggests, on the (unpublished) recommendation of the linguist Nahum Halevi Epstein, to emend 'ašer li-šelomoh to 'ašir li-šelomoh: ([the woman is speaking] "I shall sing for [to] Solomon"). One can refer to Isa 5.1. See Goitein, "The Song of Songs."

91. Today, after the delirious attribution of large chunks of the Pentateuch to female authors, one is almost ashamed to come with another such hypothetical feminine authorship in the Bible. If need be, I assure my readers that there is here no ploy to be fashionable!

92. Brenner, in a book of which she is the editor, *A Feminist Companion to the Song of Songs*, offers the following statistics: 53 percent in the female voice(s) and 34 percent in the male voice(s) (pp. 88–89).

93. Kramer, *The Sacred Marriage Rite*. Enheduanna, daughter of King Sargon (ca. 2350), for instance, wrote extensive hymns in Sumerian.

94. Lys, *Le plus beau chant*, p. 48.

95. See Goitein, "Women as Creators of Biblical Genres."

wise woman came from Tekoa to give a lesson to King David (2 Sam 14.13–14); another one is Abigail the Carmelite (1 Sam 25.29–31).

Other poetic genres are women's domain; for example, the very important funeral song (1 Sam 1.24; Jer 9.16–19; Lamentations 1; 2; 4). Furthermore, just as in Mari on the Euphrates, the prophetic oracle in Israel is not the exclusive domain of men. Scripture gives us the names of four female prophets. Miriam and Deborah may well be "bards," as Goitein pointedly says, and it is difficult to distinguish between oracle and poem as far as they are concerned (cf. Judg 5.12). But surely Huldah and Noadiah are to be counted among the bona fide prophets (2 Kgs 22.14–20, Neh 6.14). Moreover, in spite of a woman's (alleged?) exclusion from worship in the temple of Jerusalem, a woman was not denied access into it (see 1 Sam 2.22). The story of Hannah, the future mother of Samuel, is a case in point, although one will contrast it with a text like Deut 16.11, 14. Women also formed groups of singers or dancers (Judg 21.19–21; Jer 31.3–4) — a fact that may shed light on "daughters of Jerusalem," an expression recurring in the Song that designates some kind of chorus.[96]

In spite of this evidence of female creativity, one remains surprised by the great freedom displayed by the Shulammite. She is presented as taking the initiative most of the time. This is so unexpected within the biblical context in general that certain critics have thought of foreign influences upon the Canticle, mainly Egyptian or even Tamil.[97]

---

96. Note the possible parallel between the Song's "daughters of Jerusalem" and the antique Greek chorus. Based on a total of twenty-six texts with "daughter" in the MT, quite a number of them designate clearly associations of singers; the same conclusion can be drawn from texts mentioning women (without the term *bat*): they often are singers or dancers. In Aristotle's time, the chorus played the role of spectators as it represented the populace as they voice *traditional opinions*. This latter point would explain the yawning hiatus between the "daughters of Jerusalem" — possibly the outcome of the Hellenistic influence upon the Canticle — and the Shulammite. Using a Kierkegaardian vocabulary, we can say that the former group represents generality while the lovers in the Song definitely side with the particular (cf. *Fear and Trembling*, passim; see here below, p. 47, n. 114, Rosenzweig's thought). The youths in love relativize social morality. It is also possible that the presence of a chorus in the Canticle elucidates the crux of Cant 6.13 [7.1], where Versions have a "double chorus"; or as in the LXX, "like choruses"; in Pesh, "like a chorus, and like a chorus in the fields"; in the Vg, *nisi choros castrorum*. Joüon (*Le Cantique des Cantiques*) translates, "[rangées] comme un double choeur?" Buzy (*Le Cantique des Cantiques*, p. 347), "à la façon d'un choeur à deux parties." More decisive, in my opinion, is the study of Sasson, "The Worship of the Golden Calf." Sasson shows that the term *meḥolâ*, present in 6.13 [7.1], stands for an antiphonal song in two groups formed by women and musicians.

97. Rabin, "Song of Songs and Tamil Poetry"; Gottwald, "Song of Songs."

Be that as it may, it seems appropriate to stress more than has been done in general the female initiative demonstrated by folkloric poetry in Israel. When this is taken into consideration, it becomes much less surprising that the author of the Song should be a woman. For it is a woman's song from beginning to end, and it puts the heroine at center stage. "All events are narrated from her point of view, though not always in her voice, whereas from the boy's angle of vision we know little besides how he sees her," says Michael Fox.[98] He adds that the apparent absence of the author is deceptive, for she stands everywhere "behind the scenes, communicating to us attitudes about the personae... and setting many of the norms by which we are to understand and evaluate the characters" (ibid., p. 258).

In this respect, the significant text of Cant 8.12 says, "My vineyard, my very own, is for myself" (NRSV). According to Lys, it is the young man who speaks in verses 11–12, but he admits that it could be her speech.[99] The latter is, I believe, preferable. She says that her "vineyard" belongs to her, using the term *lepanay*, which is generally translated by "at my disposal" (Gen 13.9; 20.15; 24.51; 34.10; 47.6; 1 Sam 16.16; 2 Chr 14.6). The formula is already present in Cant 1.6, again in the mouth of the heroine. As André Robert says, *lepanay* can only stand in opposition to *lenôtᵉrîm* ("to the keepers," in the same verse).[100] Clearly then, the Shulammite proclaims that her "vineyard" belongs to her; she takes care of it without the help of anyone, particularly, should we say, of her male kin, father or brothers, who traditionally would be in charge of her virtue and welfare.[101]

In the Song, the Shulammite is always the one who says *'anî* (me), *napᵉšî* (my soul, me), or even *libbî* (my heart, me; cf. Cant 8.10). By contrast, "he" is frequently spoken of in the third person singular, even in her direct discourses (cf. 2.8–10); "she" is never spoken of that way by him). "He" at times invites his companions to par-

---

98. Michael Fox, *The Song of Songs and Ancient Egyptian Love Songs*, p. 309.
99. See Lys, *Le plus beau chant*, p. 302.
100. RTF, *Le Cantique des Cantiques*, p. 321.
101. Cf. Pope, *Song of Songs*, p. 690: "*If the female here asserts autonomy, this verse becomes the golden text for women's liberation*" (my emphasis). Clearly, the maiden is here proclaiming that her economic functions have been imposed upon her by others (the brothers = society at large), and she has broken all ties with economic production. The parallel with the goddess Inanna/Ishtar is here again interesting. Frymer-Kensky writes, "She [Inanna] has no true niche in society" (*In the Wake of the Goddesses*, p. 27).

ticipate in the "banquet" (banquet for the eyes, for the ears); "she" restrains her female followers, adjuring them not to stir love before it is willing. He occasionally speaks in the first person (and calls her, for instance, "my bride"), but he is clearly not the narrator, and the narrative "I" coincides with the authorial "I."[102] In summary, the maiden's presence fills the poem; she is the magnificent "I" from beginning to end. Cant 8.12 makes no exception; it simply adds *kar^emî* (my vineyard) to the list.[103] Both the absence of the father and the emphasis on the mother contribute to giving the poem a feminine flavor. Furthermore, Cant 8.13 might point in the same direction. She is invited by her lover to pursue her poem![104]

Solomon serves in Cant 8.11–12 as a foil.[105] He does not allow the ones he keeps in his harem to care for their own vineyards — their bodies, that is — but would rather have them kept by others. This is the continuation of the preceding argument (vv. 6–7) according to which one cannot buy love, for it is not a measurable quantity. "Solomon" views love in terms of one thousand and of two hundred;[106] let him keep this reckoning to himself! Let him have his vineyard kept by others if he so wishes; he will gain nothing by it, says the Canticle.

There are few male characters in the poem; apart from the fiancé and Solomon, they are indistinctly plural, "companions," "shepherds," "brothers," "guards." As is shown by the immediate context, Cant 8.12 refers first of all to those who are called the Shulammite's "brothers" (8.8–9; see also 1.6). The brothers are presented as anxious to defend their sister's chastity and give her in marriage when the time comes.[107] As is well known, in the Middle East, brothers play a major role in the betrothal and wedding of their

---

102. Cf. Keel, *The Song*, p. 88 (on 2.5c).

103. Franz Rosenzweig says that no other biblical book uses the first person singular as much as the Canticle does (*The Star of Redemption*, beginning of his development on the Song of Songs; see especially p. 201).

104. F. Landy, personal communication with author.

105. C. Bloch writes, "In the Song, even that magnificent king is no match for the lovers, who feast in splendor" (Bloch and Bloch, *The Song of Songs*, p. 11). She adds, "When she calls him 'the king,' or when he calls her 'nobleman's daughter,' they are dressing up in borrowed robes, playing at King-Solomon-at-his-court" (p. 8).

106. The socioeconomical background here recalls Esther 1 and the private-property dimension of the sexuality of the king's mate even if, as stressed by Esther 1 and implicitly by the Song of Songs, that partnership is not exclusive or enduring.

107. Another clue that the Shulammite is not married.

sister (Gen 24.29, 50, 55, 60), as well as in the protection of her virginity (Gen 34.6–17; 2 Sam 13.20, 32). It should be noted that the term *šeyyᵉdubar-bah* in Cant 8.8b (NRSV: "to speak for") means, among other things, "to ask in marriage" (1 Sam 25.39), thus leading to a better understanding of the verse, "What shall we do for our sister the day she is asked in marriage?" The young woman's response comes in verse 10: if she is a wall to "Solomon," it is not on account of her alleged immaturity! Far from being a coy virgin, she depicts herself as physically and morally fully developed and sexually alert — so much so that, here as in the entire poem, she might be confused with a loose woman. But the appearances are deceptive. She is, indeed, a free woman, but her freedom consists in remaining unswervingly true to the one she loves. To all others, she looks like an unassailable fortress, but not so to her lover, with whom she "made peace" (8.10). To him she is faithful, even though outside matrimonial bonds and social imperatives. The Song sets itself at a distance from the patronizing praises to the loyal woman (see Deut 22.13–29, for example) or to the woman as wife and mother (see Proverbs 31). Here for once the woman is praised as lover, in contrast to antifeminist texts like Qoh 7.26, 28 and Prov 9.13; 21.9, 19; 27.15.

The chasm between the Canticle and those samples of wisdom literature must not be underestimated. Qoheleth and Proverbs, Deuteronomy (in part), and Ben Sira are revealing of a rather common attitude within wisdom literature that often expresses skepticism about women in general. Aarre Lauha is justified to speak of "ein üblicher Topos der Weisheitsliteratur" in the entire ancient Near East.[108] James Crenshaw writes, "The theme of the woman who ensnares men is standard in ancient Near Eastern wisdom."[109] One thinks of Sir 26.7 and 42.12–14, but other texts representing a very broad Jewish tradition could be quoted, including Mic 7.5 and 1 Tim 2.14–15. Such an image of women is congruent with a woman's status within a patriarchal culture (see Gen 19.8; Genesis 38; 2 Sam 13.1–22). The laws of Israel speak of women as men's property

---

108. Lauha, *Kohelet*, p. 140.
109. Crenshaw, *Ecclesiastes*, p. 146; cf. H. Gressmann, *AOT*, p. 37 and *ANET*, pp. 413, 420 (Egypt); *AOT*, p. 286 and *ANET*, p. 438 (Mesopotamia); Hesiod, *Works and Days* I.372.

(Exod 20.17; see also the double standard applied to partners in prostitution and to the ritual purity of males and females). The milieu of the sages does not constitute an exception.

Within that perspective, it seems legitimate to see in the Canticle a critique of the entire societal structure as mirrored in Israel's narrative, prescriptive, oracular, and sapiential literature, in short, in Israel's culture. With respect to Cant 8.6 ("love is strong as death"), one unmistakably remembers as a foil the text of Qoh 7.26, already mentioned, that says that woman is "bitter as death."[110] The two authors do not see things eye to eye! Andrew Harper rightly perceives that Cant 8.6 is reacting against marriage as

> a mere matter of contract, and the price given for the bride [as] a subject of pride, as it still is among Orientals. Immediately and inevitably this statement of the nature of love leads on to a condemnation of the common point of view in an arrow-like phrase, which having first transfixed the gorgeous and voluptuous Solomon, goes straight to the heart of the ordinary practice of the time.[111]

All this, no doubt, gives credence to Phyllis Trible's conclusion that, side by side with the conservative second temple period's pervasive culture, there was also a "counterculture" that is, she says, exemplified in the Song of Songs.[112]

Let us note, by the way, that the reading of the poem as a piece critical of the contemporary ethos does shed light on the recurring exhortation "do not stir up nor awaken love until it please" (2.7; 3.5; 8.4). Roland Murphy is correct when he stresses that "[l]ove is personified as a power, as in 8.6... Love has its own laws and is not to be achieved artificially."[113] But the question is which negotiations are in the background. I suggest that the allusion is to the economical dealings, including the customary exchange of (compensatory) presents between the two families of the betrothed youths. The ex-

---

110. Lauha, *Kohelet,* p. 140, translates, "bitterer als Tod." He adds that "Kohelet... sich auf die Frau überhaupt bezieht" (pace Hertzberg; Galling; Scott).
111. Harper, *The Song of Solomon,* p. 58.
112. Trible, s.v. "woman" in *IDBSup,* p. 965.
113. Murphy, *The Song of Songs,* p. 137.

hortation is thus an internal commentary to the declaration in 8.7 that one cannot buy love.[114]

At this point, remember that in the ancient Middle East, marriages were arranged independently of the consent or preferences of those primarily concerned. Although sexual attraction plays an important role in matchmaking, as shown in documents of the ancient Near East, it remains that not infrequently, if love is to emerge between spouses, it is *after* the wedding. Gen 24.67 is a case in point; on the contrary, the case of Jacob and Rachel is unusual: the young man is already living with his future father-in-law and has known the damsel for years before marrying her. Thus, the allusion in Cant 8.7 to those who would buy love is a biting irony. The affection between the lovers in the Song was negotiated or bought by no one. It is perhaps the precondition to their future marriage but certainly not the outcome of any preliminary family alliance.

Something else is important to remember: there is no law in the Bible or in early Judaism against polygamy. (It is permitted, e.g., in *mKet* and *mSanh* 2.4); it was practiced by some during the second temple period (cf. 11QTemple 56.17–19; CD 4.20–5.2.) As sociologically speaking marriage and lineage/inheritance are intimately intertwined, it is normal that in agrarian societies, both ancient and modern, the focus be set on reproduction. Now, there are different possibilities offered to an Israelite male to ensure his posterity. He can divorce a barren woman and remarry hopefully a fertile one. But the exclusive character of the mutual love in the Canticle bars such a possibility. The same applies to a second option, namely, polygamy (the wives are of the same status) or polycoity (with concubines).

The absence of such preoccupation with fecundity in a poem entirely dedicated to human love is by itself not only unusual but is critical for the understanding of the poem. It disentangles two aspects that were deemed inseparable, thus liberating the erotic from the economic. Indeed, that the Song considers true love as an exclusive relationship between a man and a woman opens a wide perspective. It is understandable in that respect that some read-

---

114. Rosenzweig (*The Star of Redemption*) has correctly seen in this objurgation a claim of the Shulammite upon her own love that must not become "a case of love in general" and not be "stirred up from outside."

ers, among them Karl Barth,[115] have drawn a parallel with the myth of Genesis 2–3 and its presentation of the first humans in a monogamous relationship. More recently, Trible writes,

> The first couple [of Genesis] lose their oneness through disobedience. Consequently, the woman's desire becomes the man's dominion. The second couple [of the Canticle] affirm their oneness through eroticism. Consequently, the man's desire becomes the woman's delight. Whatever else it may be, Canticles is a commentary on Genesis 2–3. Paradise Lost is Paradise Regained.[116]

Now, it is certainly true that the Song is a celebration of the *joy of living* and of the *joy of loving* from which is absent, mirabile dictu, all sense of culpability. The guilt felt by the original couple when they became conscious of their nudity is here transcended by the delight of the "second couple" before their *différence*. But if so, instead of seeing a complement to Genesis 2–3 in the Song, as do Barth and Trible, one should rather perceive the two texts as in mutual opposition.[117] It does not suffice to merely contrast Gen 3.16 (*tešuqatek,* "your [fem.] desire will be for your husband") and Cant 7.10 [7.11] (*tešuqato,* "his desire is for me [fem.]"). Rather than just a contrasted complement, there is in the Song opposition to the formulation of Genesis 3. The Canticle is iconoclastic; I will fully develop this point below. It is only in a "second reading" that, taking her distance from the two texts, the reader can reach a tertium quid of sorts and conclude that their intertextuality frees them from being mutually exclusive and tally them as in a *coincidentia oppositorum.*

---

115. Barth said that the Song of Songs constitutes, along with Genesis 2, a second "Magna Charta of humanity" (*Church Dogmatics* 3/2, pp. 293–94). Regarding the Canticle, he added, "Here the most natural interpretation might well prove to be the most profound."

116. Trible, "Depatriarchalizing in Biblical Interpretation," p. 47; *God and the Rhetoric of Sexuality,* pp. 144–45.

117. For Barth, the Canticle brings Genesis 2's thinking to its plenitude. The feminine voice there was only implicit; it becomes explicit in Cant 7.11 (*Church Dogmatics* 3/2, p. 294). For a contrary stance, see Goitein, who writes, "[The Shulammite] unties the bondage of the ancient curse [of Genesis 3], exactly as Isaiah invalidates the curse of 'I [God] shall institute hostility' between man and serpent by letting a suckling play over a viper's son [*sic*] (Isa 11.8)" ("The Song of Songs," p. 59). Brenner herself rightly states that "the attitudes and messages of the two texts are fundamentally different" (p. 83). A middle ground of sorts is taken by Landy who writes, "[T]he Song constitutes an inversion of the Genesis narrative . . . the Song is not merely a commentary on the garden of Eden, but a reenactment, almost a hallucination of it" (*Paradoxes of Paradise,* p. 183).

I should like to reflect further on this contrast. The anthropology in Genesis 2–3 is clearly envisaged by the J literary source from a theological point of view. The thesis is that the relationship between genders is upset when the relationship with God is damaged. But the Song of Songs takes a different stance. The relationship between man and woman is now seen from a de-moralized standpoint, which allows the poet to disentangle love from guilt and to celebrate Eros without religious restraint. True, the situation thus obtained is complex. For the poem does not just take its distance from J (and from many other trends in biblical literature); it takes a different course and from the same premise arrives at an opposite conclusion.

The outcome is highly paradoxical, for it can now be said that the Song of Songs is itself theological. Lys is correct when he comes to the same judgment regarding the literal and natural meaning of the book. The Canticle is theological by virtue of its demystification of the sexual, a realm that was everywhere mythologized in the ancient Near East, for such a fundamental domain in human existence could not remain foreign to universal religious reflection. The gender relations were everywhere thought of as reflecting a transcendent model and, consequently, as being each time a repetition of a *hieros gamos*. This is particularly exemplified in the New Year rites in Babylon (the Akitu festival). To the extent, precisely, that Mesopotamian hierogamy influenced the poet in the Canticle — at least in her vocabulary selection[118] — she adopted a subversive stance against its spirit. Carnal love is no mimetic duplication of a primordial divine archetype of copulation; hence, its justification and purpose are not to be found in its generative power. All utilitarianism, even religious, is here excluded.

---

118. This theory is advanced particularly by Schmökel, *Heilige Hochzeit und Hoheslied;* Meek, "The Song of Songs," pp. 98–148; Ringgren, *Das Hohelied;* see also Pope, *Song of Songs,* who identifies the source of inspiration as the Canaanite literature from Ugarit. These authors believe that the Song is in the canon of Scriptures on account of a confusion or a deliberate annexation. The poem would actually be a booklet about sacred hierogamy, a culminating point of the New Year celebration in Babylon, for example. "Pagan" manifestations did occur in Israel, and it is thus not surprising to find in its tradition such a text as we have here. It must have been well known in popular circles. In their view, it was eventually freed of its most shocking elements for Yahwist taste and reinterpreted allegorically as celebrating the love between God and his people. To this, one must retort that the hierogamic texts center on fecundity since the ritual's object is the renewal of the year and its abundance. One finds nothing of the sort in the Canticle. Moreover, no one explains how a text revised by bona fide Yahwists still does not contain any allusion to the God of Israel or to the *Heilsgeschichte.* We shall come back to this point later.

Fecundity is never contemplated in the Song as the justification of the coming together of the human couple. True, the theme of female fecundity is not absent from the third *waṣf* in Cant 7.1–9, where one notices the exalted description of the female belly and genitalia; they evoke in the lover images of mixed wine and heaps of wheat. But all that abundance is for the sexual partner to enjoy. It emphasizes "her ability to give new life to the one with whom she shares intimacy."[119] Othmar Keel calls attention to the absence of breasts in statues of old Canaanite goddesses, the whole emphasis being "on the reproductive organs."[120] The Canticle's insistence, on the contrary, on the beloved's breasts (e.g., in 7.8 [7.9]) is one more sign that here fecundity is not the most important aim in the courtship between the lovers. And this already is extraordinary and properly subversive. The Canticle, on that score, is in advance of its own time by some two thousand years.

Furthermore, as Keel rightly stresses,[121] the all-important question of the female's virginity remains untouched upon, another extraordinary feature then as it would be down to our own times in most cultures (in the Bible, see Deut 22.13–30, from which we learn that the "coat" soiled with the blood of the defloration was kept by the young woman's parents, something still customary today in some parts of the world, in Sicily or the Near East, for example). This conspicuous absence of the main motifs in all wedding celebrations cancels out the idea that the poem is the "legend" or the accompanying script for a seasonal renewal celebration or — another tenacious theory — for a marriage ceremony. As mentioned above, some scholars speak here of *waṣf*s of sorts, that is, poems in vogue among the nineteenth-century Syrian peasants during a seven-day wedding ceremony.[122] But this theory, which seemed quite promising at the end

119. Keel, *The Song*, p. 235. Frymer-Kensky (*In the Wake of the Goddesses*, p. 57) rightly insists on the absence in the Song of father and of child. At no point is the Shulammite celebrated or demeaned as "cosmic cunt" as was Inanna, she says.

120. Keel, *The Song*, p. 246.

121. Ibid., p. 182.

122. Syrian *waṣf*s from Qasim el-Chinn were collected by Wetzstein, German consul in Damascus in the nineteenth century ("Die syrische Dreschtafel"). These are responsively sung elated descriptions by the betrothed lovers. One finds in those *waṣf*s "the whole gamut of feelings...from boundless joy to bottomless depression," say RTF, *Le Cantique des Cantiques*, p. 421. The German critic Budde was much influenced by Wetzstein in his 1898 commentary on the Canticle. But an enthusiasm of this sort must be strongly tempered for a variety of reasons. Fox, for example (*Ancient Egyptian Love Songs*, p. 232),

of the nineteenth century, must be drastically corrected, if not altogether struck out. Even if we disregard the absence of a marriage motif in the Song, a confirmation of the Syrian structure has not been found in Palestine. Besides, the Song in its given form is too short for a ceremony lasting seven days (in Tobit, the ceremony lasts fourteen days; see 13.8; cf. 8.20; 10.8).

Not a wedding song, the Canticle celebrates the noncondoned loves between a man and a woman. Not inscribed within the framework of societal approval of the union between two families of the clan, the Song is a pamphlet, that is, an "off-limits" literary production. This is the main thesis of the present hermeneutical essay. One benefit of such a thesis is its impact upon the issue of unity of authorship. As a matter of fact, it would be difficult to imagine a group of lyrical authors uniting their poetic efforts with the unique and common purpose of defying social restrictions in a language that, throughout the Canticle, remains surprisingly consistent.[123]

The shunning of social propriety in the Song is also emphasized by Keel. He points out the extent to which the Song stands apart from ordinary social structures. The institution, he notes, is simply ignored here, and this explains the striking absence of a father and descendants, that is, of past and future.[124] To this we should add that institutions, familial or other, are what gives birth to rituals. It is thus interesting to observe that the critique of custom is accompanied by an antiritualistic slant in the Song's composition. Such revolutionary moves are evident, for instance, in Cant

---

remarks that there are *waṣfs* in Egyptian love songs, but *not* in a nuptial context. By contrast, in the nuptial songs, there are none! (A fact, let it be said in passing, that gives credence to our reading rather than to Wetzstein's or Budde's.) Furthermore, as Fuerst protests, Syrian customs from the nineteenth century hardly shed light on a situation prevailing in biblical times (see *The Books of Ruth*, p. 166).

123. Exploration into language is exploration into the sociology of knowledge. Davies writes, "Literature uses language and language is a social medium; literature must thus encode the symbols and values of society" (or, it should be added, oppose the latter while subverting the former). See Davies, "Reading Daniel Sociologically," p. 347. Fuerst speaks of "continuity in authorship, or at least in the presence of traditional thought-patterns and types of literary expression" (*The Books of Ruth*, p. 165), but Fuerst thinks that some of the songs in the Canticle may have been composed "as far back as the days of Solomon" (p. 167), an unwarranted and unnecessary assumption. C. Bloch, by contrast, sees the "incremental repetition of refrains and motifs...hav[ing] the effect of binding the lyrics to one another, reinforcing the impression of artistic design" (Bloch and Bloch, *The Song of Songs*, p. 18).

124. Keel, *Deine Blicke sind Tauben*, p. 13.

3.4 and 8.2. Those texts must be read against the background of
the widespread rule according to which a bride would be transferred
during the nuptial ceremony to her fiancé's family. The latter was
called *beyt-'ab,* meaning literally "father's house." In the Canticle,
however, the motif of this ritual passage to the "father's house"
is replaced by the unexpected invitation, made by the bride to her
fiancé, to enter her mother's house.[125] Thus the roles are doubly reversed: the invitation comes from the female, and the new kinship
will be with her mother! There is no mention in the Song of the
fathers of both personae, an omission which is all the more surprising since an unmarried girl was dependent on her father prior
to becoming dependent upon her husband.[126] The reason for such
a shift is that the poem sets out, not to celebrate a couple's assent
to a socially conventional wedding, but to sing love "undisciplined,"
that is, the innocence of the erotic bond, considered from outside of
its social environment and of its matrimonial institution.[127] Ricoeur
writes:

> Eros is not institutional. It is an offense to reduce it to a com-
> pact, or to conjugal duty... Eros's Law — which is not law
> anymore — is the reciprocity of gift. It is thus infrajuridical,
> parajuridical, suprajuridical. It belongs to the nature of its de-
> monism to threaten the institution — any institution, including
> marriage.[128]

Then, in a dense page, Ricoeur develops this point and shows its
subversive character:

> It is an enigma that sexuality remains incompatible with the
> human trilogy: language-tool-institution... Sexuality, it is true,
> mobilizes language; but it goes through it, upsets it, makes it

---

125. Gen 24.67 to a certain extent corresponds to the text of Canticle: Isaac takes
Rebekah into his late mother's tent.

126. See de Vaux, *Ancient Israel,* p. 26; see also RTF, *Le Cantique des Cantiques,*
p. 385. The mother is frequently mentioned in the Song: 1.6; 3.4; 6.9; 8.2, 5. Krinetzki (*Kommentar zum Hohenlied,* p. 178) contrasts this Canticle theme with Egyptian
parallels, where the mother serves as a useful intermediary in the development of the narrative. Here, the mother is "Urbild des Mädchens hinsichtlich seiner Weiblichkeit" (p. 257
n. 231).

127. Landy writes, "[T]he absence of the father is also that of the authoritative
patriarchal society outside the Song" ("The Song of Songs," p. 314).

128. Ricoeur, "Sexualité: la merveille, l'errance, l'énigme," p. 204.

sublime or silly, reduces it into fragments of murmur or invocation; language ceases to be mediation. Sexuality is Eros,
not logos...It is supra-instrumental as its instruments must
go unnoticed...Finally, whatever is said of its equilibrium in
marriage, Eros is noninstitutional.[129]

Let us return to the Shulammite's brothers, whose hostile role has
been pointed out. Their very presence in the poem is striking. Various males, such as father, husband, priest, prophet, judge, or city
elder, whose presence would be expected here are conspicuously absent. Others, when they come forth in the picture, only serve as foils.
These include the vain Solomon and the watchmen on the walls, who
do not hesitate to mistreat the maid as a loose woman or worse.
The brothers are no exception. All this no doubt contributes to a
setting in which the love between the maiden and the "shepherd"
is repeatedly upset and thwarted. He must flee; she cannot come to
him; when they get together, it is only for a short while; they are
granted no rest, no enduring peacefulness, no routine. They meet
by night, in spite of "city watchers," guardians of morality on the
search for delinquents; they must brave the matchmaking brothers
of the belle. Their caresses take place under the starry sky; their tryst
is in the woods, outside the city or village limits. There are here none
of those things that make a couple's life comfortable, not even a wedding bed. Incidentally, let us note that in Cant 5.5–6 (cf. 2.10), the
girl's bed *almost* becomes their love nest. At the last minute, this
piece of furniture that is habitual in a "regular" household — and
which, therefore, would have signified a compromise of sorts with
the societal — is rejected by the shepherd, who instead escapes (5.6;
see below p. 118).

---

129. Ibid., p. 208. Regarding the effect sexuality has on language, one thinks of the
pleonastic superfluity present in a sentence such as, "Let him kiss me with the kisses of
his mouth!" (Cant 1.2), for example. Also, see Gerleman (*Rut — Das Hohelied*, p. 120,
on Cant 2.6), "The drama of love according to the Canticle is indifferent to customs and
morality. What is more, the Song affirms with calm the priority of love over any social reg-
ulation and over any blood kinship (and even over any preliminary marriage condition)."
Heinevetter (*"Komm nun, mein Liebster"*) speaks of "Reglementierung der Liebe in der
Stadt," which he contrasts with the "Liebe in freier Natur" (for instance, p. 189). He
correctly sees in the Canticle "a sexuality unencumbered by moralization, a non-Oriental
role of the woman [under the influence of Hellenism], a return to the magic of nature"
(p. 217).

Irreverence and Defiance

The poet wrote about romance, about Eros that knows no law. If it is "an offense to reduce it to a compact, or to conjugal duty," as says Ricoeur, it is a graver offense to camouflage its dynamics, to tame its wildness, to allegorize its discourse.

Singing Eros is never innocent, especially where love is regulated by guardians of public morality — who happen here to belong to the male gender — for there is in every society a proper and improper way to deal with love.[130] An accepted and condoned language to speak of it exists and claims exclusivity. The genius and the attractive power of the Song of Songs consist in adopting a sanctioned language, while subverting it from within. One aspect of this kind of subversion, as we saw above, consists in "demetaphorizing" prophetic discourse and adverting it to the description of the nonfigurative love between the shepherd and the vineyard keeper.

Here is the touchstone for allegoresis: the metaphor at the text surface is taken as pointing out an alleged deeper metaphor, rather than a nonfigurative reality.[131] But this does not work for the Song of Songs. Since many passages of the Song obstinately resist allegorization, allegorizing must force them into prefabricated molds. About Cant 8.5, for example, where one finds the term ʿorar^etîka ("I awakened you," in the mouth of the Shulammite), the school not surprisingly deems the text wording "impossible." As Marvin Pope writes ironically, "The text as received would, in keeping with the allegory, represent Israel as arousing YHWH under the apple tree where His mother conceived and bore him!"[132] The allegorizing school must consequently alter the traditional Masoretic vocaliza-

---

130. True, women as much as men (and sometimes a great deal more than their male companions) are censorious of "cheap women." But the Weberian distinction between authority and power applies here. It is expected that a "feminist" document, as it were, would emphasize *patriarchal* guardianship of societal propriety.

131. One can also express the difference between metaphor (or what the "parable" represents in the NT) and allegory in the terms of Bultmann: "In my view the difference between the nature of similitudes and parables on the one hand and allegory on the other is most clearly formulated by saying that the former involve the transference of a judgment (derived from some neutral field) from one sphere to another which is under discussion. But allegory does not involve such a transference of judgment, but is concerned with disguising some situation in secret or fantastic forms so as to serve prophetic and other purposes" (*History of the Synoptic Traditions*, p. 198).

132. Pope, *Song of Songs*, p. 663.

tion of the text in order to put the discourse in the young man's mouth! In short, not only are the purpose and message of the Canticle badly missed, but its poetics becomes purely functional, with a term-by-term allegorical equivalence that in truth kills poetry.

In the present essay, I am proposing a reading that presupposes another understanding of the vehicle and the tenor. The Song of Songs is conveying a message; I mean, the Canticle is no aesthetical witty flirtation for the use of leisurely and somewhat blasé courtiers at the Jerusalem royal palace or elsewhere. Witty flirting uses a shallow and precious language, purposely remaining at a superficial level, where the unswerving mutual faithfulness of the lovers has no place because it is from a literary point of view uninteresting. The vehicle of witty flirting is pompous and florid; the tenor is characterized by an "unbearable lightness" that all but empties its content. In contrast, the Canticle's tenor is "loaded" with ultimate importance. Its object is the most fundamental, enduring, and existential human motivation. It is "love as strong as death." Its vehicle is no witty flirting, the very thought of which incensed Rabbi Aqiba. The poet defies religious and societal propriety with a song celebrating the sovereign freedom and ultimate triumph of Eros. Therefore, she daringly works the mine of prophetic language, especially as it deals with the relations of love between God and people. She, however, shifts from a "vertical axis" (divine-human, human-divine) to a "horizontal axis" (human-human).[133] It could perhaps be said that she shuns Agape and magnifies Eros, but more pointedly, as we will see below, she protests against the disembodiment of the one as if it had nothing to do with the other. On the contrary, she says, Eros is a reflection of Agape. "Carnal" love is also "spiritual" love. Eros is the "sacrament" of divine love (to use a liturgical language on the model of early Christianity's use of the Canticle).[134] Eros does not need justification in order to be. Eros is a "given" of creation. It is

---

133. Volz also insists on the "verticality" of the divine love in prophetic discourse. About Isa 49.15, for example, he writes, "That love is greater than motherly love, stronger than the strongest human experience, more intimate than the most intimate natural bond" (*Jüdische Eschatologie*, p. 102). The Song of Songs, in a contrasted parallelism, reminds us that "Mutterliebe" and "menschliche Empfindung" are not only worthy terms for the prophetic analogy but are the "sacraments" of the divine love. In other words, the manifestations of human love are the privileged loci where the miraculous intimacy between God and humans is experienced as habitual.

134. See above a couple of examples along that line, p. 5.

not acquired or bought (Cant 8.7). It is always already there. No one can live without love. To love is to live. Hence, no living is deprived of love, which means that no one is deprived of the care of God; no one is ignorant of God. John once exclaimed, "God is love."

Summary and Conclusion

Having arrived at the conclusion to this introduction, I return to my initial statement: the Song of Songs' textus receptus puts its readers in a highly paradoxical hermeneutical situation. In fact, we are dealing with a case standing out in biblical hermeneutics. To wit, the "trajectory" of the Canticle, its *Wirkungsgeschichte,* might be retraced as follows: first, the author of the Song defigurativizes, one might say, the language the prophets accredited for the description of the vertical relationship between Israel and God. Thus, in a fashion, the Song restores the language to its first, original, nonfigurative meaning and makes that language once again available for the horizontal description of the love between a man and a woman. It is on that plane that the poet's similes and metaphors — her refigurativation — must be read. A second step takes the author even further. In her poem she magnifies luxury, nature, courtship, eroticism, all things that prophets and sages found objectionable (one can compare, with Keel, Prov 7.8 and Cant 4.14 and 1.13; Isa 3.16 and Cant 4.9; Hos 4.13 and Cant 1.16–17).[135] In summary, language has come full circle, from the horizontal plane to the vertical through prophetic metaphorization and to horizontal again through poetic defigurativation and refigurativation.

The composer-writer is thus herself a reader; we as readers of the Canticle read the work of a reader:

---

135. One of my students, Phyllis Toback, wrote in a paper of December 1994, "Even in [the story on] the Garden of Eden there is not the same interest in lush description. The only other place I can think of which contains such description is in *the portrayal of the ornaments for the Tabernacle or the building of the Temple*" (my emphasis). Let us also note that while a strong tradition in Israel used nature to illustrate a particular teaching, the Canticle refers to nature as a signifying *subject.* Strikingly the divergent approaches to nature are again conspicuous in the way Jesus refers to animals and flowers in the field as teaching a lesson, while Qumran uses nature with a quasi-allegorical meaning (see 1QH 8).

> The writer's interlocutor, then, is the writer himself, but as reader of another text. The one who writes is the same as the one who reads. Since his interlocutor is a text, he himself is no more than a text rereading itself as it rewrites itself. The dialogical structure, therefore, appears only in light of the text elaborating itself as ambivalent in relation to another text.[136]

The dialogical quality of the work is eminent. True, the readers are never overtly addressed by the Canticle as "you," but the address is never covert either: the "you" is implied in the third person of the narrator.[137] Furthermore, the poet has multiplied dialogical devices: the lover speaks to the beloved; the beloved to the lover; they both speak to "companions," to "daughters of Jerusalem."[138] This way, the reader is not permitted to stay out as an onlooker (a Peeping Tom?). The reader is among the male friends, among the female chorus, and is exhorted not to precipitate the action ("do not stir love . . ."), not to hide the lover from the beloved, but to participate in their mutual quest. The reader is eminently *active*.

This concatenation of readings explains the successive transformations that occurred through the writing of the Song of Songs and through the reading of the resulting work, for historically there occurred one more veering move, unforeseen by the author. What the original composer of the Canticle wrote with a critical and liberating intent became forcibly reintegrated by puritan readers of the text into the habitual religious mold, itself a reflection of a conservative mentality. To the Eros of the poem was artificially substituted a disincarnate Agape, a noncarnal love on an alleged "spiritual" level. By such means, the subversive spirit of the work was tamed into a mystical hymn in which the male character is no longer a man

---

136. Kristeva, *Desire in Language*, pp. 86–87.

137. Note with Boyarin (*Intertextuality and the Reading of Midrash*, p. 121), after Emile Benveniste, that the first person also, which pervades the Canticle, presupposes a "you."

138. Hence the importance of the presence of secondary characters in the Song. As Ricoeur rightly stresses, "[Au] dialogue entre 'je' et 'tu' . . . il manque à ce face à face la relation au *tiers* qui paraît aussi primitive que la relation au toi. . . . [L]'autre figure seulement comme un *tu* reste tronquée. . . . [I]l manque [en particulier] la référence à l'institution même du langage, dans laquelle s'encadre la relation interpersonnelle du dialogue. En ce sens, le *il/elle* représente l'institution dans la mesure où celle-ci englobe tous les locuteurs d'une même langue naturelle" (*Le Juste*, p. 35, my emphasis). Such a flaw is absent in the Canticle.

and the female character is no longer a woman. Eros was steril-
ized! Jacques Winandy is possibly correct when he says that already
the final redactor, particularly by means of specific interpolations,
did mute the love song into a sapiential piece describing Solomon's
fondness for wisdom.[139] At any rate, the superscription "Song of
Solomon" is suspect, as we saw above. It may be that we must also
read, with Robert, Tournay, and Feuillet, the appendices of 8.13–
14 as identifying the Shulammite with Wisdom.[140] If so, they would
slant the general theme of the poem.

The case of the Canticle presents us, therefore, with a prime example of the problem posed by the canonization of documents. Such
a process was a conservative measure in more than one way. Meant
to save texts from oblivion and/or alteration, it was also the prod-
uct of powerful resistance against innovations and "unorthodox"
formulations. Canonization was also assimilation. Not only was a
selection made that excluded "unworthy" documents (which thus
became *separîm ḥiṣônîim* or "outside books"), but some of the traditions that entered the canon were from the start adorned with an
interpretation acceptable according to customary norms. The Song
of Songs is a case in point. Thus, albeit in the Bible we do also find
a subversive literature of protest against reactionary complacency at
the oppression of foreigners, women, and disfranchised classes of the
population, some of those documents found their way into the canon
only because they were reinterpreted by guardians of orthodoxy in a
sense with which they could agree![141]

The issue reveals its sharpest edge if we focus on the canonized status of the Canticle from the vantage point of its *function*.
Whereas, for instance, biblical narrative is "sacred story" because

---

139. Winandy, *Poème d'amour*. One thinks of the insightful judgment of Freud, *Moses
and Monotheism*, pp. 283–84: "[T]he text has been subjected to revisions which have
falsified it in the sense of their secret aims, have mutilated it and amplified it and have
even changed it into its reverse." This insight applied here to the textual transmission of
the Canticle should not induce us to imagine an "original pure text" that never existed.
Freud's critique here is pertinent when we assess the trajectory between authorial purpose
(inasmuch as it can be detected) and a certain interpretive distortion of such subversive
purpose into an apologue of established social values. So the issue is not the shift from
"pure" to "distorted" but from a literary genre to another at the antipode of the former.

140. RTF, *Le Cantique des Cantiques*, pp. 351–52. Keel (*The Song*, p. 39) says that
as "to [from] David" means "belonging to liturgy," so "to [from] Solomon" means
"belonging to the joys and the wisdom of life."

141. Already in the NT some metaphors of the Song were used in a way that facilitated
their allegorical interpretation; see John 3.29; Eph 5.22–23; Rev 18.23; 21.2, 9; 22.17.

of its threefold function as traditional, authoritative, and liturgical (through reenactment), the Song of Songs' literary genre hardly satisfies any of them (in contrast with Psalms, for example). The attribution of the Canticle to wisdom literature through the mention of Solomon in its title is due, I suggest, not just to the object of the poem but also to a certain uneasiness with the classification of it on the part of the canonizers. Not narrative or prophetic, psalmic or liturgical, prescriptive or apocalyptic, the Song of Songs would be accepted as sapiential.

But a methodological distinction must be made between different aspects of wisdom, primarily between its generic and its pragmatic sides. As a broadly encompassing reflection on a vast existential field, wisdom is interested in everything that pertains to human life (including love, needless to say). But not every formulation of such interest may be called generically wisdom. To characterize a given psalm as "sapiential" stresses a philosophical aspect of what is generically poetry. Conversely, an adage may be formulated in a way that makes it akin to the oracular, for example: "Riches and glory are with Me, that is, the durable goods and righteousness" (Prov 8.18). The mixing of genres is a well-known phenomenon in the Bible. It remains, however, that just as Prov 8.18 is generically no oracle, the Canticle is generically no wisdom.[142]

Precisely the same distinction between the pragmatic and the generic applies when we learn from Egyptian love songs that some of them claimed to be "proverbs" or "wisdom songs." Their ostensible purpose was to teach practical ways on the basis of religious principles. What this means is that occasionally Egyptian love songs reflected philosophical-religious stances that qualified them as "sapiential" but certainly did not transform them into treatises of ethics. They have merely been attracted within the magnetic field of wisdom, so to say.

Now, according to a principle already encountered in the realm of intertextuality, genre mixing entails interaction between charac-

---

142. It is only when interpreted allegorically that the Song of Songs may be seen as praising sapience or finding a niche in liturgy (being eventually attached to the festival of Passover in the synagogue or to the baptismal liturgy in the church). The same distinction applies between the Canticle and Psalms, for, as says Westermann, "a Psalm does not spring primarily from an idea, but from an event; in every Psalm something happens, and what happens is the first concern of exegesis" (*The Living Psalms*, p. 14).

teristics discretely attached to specific genres. In the Song of Songs, lyricism and sapience react upon one another. The poetic is permeated with a (countercultural) pedagogy, and the doctrine never loses its quality of celebrative hymn. This is no chance occurrence, for the paean to Eros belongs intrinsically to a message of protest, which indeed the poetic enhances to a perfect gem. In hindsight, no philosophical treaty on the bliss of Eros could rival the poetic vehicle of the Song of Songs.[143] No speculation evoking another world, it sings Eros's qualities from the inside, describing the beauty and the delight, the goodness and the pleasantness, the "desirability" and the wisdom, of the world of love. It is meant to open the eyes and all the senses, to give intelligence and create a feeling of immortality. Perversion and its accompanying curse occur only when love is sung in inns and taverns!

This message, however, offended. Its challenge to the societal sense of proprieties readily became an embarrassment to the Jewish and, later, to the Christian establishment. One possible response was, of course, to reject the poem wholesale. We learn from rabbinic literature that this radical solution was considered by some. An alternative approach was offered by Rabbi Aqiba, who saw in the Song the finest expression of divine and human revelation, for in celebrating love, it says who God is, who Israel is, and what the nature of their relationship is. To underscore this, Rabbi Aqiba saw in the Canticle a Midrash of Exodus, not that he "invented" that method ad hoc for this particular purpose, however. Nor was it supplied by him only in cases where the plain meaning would be judged intolerable, although, as is evident in Rabbi Aqiba's successors, allegory is a handy and effective means of clearing the scandal that results from literal reading. It seems that the more a love scene is daring, the more it demands to be interpreted mystically. Origen, we saw above, set forth the rule that "[t]he Scriptures cannot tell us anything unworthy of God, and so where something is unworthy of Him, it must be interpreted spiritually."[144] Thus, if something unworthy of

---

143. Koch writes, "[M]odern western society formulates its final truths in prose, whether in philosophical treatises or in church proclamations, and the poems are in our opinion only the symbolic expression of these. But the ancient Orientals were only able to express the profound questions about human existence in poetry" (*The Growth of the Biblical Tradition,* p. 97).

144. Daniélou, *Origène,* p. 149. He refers to the book by Prat, *Origène, le théologien,*

God is found in the Song, a figurative interpretation is automatically imposed.

The obvious flaw in such a principle is the apriority it presupposes as regards what is or is not "worthy of God." Furthermore, once this step is taken for saving a text from giving scandal, it becomes almost unavoidable that we require the author to exhibit his or her credentials. Not only must the work be cleared, but its creator must pass the censor's test of propriety. When the message becomes disquieting, an immediate reassurance can be conveyed by the identity of its author: nothing really offensive, nothing subversive, can come from Solomon, the king-administrator, the judge that splits the difference — or the child — in two equal shares, the patron of wisdom, that is, of moderation and dispassion (the greatest virtue as extolled also by all the philosophers of Greece and Rome). By contrast, no lengthy demonstration is needed to show that, in a patriarchal society, female authorship raises suspicion. With the help of elapsing time, it became easier to obliterate the authorial gender. Thus, the composer was reintegrated within the ranks of well-known, hence less threatening, literary guilds. Originally an erotic hymn composed by a faultfinding female, the poem was transformed into a collection of wisdom aphorisms, that is, precisely the opposite of a subversive piece. No strategy, I repeat, could be more efficient in this respect than to introduce the booklet with an attribution to the prince of apologue, Solomon. Such attribution was all the more fitting as the poem itself designates the female key character as "the Solomon-ess."[145] Solomon is, in the second temple period, the patron of scribalism. He is also in popular imagery the "macho" par excellence, whose harems testify to legendary masculine

---

p. 179. Yet let us note that there is no complacency toward eroticism in the Song. Even in the ravished and reciprocal descriptions of the anatomy of the opposite sex, "their eyes never pass over intimate parts of anatomy nor dwell on them (5.14; 7.2–3 [1–2])," says quite rightly Murphy (*The Song of Songs*, p. 102). This is why, moreover, the modern exegete must respect the ambivalence of the metaphors and must not smother it under a "clinical translation" (ibid., p. 102 n. 395).

145. In 1957, Goitein tried to pull back the Song of Songs to the Solomonic times with the argument that the Persian era — another alternative — was not an ideal one regarding women's status. On that, he is right, but my point of view stresses the satirical stance of the Song of Songs and thus renders possible a late date of composition (when such polemic was necessary), as is linguistically probable in the first place. From an ideological point of view, Müller ("Poesie und Magie in Cant 4:12–15," pp. 160–61) says that the setting is typical of an age of political irresponsibility. It manifests itself either in a skeptical despair (Qoheleth) or in hedonism (the Canticle).

prowess. Thus, by a stroke of the calamus, the female author of the Song of Songs was dispossessed, and her property passed to a scribe, that is, to a representative of conservatism! The substitution did not convince only prescientific readers; modern critics do not fundamentally question the reassignment of the Canticle. Moses Segal, for instance, speaks of a *school* of popular love poetry; Robert Pfeiffer, of a *professional* poet; and so forth.[146]

It suffices, however, to bypass the artificial superscription (Cant 1.1) in order for the plain meaning of the book to be unmistakable. In fact, the Solomon of the Canticle is reduced almost to the risible dimensions of Ahasuerus in the Book of Esther. Furthermore, the poet portrays the male family members and familiar guardians of women's chastity (the "brothers" and the "night watchers") as largely outdone by events over which they have lost control. The female lover is the active partner in scene after scene, as Queen Esther is the centerfold in the story that bears her name. But there is more. As signaled above, the rhetoric of the Song is even more irreligious than in the Book of Esther. One does not find here any moral exhortation, any reminder of the *Heilsgeschichte,* any national theme, any divine invocation (no prayer, not even a fast as in Esther), any allusion to the sacredness of Zion or the land. Carol Meyers summarizes this phenomenon in a brief, but accurate, judgment; the Song, she says, is "the most 'unbiblical' of all biblical books."[147]

The defiance by our author reaches its summit when sacrosanct formulas, oaths for example, are ironically parodied. Although here also asseverating phrases appear using the phraseology of conjurations, these are shockingly "secular," invoking wild animals of the field, a totally blasphemous utterance. The ancient world took it for granted that an oath is sworn in the name of the gods.[148] In this re-

---

146. Segal, "The Song of Songs"; Pfeiffer, *Introduction to the Old Testament.*

147. Meyers, *Discovering Eve,* p. 177. See also Alter, *The Art of Biblical Poetry,* p. 186: "It is only in the Song of Songs that there is no one giving instruction or exhortation, no leader or hierophant, no memorializer of national experience, but instead the voices of two lovers."

148. True, in the Bible, it happens that one swears an oath by someone, "You live and your *nepheš* lives!" (2 Sam 11.11) or by the *nepheš* of the king (1 Sam 17.55) or of a prophet (1 Sam 1.26), but never by an animal! The Targum piously translates, "by the Lord of Hosts and by the Strength of the land" (*CantTg* 2.7). Revealing a similar embarrassment with the formula in the Canticle, Fuerst "translates" it, "by the spirits and the goddesses of the field" (see Cant 2.7; 3.5; 8.4) with a note, "or 'by the gazelles and the stags'" (Fuerst, *The Books of Ruth,* p. 13). Noticing the absence of the formula in

spect, the homophony between the poet-selected terms, on the one hand, and genuinely religious expressions of oaths, on the other, must be emphasized. Cant 2.7 (repeated in 3.5; cf. 8.4; 5.8) says, "I adjure you, O daughters of Jerusalem, by the gazelles or the hinds of the field." The Hebrew has *bis*^{e}*ba'ôt 'ô be'ay*^{e}*lôt hassadeh*. Clearly, *seba'ôt* is the same word as in the well-known Yahwistic expression *YHWH seba'ôt*, except that the term there designates the "armies" in heaven (and on earth?). As to *'ay*^{e}*lôt*, it looks both morphologically and etymologically like *'él, 'elôah*, God. Finally, *sadeh* is in assonance with *šadday; 'ay*^{e}*lôt hassadeh* evokes *'él šadday*, "God Almighty."[149] The verb in the first hemistich, "to adjure, to charge under oath," is no less surprising at this place. The Koehler-Baumgartner dictionary indicates at *šb*^{c} (swear, etc.):

> The preposition *be* [by] after *šb*^{c} indicates the valuable thing that is pledged in case the oath is not kept: God swears by his life, Jer 51.14; Am 6.8 ... With *be* apposed to names the god who is witness and sponsor of the oath: *b'elohim* Gen 21.23; 1 Sam 10.15; Isa 65.16; Jer 5.7! ... Hifil [causative] with *be*, Gen 24.3 ["by YHWH, God of heaven and earth"]: 1 Kgs 2.42 ["by YHWH" under death penalty]: Neh 13.25 [after inflicting corporal punishments, Neh demands an oath by the name of God]; 2 Chr 36.13 ["by God"]; [and the texts of the Canticle that we are here discussing].[150]

One cannot imagine more solemn and performative oaths.

I claim that no one in the Israelite audience of the poem could have missed such transparent allusions. The formulation could not

---

8.4, Keel suggests that it is perhaps due to objections raised against oaths invoking other gods than YHWH (*The Song*, p. 264). Cf. also Heinevetter, *"Komm nun, mein Liebster,"* pp. 179–80. As expected, Heinevetter sees in this motif a polemic against city culture and a daring return to polytheistic metaphors (see below p. 84, n. 4).

149. The LXX has *en tais dunamesin kai en tais ischusesin tou agrou* (by the field power and sway); a comparable text is found in VLat. The *CantTg* has "by the lord of the armies and by the power of the Land of Israel." Furthermore, the word is read, according to the rule called *tartei mashma*, with the double meaning of "hosts" and "gazelles." Murphy (*The Song of Songs*, p. 137) says, "The reference to the gazelles and hinds seems to be an imitation of an invocation of God." In RTF, *Le Cantique des Cantiques*, p. 108: "The poet can evoke in this conjuration formula the divine name *'elohey sebaot*, 'God of the armies,' by avoiding to mention it explicitly and by only suggesting it through a play of words with *'ayelôt* and *sebaôt*." For Harper (*The Song of Solomon*, p. 58), true love must be as spontaneous as gazelles and goats.

150. KB, p. 943.

be construed as a slip of the tongue or as a mere poetic substitute for the customary religious content of an oath; besides, the occasion was neither casual nor perfunctory.[151] The shift was too substantial; it readily raised the issue of intent or, if you will, of tone. The answer to which is provided by the general atmosphere of the poem. Just as "Solomon" is used ironically in the book as if the author was putting out her tongue at the "establishment," so do the formulas of conjuration parody the religious language and make fun of it.[152] The same satiric spirit applies to most everything handled by the author; it applies, for instance, to the obvious imitation of Lev 26.12, "I became your God and you became my people," in Cant 2.16; 6.3; see also 7.10 [7.11], "My beloved is mine and I am his."[153]

The composer of the Canticle did not make it her business to praise the chaste love between Israel and her God or between Israel and Wisdom personified. There is not a single word about *ḥokmâ* in the Song. What the poet is doing here is shedding her societal chains; she is shouting her freedom from gender stereotypes. She is daringly mocking consecrated definitions and formulas. She is throwing in the faces of the "magistrates" her rejection of Agape devoid of Eros, by which they have castrated religion and mores. She is magnifying romance in terms that parody their theological jargon, terms that deceivingly echo things tamed and familiar, things annexed and made comfortable. The Song of Songs is carnivalesque: kings, bishops, magistrates, are caricatured and made fun of. Mikhail Bakhtin's description applies here,

> The laws, prohibitions and restrictions which determine the system and order of normal, i.e., non-carnival, life are for the period of carnival suspended; above all the hierarchical system and all the connected forms of fear, awe, piety, etiquette, etc. are suspended, i.e., everything that is determined by social-hierarchical inequality among people...[A] special

---

151. As says Krinetzki, calling attention to the great number of *hapax legomena* (*Das Hohe Lied*, p. 44), how could this be in a poem that is not folklore but a *Kunstdichtung?*

152. Another purpose consistent with the Song's general tone was to celebrate nature and the freedom of the animals of the field (see above, p. 56, n. 135).

153. See Deut 26.17–18; 29.12; Hos 2.4; Jer 7.23; 11.4; 24.7; 31.33; Ezek 34.30–31; 36.28; 37.23, 27. See also the fifth-century Egyptian document, the "Contract of Mibtahiah's Third Marriage:" "she is my wife and I am her husband from this day for ever" (*ANET*, p. 222).

carnival category goes into effect — the *free, familiar contact among people.* . . . With this is connected yet a [further] carnivalistic category — *profanation:* the carnivalistic blasphemies, a whole carnivalistic system of lowering of status and bringing down to earth, the carnivalistic obscenities connected with the reproductive power of the earth and the body, the carnivalistic *parodies of sacred texts and apophthegms,* etc.[154]

A categorical term fitting for the Canticle is Midrashic intertextuality. Every passage in the Canticle refers to well-known Israelite traditions and cannot be interpreted independently of them. While allegoresis claims to unveil the correspondence between signifiers and signifieds, the correspondence I indicate below is between texts and texts, that is, signifiers and signifiers, proper to Midrashic intertextuality.[155]

Now, the hermeneutical tally of signifier and signifier requires that they mutually read each other. In my exposition of the Canticle's intertextuality, it might appear that the reading is one-sided: from such or such prophetic text to the Song of Songs, not conversely. But the mutuality of signification is not ignored, and it cannot be. The very use of prophetic metaphors for the singing of the loves between a man and a woman reflects back upon the prophetic sources, shedding new light upon them. Prophets insisted upon the relationship between God and Israel as metaphorically nuptial.[156] No sooner has that metaphor traveled back down to characterize the relationship between a man and a woman in the Song that it ricochets again and human Eros is endowed with a vertical dimension that ennobles it and makes of it the prime translation in life of the *imago Dei.* When this is realized, it becomes clear why prophets chose *that* metaphor in the first place. If at times one detects some kind of irritation on the part of the poet with prophetic doomsday predictions,[157] it re-

---

154. Bakhtin, *Problems of Dostoevsky's Poetics,* p. 101 (my emphasis). As to "carnivalistic obscenities connected with the reproductive power of . . . the body," the Song of Songs does not qualify. Its language is, on the contrary, devoid of triviality. It is the allegorical interpretation of the Canticle that paradoxically gives credence to an obscene dimension of the poem!

155. Cf. Boyarin, *Intertextuality and the Reading of Midrash,* esp. pp. 110, 115.

156. The latest book on the subject is by the Dutch scholar Stienstra: *Yhwh Is the Husband of His People.*

157. Hos 2.4, for example; contrast with Cant 2.16; 6.3.

mains that, fundamentally, prophets and the poet build on the same foundation: God as love.[158] It is this back-and-forth movement between two generically unrelated semantic fields, God and love, that succeeds in transcending their mutual otherness and tallies them so closely as to change them from a trope to an equation, "God *is* love."[159]

The miracle is thus made commonplace. Where there is love, there is God. The habitual is easily equated with the trivial. But there is nothing trivial in the passion of God for his creation, which in turn structures the erotic experience itself. Were it not for the existence in the Bible of the Song of Songs, one could only say that the divine-human nuptial metaphor did reflect back upon the way the Israelites viewed marital relationships. Canticle broadens this to include all human relations of love, even outside (meaning here: before) marriage and without societal license. Thus, the reader is led to the conclusion that wherever there is love between two human beings, there is God. That is why the Song compares the maiden in love with the sacred chariot carrying the ark of the covenant! Again here it would be insufficient to attribute the simile to mere poetic whim.

Daringly, the Song describes the lovers as living in "Paradise Regained" so that Genesis 3 cannot any longer be read but intertextually.[160] Who could still read Gen 3.16 and forget about its reversal in Cant 7.10? This proceeding is not novel. Isaiah 7, for example, also rereads Genesis 2–3 and reverses the thrust of the original: Emmanuel will choose the good; his food will be abundant without effort, for the land's fertility will be miraculous on his and the remnant's behalf. Along the same line of thought, one finds the same reversal in Isaiah 11: peace again obtains between the serpent and the woman's progeny (q.v. Gen 3.15). "Eden" is not only behind us but also before us (Isa 11.9). Similarly Isa 26.19 is the reversal of Gen 3.19; 66.7–14 is the reversal of Gen 3.16. In similar fashion,

---

158. Or, at least, love as existential and relational revelation of God.

159. Kristeva (*La révolution du langage poétique*) speaks of "transposition" (of one system of signs to another) within the signifying process, thus potentially *altering* the former one. For this to happen, there must exist between the two systems a common *pulsionnel* (drive), although the latter may be daringly bringing together previously unrelated texts (all the more so when the drive can be identified with a standpoint marked by a different gender or sociological context).

160. See above Trible citation (p. 48).

Jeremiah rereads his Hosean model. The luxuriant vine of Israel in
Hos 10.1 has become, in Jer 2.21, a wild vine (cf. also Isa 5.1–7).
The dear olive tree of Israel in Hos 14.7 is destroyed in Jer 11.16.
For that matter, a prophet may reverse the sense of a previous oracle
of his own; Jeremiah 16 is reversed in chapter 33.

Thus, intertextuality makes the nonreligious Book of the Song of
Songs a profoundly theological text, indeed the key that unlocks
Torah, according to the rabbis of old, the revelation of revelations
according to the great Rabbi Aqiba. Such a conception is very much
akin to Jesus of Nazareth's declaration that the whole Torah is about
love.[161]

This concludes the introduction. In what follows, I will read the
Canticle in the traditional order of chapters and verses, although it
must be underscored that I have no intention of writing yet another
commentary on the Song. I will assay to show in a systematic way
the contesting character of the poem. My leading thread will be the
hermeneutical principle spelled out in this introduction. I will consistently shun any recourse to allegory, for the Canticle is no esoteric
or camouflaged vehicle of a cryptic message. According to allegory,
a dog is not a dog, and a cat is not a cat. Each term of the discourse
is only the bark around the tree, the shell around the pearl, the crust
around the ore of gold. In fact, allegory is essentially dualistic; it
projects upon the text its disdain for the flesh, prison for the soul.[162]
But, the Song of Songs cannot be read that way. Its allusive character is of another sort, found not beneath the letter but at the level
of its discourse. For, instead of bursting in pieces with the explosion
of a "spiritual" core it could not keep imprisoned, the letter on the
contrary is the whole message — but with a twist: the author uses
the language impregnated with religiosity of prophets, sages, priests,

---

161. Interestingly enough, Rabbi Aqiba is reported (by *Mek* on Exod 15.2) to have
read 'almot (maidens) in Cant 1.3 as 'al mut ([love] unto death). This spelling occurs in Ps
9.1 and 48.15, but Rabbi Aqiba was rather tallying this verse of the Song with Ps 44.22
[23], "for Your sake we are killed all the day." Rabbi Aqiba came to the love of Torah
through the love of a woman, and he died for the love of God's sake (*j. Berak* 9.5), thus
"transforming his execution into a consummation of erotic love for the beautiful King,"
as says Boyarin (*Intertextuality and the Reading of Midrash*, p. 127).

162. Regarding Origen's commentaries on the Song of Songs, distinguishing as they do
between carnal and spiritual love, Ricoeur writes, "It is undeniable that the initial hiatus
[between the two kinds of love] is uttered in the Platonic dualistic terms of intelligible and
sensible... [i.e., on] two ontological levels" (LaCocque and Ricoeur, *Thinking Biblically*,
chapter 9 on the Song of Songs).

psalmists...and she uses it with *irreverence*. The Song of Songs is full of biblical reminiscences; on this score, Robert, Tournay, and Feuillet were right, but they used a wrong hermeneutics because they misjudged the esprit in which the borrowing was made by the defiant writer. As for me here, I do not claim to come with an exhaustive list of the biblical allusions in the Canticle. I only want to submit to the reader's judgment an applied methodology for the interpretation of the Song. Today we have full-fledged exegetical instruments of flawless scholarship at our disposal,[163] and I do not feel the urge to add to those works yet another, which would probably fall short of its predecessors. The following is an exercise in biblical hermeneutics.

---

163. Mentioned in part in what precedes, especially in the footnotes. See the bibliography.

Chapter One

CANTICLE 1 (1.1–17)

Our inquiry starts with 1.4,[1] where the shepherd is addressed in the second person singular, then spoken of in the third person (as a king), then addressed again in the second person (a familiar process in Hebrew poetry; see Psalm 23):

> Draw me after you, let us make haste.
>   The king has brought me into his chambers.
> We will exult and rejoice in you;
>   we will extol your love more than wine;
>   rightly do they love you. (Cant 1.4 NRSV)

To recall, our purpose here is not to offer an exegesis of the verse but remarks on the intertextuality of the composition. Hence, whatever may be the possible alteration of the MT[2] or the relevance of using terms like "king," "chambers," and the like,[3] we must point out the vocabulary of this verse that is reminiscent of priestly and prophetic texts. Thus, "Draw me after you" recalls Jer 31.3: "I have loved you with an everlasting love; therefore with lovingkindness I have drawn you" (NKJV). Note the presence here and there of the

---

1. Let us note with Rosenzweig that the Song of Songs is the only biblical book to start with a comparative, "better than wine." This "better than" follows suit to the "very good" that ended the narrative on creation, he states (*The Star of Redemption*, p. 201). Such paralleling of Genesis and the Canticle is repeatedly echoed in this present essay.

2. Cf. the proposal of Gaster ("Canticles i.4," p. 195) to read, instead of *meyšarîm ahebuka: mimeyraš ahabeka; meyraš* in Ug. = *yn* = Aram. *meyrat* = Heb. *tiroš*. Hence, "We shall sing your love more than wine, your caresses more than new wine."

3. "The king" designates the youth; the word is a term of affection (Fox, *Ancient Egyptian Love Songs*, p. 98). The "chambers" are none else but the bowers where the lovers meet, but they are more sumptuous than the chambers of Solomon, continues Fox (cf. 1.6–7; 2.4; 3.7–11). The lovers meet in gardens, vineyards, orchards, etc. The girl herself may be compared to a garden.

same vocabulary of love (*ahab[â]*) and of the same setting of exultation. In Jeremiah, God is the speaker: in the Song, characteristically,
it is one of the two lovers. Elsewhere in Scripture, "the king" might
be in reference to God the Lord, but here it is the lover who is called
by that term of endearment. The "chambers" in the Song conjure
up the other contexts where the word *ḥeder* appears; it designates
an inner room, especially a bedroom (cf. here 3.4). It can allude
to royal chambers (cf. Judg 3.24; 15.1; 16.9, 12; Ps 105.30) or to
private apartments (Joel 2.16; Ezek 8.12). 1 Kgs 1.15 offers an interesting parallel with our text, as the term under consideration is
accompanied there too by the same verb "to go in" (and also by the
"gentilic" *haš-šunammît*, of which we shall have to say more below;
see pp. 144–46; cf. 7.1).

Speaking of "royal chambers" is not without evoking also other
chambers in the building next door to the palace, namely, the temple
(cf. 1 Kgs 6.15; 2 Chr 21.11; Neh 10.39 [the term is different
from *ḥeder* in these texts but designates the same reality]). Besides,
"exultation" and "rejoicing" in the Bible designate almost always
cultic responses to the proclamation of salvation.[4] A similar situation obtains with the mention of "remembrance" (NRSV: "extol"),
generally in celebration of the acts of YHWH (Isa 63.7; Ps 45.18;
71.16; 77.12). There is thus consistency in the rest of the verse when
we come across the mention of *meyšarîm*, which means normally the
"righteous ones" and thus parallels the ones who "delight in you,"
or "desire you" in the same verse, and is translated with respect to
the context by "rightly" (cf. Pss 58.2; 75.3). In verse 3, the subject
of the action of "desiring" was the *ᵃlamôt*, "the young women,"[5]
and the contrasted parallel thus drawn between "maidens" and "the
righteous ones" (so Pesh; see also KJV here) increases the sense of
irreverence.[6]

---

4. For *gîl*, see Isa 35.1–2; 49.13; Zech 9.9; etc.; for *samaḥ*, see Isa 9.2; 25.9; 46.10;
Zech 10.7; Pss 32.11; 40.17; 63.12, etc.

5. In the Jeremiah text, one finds "virgin Israel." Cf. here below p. 71, Boyarin's emphasis on that reversal of symbolism in the Canticle. The case, by the way, is not unique.
Suffice it to compare literal citations of Joel with their reversed meaning in Jonah: Joel
2.13 in Jonah 4.2; Joel 2.14 in Jonah 3.9; Joel 2.17 in Jonah 4.10–11; Joel 2.12,15 in
Jonah 3.15.

6. Jer 31.3–4 is used again in Cant 6.13 [7.1]. As will be obvious all along, some
traditional sayings haunt the poet, and she returns to them repeatedly.

The allusions to the temple continue in the following verse (1.5), where the "curtains of Solomon" recall the priestly usage of the term *curtains* in the Pentateuch designating the "curtains of the tabernacle" (cf. Exodus 26; 36). It may even be that blackness, which the maiden says is the color of her skin, and which also is what the name *Qedar* evokes (v. 5),[7] is called for by the curtains' color, as some of them at least were made of goat skin (Exod 26.7).[8] Here, as elsewhere in the poem (cf. below, pp. 137–43, for example), the maiden compares herself or her lover with sacred objects of Israel's worship. Later on in the Song, such allusions will become more and more daring and iconoclastic.

Strikingly, the proclamation of the maiden's dark skin is followed in the next verse by the exhortation to the other women not to look at her, as if she were disfigured by her blackness: "Don't look at me, for I am dark." In reality, we know that she is most beautiful, but her beauty is unconventional. According to societal standards a nice-looking woman should be fair (so are doubtlessly the "daughters of Jerusalem"). But she is rustic and ruddy like a peasant; it takes some time and some reflection for the maidens around to call her the fairest among women (5.9, perhaps ironically; 6.1, in all earnestness). Note that there is here perhaps an echo of the second temple rivalry between the bourgeoisie of Jerusalem and the commoners of the "province," as is illustrated, for instance, in Zech 12.7–9. In the Midrash, "daughters of Jerusalem" designates the Gentiles (see *Mek Exod* 15.2)! Daniel Boyarin, who quotes that Midrash, also calls attention to the reversal of symbolism in the Canticle (esp. 1.3), where the maidens are "desiring subjects and not…desired objects," and he astutely asks, "Does this render ancient Hebrew society any less patriarchal? I rather doubt it, but it does perhaps further unsettle 'literature' as a univocal reflection of other social practices."[9]

---

7. The root of *Qedar* means "to become dark," even "dirty," "turbid" (cf. Job 6.16; Jer 8.21; 14.2). Rashi adds that the tents of Qedar are dark because they "constantly lay exposed to the elements."

8. So RTF, *Le Cantique des Cantiques*, p. 71.

9. Boyarin, *Intertextuality and the Reading of Midrash*: see p. 118 (quotation of the *Mekhilta*), p. 123 (on the maidens), p. 158, n. 23 (the rhetorical question). More on Cant 1.5 below, in my discussion of Keel's commentary (p. 198).

There is between our text and Job 30.28, 30 a striking kinship. Job also sees his own skin becoming dark (*qodér*) but not through the action of the sun (*ḥammâ*). "My skin," he says, "became black" (*šaḥar*)! The lady's "blackness" is, besides, somewhat dialectical, especially when we turn to 6.10 where she is "like the white one" (*kallebanâ*), although also "like the hot one" (*kaḥammâ*), as she appears as the dawn of day (*šaḥar*).[10] Texts of Job were probably on the poet's mind, for the verb *šzp* appears again only in Job 20.9 and 28.7!

The fact that physical beauty is not foreign to the matter of being socially accepted is emphasized by the Song's pointing to the cause of the Shulammite's unconventionality: she has been rejected by her own family (v. 6a) and, expectedly, left by herself (v. 6b). If we transpose this idea into our modern world, a Gypsy woman may be of great beauty, but prejudice throws a veil upon her, as it were, so that we might see only an outcast. Regarding the Shulammite, it is important to realize that, more than ever, "beauty is in the eye of the beholder."[11] It is the mutual love between her and her lover that elevates her from the contempt of others to the stars; it is also because she is transcended by love (given and received) that the "daughters of Jerusalem" bow before her "fairness." (One finds the same literal inconsistency in 5.11: the shepherd's head is pure gold, and black like a raven!) The skin's shade plays here, evidently, but a little role. What is stressed is the transfiguration through love. That is why, playing on another keyboard, the maiden is shown to us as dispossessed in 1.6b, at the beginning of the "affair," and in full possession of herself at the end in 8.12, "my vineyard, my very own, is before me." In the words of Francis Landy, "she may... be her own through being his."[12] The critic adds, "the Pastoral accomplishes... a complete inversion of social values... if taken literally, [it] incites revolution."[13]

---

10. See Salvaneschi, *Cantico dei cantici*, pp. 46–48. Falk rightly emphasizes the whiteness of the moon. It is called *lebanâ* in the text, "the white one" (*Love Lyrics from the Bible*, p. 186).

11. The Targum reads the maiden's blackness very negatively: it came to her from sinning with the golden calf!

12. Landy, *Paradoxes of Paradise*, p. 156.

13. Ibid., pp. 144–45.

The black girl confesses, "my own vineyard I have not kept" (v. 6). The association of vineyard and Israel in Hebrew Scriptures does not need demonstration (one thinks of Isaiah 5; Psalm 80); suffice it to look at the allegorizing commentaries. Similarly, the verb *natar*, "to keep," say André Robert, Raymond Tournay, and André Feuillet, "is only used for speaking of God: He keeps his anger forever [*sic*]."[14] True, the verb is used in Arabic for the keeping of a vineyard, but what interests us here is the religious connotation of the word in Israel's usage. We will keep it in mind in our conclusion to this passage.

At this point, however, we must call attention to a "source text" of great importance for the Canticle, namely, Hosea 2. Here also vineyards are featured: the wild animals devour Israel's vineyards as a result of being abandoned by her husband, YHWH (v. 14).[15] This motif need be remembered when we turn to Cant 2.15 (the "little foxes"). After a while, however, the vineyards are restored by God's grace; he again becomes Israel's husband (Hos 2.16–19). So it is clear that the theme of the vineyards is metaphorically referring to loving relationships. Even for that matter the poetic choice of setting the dramatis personae in a pastoral environment and of depicting them as shepherd and vineyard keeper is not foreign to the author's general purpose of imitating the traditional metaphoric roles of God vis-à-vis his people Israel.

In Hosea 2 also the question is of lovers as in our Canticle text. But in the prophetic oracle, the lovers are idols and Baals with whom Gomer/Israel has committed adultery. In the Canticle, "lovers" are shepherds, companions of the male character in the poem. As a pendant to the theme of the "daughters of Jerusalem," they play a somewhat ambiguous role, until such time when they are invited to the feast of love (Cant 5.1). Meanwhile, maidens and young men are involved in the mutual quest of the two lovers, a theme that is central in the Song of Songs. Once again, Hosea 2 is a source text. One reads in verse 7 [v. 9]: "she [Israel] shall look for them [her lovers], but she shall not find [them]."

---

14. RTF, *Le Cantique des Cantiques*, p. 74; in fact, the texts, only some of which are cited by RTF, say that God does *not* keep anger forever.

15. *j. Erub* 3.9 has Israel ejaculating, "What made guard the vineyards? It is because of not keeping my own vineyard!"

As to the male hero in Cant, he is a shepherd, and the allusion is transparent to the very common divine metaphor in Scriptures emphasizing the loving care of God for his people (cf. Ezekiel 34; Isa 40.11; 49.9; 63.11; Jer 23.3; 31.10; Zech 9.16; 10.2–3; 11.1–17; 13.7–9). In the Song, "shepherd" is no more a figure designating God, but the term has retrieved its proper, that is, nonreligious, sense. In the process, it is no longer YHWH who "makes [her] lie down" in green pastures (Ps 23.2 and esp. Ezek 34.14–15), but the lover.

We will not leave Hosea or Ezekiel without noticing that YHWH is the one who takes the initiative from start to finish (cf. Hosea 2; Ezekiel 16). The reversal in the Canticle, where mostly the female holds the speech, is all the more striking. In short, the meaning of the expression here is the following: with an ironical twist, she says that, although assigned as keeper of many vineyards, she did not protect even hers. (Not surprisingly, another reading is preferred by *j. Erub* 3.9: "What made me guard the vineyards?" says Israel. "It is because of not keeping my own vineyard." [God doubled up, so to speak, his demands because Israel did not keep even the simple former ones. Or, not subjecting itself to God's rule, Israel will be submitted to nations.])

"At noon" when the day heat is the greatest, the shepherd gives rest to his flock (Cant 1:7), thus emulating God's ministering to those whom he keeps. In this respect Ps 121.6 comes to mind. But another text is still more relevant; it is found in Isa 49.10. Here, not only is the prophet alluding to the heat of the day and to the "smiting" sun, but he promises that God will lead his people to the springs of water, a motif that is well represented also in the Song of Songs. Now, however, it is not God who "leads in right paths" (Ps 23.3) but the shepherd-lover who makes sure that she is not lingering with her veil beside the flocks of his companions.

The rest of verse 7 is not clear. If we understand the verb *'atah* (as in Ps 104.2 or Ezek 24.17, 22) with the meaning "to cover" (with a veil, for instance), then Gen 38.14 comes to mind, although here the term for veil is different (*ṣa'îp*). Now, Gen 38.14 has taught us what a veiled woman may be taken for. For the free-spirited heroine of the Canticle (and the poet behind her), the risk to be mistaken as a prostitute is constant. Several texts hereafter will allude to this danger in still more dramatic terms (see, for instance, 5.7). Meanwhile, the veil here probably serves as an identity-hiding device from the shepherd's companions. The text thus stresses the clandestine nature of the couple's love.

But, after August F. von Gall (followed by G. R. Driver), the Koehler-Baumgartner dictionary (s.v.) distinguishes ʿatah II from ʿatah I, the former on the model of Arabic ʿata, "delousing"![16] This makes good sense both here in the Canticle and in Isa 22.17;[17] the similarity is still stronger with Jer 43.12 about Nebuchadnezzar's easy conquest of Egypt as predicted by Jeremiah. The Babylonian king will take over Egypt(ian booty) as one delouses one's garment! In Cant 1.7, the shepherdess would say in the same vein that if her lover is not to be found, she will have to pass her time delousing her garment (something like twiddling one's thumbs, says John A. Emerton).

Be that as it may, the similarity of vocabulary between the Song of Songs here and Jer 43.12 goes even further. Not only is the verb ʿatah used here (once) and there (twice), but also rʿh. Remembering that alliteration "is a persistent and elaborate feature of both Hebrew verse and prose,"[18] there is possible assonance between mṣrym (Egypt) of Jeremiah and bṣhrym (at noon) of the Canticle; again between bšlom (in peace) there and šlmh (lest?) here; perhaps even the word haggîdah in the Song ("tell"; v. 7a) is reminiscent of the term bigʿdo in Jeremiah. The image of delousing has been picked up by the poet in Song 1, where it would appear as tastelessly trivial were it not precisely for the parallel it draws with the prophetic metaphor.

Retrospectively, we can now return to the mention of blackness in verse 5 above. The defiance of the author, although not set on a racial plane, is quite strong. She is dark, for she works outdoors, and might be confused with a servant.[19] The contrast with city dwellers keeping their complexion fairer (the recurrent bᵉnôt yerûšalayim) is repeatedly made in the Song. The "daughters of Jerusalem" belong

---

16. Cf. von Gall, "Jeremias 43,12"; Driver, "Lice in the Old Testament."

17. See now Emerton, "Lice or a Veil" and his discussion of Isa 22.17, as well as the other texts with ʿatah II, including Cant 1.7.

18. In the words of Landy, "The Song of Songs," p. 307; or, as says Roman Jakobson, "Words similar in sound are drawn together in meaning" ("Linguistics and Poetics," p. 43).

19. Cf. Lys, Le plus beau chant, p. 71. Also, cf. GenR 18.5, "When Nehemiah came up from the land of exile [to Zion, he found that] the women's faces had been blackened by the sun, so that [their husbands] had gone and married strange wives."

with the guardians of the city, with the brothers of the belle, and with all pillars of society who have a low tolerance for what they do not consider as customary or proper. Landy rightly says that the Shulammite is "the living presence of the irresponsible, untamed part of the daughters of Jerusalem."[20] These are jealous of their own purity, and "to the pure all things are impure."[21]

The kinship with religious texts like Isa 49.10, however, offers still another direction to our reflection. God protects his own from the smiting sun (see also Jonah 4), but the Shulammite precisely is blackened by the sun. It is understandable, therefore, that she would become suspect of displaying a sign of divine displeasure. If so, she proudly meets the challenge with boasting about the darkness of her skin. Defiantly, she makes a long nose at those who thought of punishing her by making her the keeper of vineyards. Her own vineyard she has not kept! By sending their sister out to the fields, the brothers gave her motive and opportunity to lead a free existence.

One will note the superficiality of societal judgment against the Shulammite. The darkness of her skin stirs among those of her own kin reprobation and a banishment of sorts. She is chided by opinionated people whose feelings are a mixture of social propriety and religious superstition. It is indeed against that background of pettiness that the poem unfolds as a song to liberty. Along that same line, it is striking that verse 5 starts with the root *šḥr* and ends with *šlm,* a combination that corresponds to the composite divine name "Gracious and Nice" (*šḥr-w-šlm*) in Ugarit. For Daniel Lys, the Song demythologizes this Canaanite expression: the Shulammite is *šeḥorâ* (black), not *šaḥar;* the shepherd is *šelômôh* (Solomon), not *šalim.* Here again, the iconoclastic quality of the poem will not be missed.

Cant 1.7 closely resembles a Pentateuchal text, of which it is almost a pastiche: Gen 37.16. In the Genesis text, one reads, *haggîdah-na' lî eyphô hém rô'îm* ("Please, tell me where they are pasturing"); in the Song, *haggîdah lî . . . eykah tir^e'eh* ("Tell me where you are pasturing"), and the missing *na'* (please) of the former text is replaced by the periphrasis *še'ah^{a}bah nap^{e}šî* ("whom my soul has loved"; cf. 1 Sam 20.17). In the Genesis text, Joseph is speaking to a

---

20. Ibid., p. 144.
21. Ibid., p. 146.

man he met when on his way to join his brothers. He addresses him
with the paragogic form *haggîdah,* "tell!" The author of the Song
puts the same words in the mouth of the maiden with the same form
of the imperative. The imitation of Genesis is striking. Simply, the
maiden has taken the place of the patriarch! She speaks as he did,
and she, like Joseph, hopes that her wandering is over (see especially
the Versions to the Canticle text). The motif of the veil (if such is the
case here) would not be without reminding one of the famous robe
of Joseph. But here, from the pride of the patriarch the vector has
rather shifted to the veil of Tamar in the infamous scene with Judah
(see Genesis 38).[22] In the reuse by the Canticle, neither Joseph nor
Judah comes out very admirably!

As regards 1.8, it may well be that Michael Fox is right.[23] The
boy, he says, is teasing the maiden, in turn implying that she should
know where he "grazes and causes to lie down." We have here a
wordplay based on the very ambiguity of the terms used, but she initiated that type of double entendre in her inquiry, leaving the verbs in
suspension in verse 7. That she knows the answer to her own question is shown, for example, in 2.16. But there is more. The plural
mišᵉkenôt (tents) appears some nineteen times in the Hebrew Bible
and often designates the temple or the land (Pss 43.3; 46.5; 84.2;
132.5, 7; Isa 54.2). In the Song, the erotic has taken over the sacral.

The irreverence of the author is perhaps more dramatic or graphic
in the following verse, which compares the belle with a mare in
Pharaoh's cavalry. The simile is familiar in Egyptian love songs,[24]
but unexpected in Israel! The motif of the exodus from Egypt with
its concomitant humiliation of the Egyptians is central in Israel's
theological reflection; but now we are invited to admire the proud
majesty of Pharaoh's pursuing chariots—unless the prevailing irony
of the Canticle be again at work here. Then one might, for instance,

---

22. The *TOB* combines the two meanings (wandering and veiled) and renders the expression, "pour que je n'aie pas l'air d'une coureuse" ("so that I don't look like a slut,
a 'runner' after men"). In a personal communication, Landy evokes "an immensely ram-
ified intertextual web" developing around the story of Tamar, in Genesis 19, Judges 14,
2 Samuel 13, Ruth, and "most obviously [Cant] 7.8."

23. Fox, *The Song of Songs and Ancient Egyptian Love Songs,* p. 101.

24. See *ANET,* p. 469, song "f" (from papyrus Beatty I): "Would that thou wouldst
come (to the sister speedily) like a horse of the king." Here, as fitting the context, the lover
is compared to a "steed...picked from a thousand." In the Canticle, however, the horse
has become a mare as it represents the Shulammite.

see in the present image a very unconventional and unsettling depiction of a mare set amidst Pharaoh's chariots: "The female horse set loose among the stallions of the chariotry does violence to the military effectiveness of the charioteers," says Carol Meyers.[25]

Verse 10 might be seen as just another ejaculation about the beauty of the maiden, but a philological phenomenon is rather arresting. What is generally translated by "comely" is in Hebrew a verb that appears in this *pa'el* form only here and in Isa 52.7 ("How comely are the feet of the messenger"). True, the parallel may be accidental, but interestingly the prophetic metaphor provoked the same kind of reaction as we saw arising about the Canticle similes. Christopher R. North, on the Isaianic text writes, "but feet are hardly beautiful."[26] In fact, in one case as in the other, the qualification does not refer to the object itself (neck, feet, breasts) but is descriptive of the impression/feeling the object stirs in its beholder.[27]

The cohortative form *na'*a*seh*, "we shall make" (v. 11), in the first person plural has struck as strangely familiar all students of the Bible, at least since medieval times. Rashi drew a parallel with Gen 1.26 ("let us make man"). Perhaps in 1.11 as well as in Gen 1.26 the backdrop notion is of *selem* (image). The image of the maiden will be adorned with gold and silver — a far cry from the priestly narrative celebrating the human being created in the image of God. Still within the priestly source and, for that matter, anywhere else in the Bible, the only other place that contains such description as we have here of jewels, gold, and silver is the portrayal of the ornaments for the tabernacle or the building of the temple (Exodus 25–27; 1 Kings

---

25. Meyers, "Gender Imagery," p. 217. On the plural *merkabot* and its association with the divine glory on the model of Ezekiel 1 and 10, cf. 4QShirShabb, fragments 1.20–22:

> line 2 ("the seat of the throne of his kingship")
> lines 3, 5 ("the chariots of his glory")
> lines 4, 11 ("chariots"); cf. col. V li. 6.
> line 8 ("the image of the throne-chariot")

Cf. also col. II lines 4, 5, 6.

26. North, *The Second Isaiah*, p. 221.

27. Perhaps due to their very audacity, the metaphors in the Canticle serve as a magnifying glass through which to look at the metaphors in Scripture in general. When we read in Israel's hymns or oracles that God is king, father, shepherd, the stress is, not on the divine gender, but on the kind of awe the divine presence inspires in the Israelite. God as king means that God reigns, so exactly the same message might be conveyed by the proclamation that God is queen (as was said in Babylon of Ishtar), and God is father does not say more or less than God is mother (cf. Isa 49.15; 54.6).

6–7). Such a tally should not surprise us here more than it does in Ezek 16.9–14, for instance. Note that there too the young woman is adorned in splendid array (vv. 11–12). True, in both texts, one could hesitate between association with the temple riches and with the dress of a princess (cf. Ps 45.15), but Moshe Greenberg is certainly correct when he says that "much of the cloth of the Tabernacle consisted of such work (Exod 26.36; 27.16; 28.39, etc.)."[28]

Starting with 1.12, the discourse becomes again the maiden's. The New Revised Standard Version translates the text, "While the king was on his couch," a rendering which jibes with the Versions and with the traditional Jewish understanding. One could also think of the king "reclining" (at the table). But Robert, Tournay, and Feuillet call attention to a parallel in 2 Kgs 23.5, where the word *mesib* designates "the surroundings" of Jerusalem. Then its association with perfumes makes us think of the precincts of the temple in full activity. Identifying either one of the lovers with the king (see above 1.4 and below 7.5 [6]; cf. language of 5.10–16) or with the temple (already in 1.4–5) is a recurrent feature in the Song. Almost each time this occurs, though, the Versions and modern scholars feel ill at ease, for obvious reasons. It is not without surprise and even discomfort that the reader finds the shrine transformed into a tryst of love and the sacred nard into "the scent of a woman" (4.13–14), while in 1.13 the henna (or "myrrh") is counted among the charms of the man (3.6; 4.6, 14; 5.1, 5, 13).[29]

The scene continues in verse 13, not with an elevated description of the divine presence in its abode, but with the shepherd (*dôdî*) lying, like a sachet of myrrh, between the breasts (*šaday*) of his beloved, where he shall spend the night! With the exception of two other texts, one of which is enshrined in another risqué chapter of the Bible, namely, Ezekiel 23 (v. 21), the word *breasts* never appears in the form *šdy* ("the breasts of," read: *šaday*), which could be confused by alliteration with "Shadday," the Almighty![30] In the Canticle, on the contrary, that consonantal spelling occurs in 1.13; 8.1; and 8.10. Ezekiel 23.21 imposes itself as a parallel to our verse. Strikingly, Ezekiel puts *šadîm* in an alternation with another word for the

28. Greenberg, *Ezekiel 1–20*, p. 278. Cf. Zimmerli, *Ezekiel,* vol. 1, pp. 340–41.
29. More on this verse below, in my discussion of Keel's book (p. 195).
30. The other occurrence, an "innocuous" one, is Ps 22.10.

same body part, *daddîm,* a word very close to the recurrent *dôdîm* in the Song of Songs. Besides, it is interesting that etymologically the divine name Shadday, "the mountainous," is *tdw/tdy* (breast), in Arabic *tdy.*[31]

Not surprisingly at this point, Hosea 2 is again in the background. In verse 2 [4], the prophet had said of his unfaithful wife that she wore "her adultery between her breasts," alluding probably to an outfit or ornament indicating harlotry. In the Canticle, as among prophets like Hosea and Ezekiel, there is a contrast between the attire that the girl dons upon herself, which is construed, truly or wrongly, as of a harlot, and the clothing of the (divine) groom or even his intimate presence in the form of a sachet of myrrh, which is a priestly ingredient par excellence (Exod 30.23; Matt 2.11; John 19.39).

In a swift exchange of comparable terms of endearment, the man is speaking in Cant 1.15, and the woman in 1.16–17. Her eyes are (as) doves, and thus the allusion to Ps 68.13 [14] that started verse 11 above is complete. Ps 68.13 [14] reads (about the spoils after a great victory), "the wings of a dove covered with silver, its pinions with green gold" (NRSV). From the psalm to the Canticle, the poet went a long way! Besides, the text of Isa 3.16–24, already mentioned (p. 56), serves as a model for this verse. According to the convincing argument of Othmar Keel, the glances of the maiden are doves, meaning "messengers of love."[32]

The shepherd also is most handsome, especially, it seems, when evoked lying in bed. The image is for the author occasion to be both specific and allusive. The couple, as I insisted in the introduction, do not constitute a "household." Like foxes, they have only holes to hide themselves. The material their "bed" is made of — like the "fruit of majestic trees, branches of palm trees, boughs of leafy trees, and willows of the brook" for the confection of the *sukkâ* (Lev 23.40) — provides them with a roof above their heads that is but cedars and cypresses (v. 17; more on this topic below p. 81). We are a far cry from a wedding ceremony. The Canticle celebrates loves that are "sans toit ni loi" (without roof or rule). For this purpose, there

31. Cf. F. M. Cross, *Canaanite Myth and Hebrew Epic,* p. 55; Cross adduces the example of the American Grand Teton range (p. 55 n. 44).
32. Keel, *The Song,* p. 71.

was no better way than to parody established mores and propriety, law and order, in a carnival-like fashion (see p. 64).

The text of verse 16 uses the term *ra'anâ*, a feminine form of *r'nn*, that appears some eighteen times in the MT and mostly in the polemical expression "under all green trees" (Deut 12.2; 1 Kgs 14.23; 2 Kgs 16.4; 17.10; Isa 57.5; Jer 2.20; 3.6, 13; 17.2; Ezek 6.13; 2 Chr 28.4). There are, however, some positive uses of the term in the Psalms (52.10; 92.11, 15) and in Hos 14.9 and Jer 17.8. Whether in positive or negative contexts, *ra'anan* is uniformly figurative, and its contexts are uniformly religious. Cant 1.16 is the only instance of a nonreligious use of the word.[33]

In the last verse of chapter 1 (v. 17) the temple of Jerusalem is again very much in the background. There is no inconsistency in the shift from the image of verse 16 to the one of verse 17. The lovers have no roof above their heads, and their bed is made of moss, but this pastoral setting is daringly a *bayit*, a common word for the temple in the Bible. In our verse, the term appears strangely in the plural. Ariel Bloch is surely right when he sees in "our houses" the places where the lovers meet.[34] Like the shrine in Zion, *bateynu* are made with *'arazîm* and *berôtîm*, "cedar and cypress." These two tree essences are replaced later on in the Canticle by "Lebanon," the place of their most characteristic provenance. They are the material used by Solomon for the building of the temple-palace, so "Lebanon" becomes a common metaphor for the temple in Jerusalem (1 Kgs 5.8 [22], 10 [24]; 6.15, 34; 2 Kgs 19.23=Isa 37.24; Jer 22.6–7, 13; Ezek 17.3, 22–23; the Targum on our text has "Lebanon and incense"). As to the cedars, they are called "of God" in Ps 80.10 [11] and "trees of YHWH . . . that he planted" in Ps 104.16.

Upon our arrival at the end of chapter 1 of the Song of Songs, a conclusion is fitting. First, strikingly, a large part of the discourse is set in the female's mouth. She is certainly the centerfold. She declares herself free from the constraints of fashion and custom. Clearly, her love for the shepherd is all that counts for her. The irritation of her own siblings has proved to be counterproductive for them but rich in new opportunities for her to exercise her liberty.

---

33. More on this verse below, in my discussion of Keel's commentary (p. 198).
34. Bloch and Bloch, *The Song of Songs*, p. 147.

The female expresses that much in a language that deserves our utmost attention, for the imagery is permeated with "biblical" reminiscences. The poet uses the well-known language of prophets — their talk of shepherding, of leading the flock to shaded and watered spots, of protection against the "smiting" sun, and the central event of Israel's escape from Egypt. And the poet also uses the priestly descriptions of the temple in Jerusalem. But now, the shepherd is just that, a shepherd; the nard is a woman's perfume; and the temple chambers are trees of the forest extending their branches to cover clandestine loves!

Canticle 1 has thus accumulated cameos and sketches with the purpose of creating the atmosphere that prevails in the Song. Poetic creativity is here — at the image of the lovers, heroes of the poem — almost too rich, unbridled, and unruly. Already at the rhetoric level, there is some kind of derision of the chastened language of contemporary scribes.

Chapter Two

CANTICLE 2 (2.1–17)

⟨decorative divider⟩

Canticle 2.1–7

The terms *ḥᵃbaṣelet* and *šarôn* of Cant 2.1a appear in Isa 35.1–2!
Let us note also there the verb *yesusûm* that the Canticle trans-
poses through alliteration into *šôšannâ*. The eighth-century prophet
was speaking of the blossoming of the desert ("[They] shall be glad
... The desert... shall blossom as the rose... The glory of Lebanon
shall be given to it, the majesty of Carmel and Sharon"). The image
in the Canticle is completed with the mention of a *šôšannâ* and of
ᵃmaqîm (valleys), both stressing the concavity of the figure, for the
šôšannâ is a large flower in form of a cup.[1] In fact, Othmar Keel insists that the flower in question is the (large) water lily or lotus, in
the shape of which, he emphasizes, was the brim of the molten sea
in the temple (1 Kgs 7.26). Keel then continues, "[This matter] de-
termines how one envisions the young woman in the Song," and he
rejects the patriarchal imagination of the woman here as "a chaste
and modest maiden" displaying "the purity of the lily."[2] One will
contrast this healthy reaction with what these images represent for
Giuseppe Ricciotti and Paul Joüon. Ricciotti understands that the
heroine "behaves as a virtuous wife," for, adds Joüon, she is but a
little graceful flower![3] There is nothing particularly coy in advertising
one's concavity and curves.

The discourse is in the man's mouth. He first quotes her saying, "I
am a rose of Sharon, a lily of the valleys" (NRSV). He then continues

---

1. Dalman, *Arbeit und Sitte in Palästina*, vol. 1, pp. 351–60.
2. Keel, *The Song*, p. 78.
3. Ricciotti, *Il Cantico dei Cantici*; Joüon, *Le Cantique des Cantiques*.

by starkly contrasting his beloved with the other women (*habbanôt;* v. 2). The word *banôt* has been encountered in 1.5, where it designated the "daughters of Jerusalem." The latter are certainly included by implication among those females that are just thorns in comparison with the "lily of Sharon." Although there exists between the Shulammite and the *banôt* a complicity of sorts through their belonging to the same gender, the similarity stops there. The other *banôt* are "of Jerusalem." They have no share in the Shulammite's freedom. They judge and condemn, but it is out of bitterness; they are only thorns, not flowers.[4]

That which, in the following verses (vv. 3–4), is said about the shepherd among the other young men amounts to the same conclusion of incomparability. He is the only fruit tree in the forest. To say that his virility is alluded to here is a probable but insufficient proposition. He is unique — at least to her and to her palate (v. 3).

Cant 2.3b appears to be innocent enough. But the *ṣēl,* "the shade," designates the protection granted by YHWH in religious vocabulary (cf. Pss 17.8; 36.8; 57.2; 63.8; Isa 49.2; 51.16). More striking for us here is the text of Hos 4.13, speaking negatively, as usual among the prophets, of the shade of trees in which Israelites offer sacrifices. A confirmation of the allusive meaning of the image is found in the fact that an apple tree provides actually a very poor shadow against the heat of a summer day. The metaphor is thus stretched and disregards reality. But if there is protection of the belle, it now comes from the paramour ("With great delight I sat in his shadow"). Delight is no longer in the cultivation of idols (called *ḥamûdîm,* literally "delights" in Isa 44.9; see the same idea in the use of the word *ʾᵃšîšôt* in 2.5). In hindsight, the allusive language in 2.3b, combining as it does (YHWH's) protection and delight (of idols), explains why the traditional Jewish reading saw in 2.2–3a the mutual incomparability of Israel in God's eyes and of God in Israel's. Mutually incomparable are now the shepherd and his beloved.

---

4. Heinevetter delays, expectedly, over this motif. The "daughters of Jerusalem" are the Shulammite's antipode. They represent the city, where one helplessly errs about (3.1–5) and is submitted to its violence. The city is no home; home is where there is love (*"Komm nun, mein Liebster,"* p. 182): "The experiences made in the garden of love encompass the fight with societal reality" (p. 185).

The iconoclasm continues, verse 4, with the belle being brought to the house, not of YHWH, but of wine, a symbol of Eros in the Song (1.2, 4; 4.20; 5.1; 7.10; 8.2). There, she does not put herself under the protection (or the shadow) of God's wing (Ps 63.7; cf. Pss 17.8; 36.7; 61.4), but the shepherd spreads upon her his *degel*, "banner."[5] Apart from here, the noun appears exclusively in P (Num 1.52; 2.2–3, 10, 17–18, 25, 34; 10.14, 18, 22, 25), where it designates standards of the Israelite camp around the tabernacle! Equally striking is the text of Ps 20.5 [6], where the same word in verbal form is used: "In the name of our God, we shall set up our banners." The shift in meaning when we pass to the Canticle needs no comment!

Hos 3.1 is the source text for the following verse (v. 5). Like in Hosea, the Canticle expounds *'ahᵃbâ*. The prophet was commissioned to love a "woman who is the beloved of another," for his mismatched marriage reflected the "love of YHWH" for his people, a people adulterous, engaged in full-fledged idolatry with divinities that are *'ôhᵃbey 'ᵃšîšey/'ᵃšîšôt 'ᵃnabîm* (lovers of cakes of raisins; Keel says that "forms may have been used to impress the image of the goddess on them").[6] This will make Ephraim sick (*ḥolî*), Hos 5.13 adds, and Cant 2.5 picks up the idea. In Hosea, however, it is an evil sickness, the outcome of ethical and religious backsliding, while the belle's illness in the Song becomes her pride and is a flame carefully made up. So, if hers is also a sickness of love, it is a far cry from what the prophet spoke about, and it will not be healed by any king of the Assyrians!

The sick must be sustained, hence the use of the verb *smk* in this verse. A look into Ps 3.5 [6] ("The LORD sustains me"); 51.12 [13] ("Sustain me!"); or 145.14 ("The LORD sustains all who are falling") suffices to mark the distance with the borrowing reuse.

I am not sure whether Cant 2.6 is one more allusion to theological discourse. If it is, the embarrassment of traditional Jewish interpretation shows the way. Proceeding from the understanding of God's left hand/arm as indicative of his attribute of justice versus his right hand, the attribute of compassion, Middle Ages commenta-

---

5. Surprisingly in the New Revised Standard Version, "his intention"! The root *dgl* is found again in 5.10 and 6.4, 10.

6. Keel, *The Song*, p. 85.

tors, hesitantly it is true, see the same contrast expressed here. But, at any rate, the Shulammite celebrates the exclusive loving attention of her lover. On that score, his affection is superior to God's, for the shepherd's "left hand" and "his right hand" cajole and embrace!

The defiant refrain in verse 7, the adjuration by the gazelles or the wild does, has been dealt with in the introduction above (see p. 63). The oath formula, normally with the name of God, has been here twisted into an invocation of animals of the field. *YHWH ṣeba'ôt* has become *ṣeba'ôt;* while *El Shadday* has been changed into *'ayᵉlôt hassadeh.* Note here again Hosea as "donor field" and the Canticle as "recipient field."[7] Hos 2.18 promises a divine covenant with "the wild animals, the birds of the air, and the creeping things of the ground" as a prelude to the consummation of the intercourse between "husband" and "wife." Within such a context, it may well be that the exhortation not to stir up love before it is ready must be understood in the sense of not disturbing the fulfillment of love (if so, the will to shock is obvious).

Along that perspective of irreverence, the rest of the formula in verse 7 is also a parody. "Do not stir up or awaken love until it is ready" is an implicit criticism of societal mores, according to which very young teenagers were married by matchmakers, without the consent of the children and whether or not there was mutual attraction between them. Parody is also found here in the light of scriptural parallels. Isa 51.17 reads, "Awake, awake, stand up, O Jerusalem," and 52.1, "Awake, awake, put on your strength, O Zion," a quasi-verbatim repetition of 51.9, "Awake, awake, put on strength, O arm of the LORD." Note in passing that the two forms of *'wr* that are present in the Canticle (*ta'îrû* and *te'ôrᵉrû*) echo those in Isaiah (*'ûrî* and *hit'ôrerî*). In the Ugaritic *Baal* 2.4.39, expressions like "wake up, arouse" (*'wr*) and "love" are put together: "See, El the king's love stays (*yḥssk*) thee, Bull's affection sustains (*t'rrk*) thee" (*ANET*, p. 133). In the Song of Songs, the devotional discourse is redirected towards another purpose with a smack of scandal.

---

7. Those terms are used by Kittay and Lehrer in their collective work "Semantic Fields and the Structure of Metaphor," 1981.

Canticle 2.8–15

A new section starts with Cant 2.8 ("Listen! My beloved! Behold, he comes, leaping upon the mountains, skipping upon the hills"). The Shulammite's speech runs till the end of chapter 3. Verse 8 is unmistakably an echo of Canaanite mythology about young Baal Haded, leaping upon "mountains and hills." These elements are "standard poetic parallels, both in the Bible and in Ugaritic," says Marvin Pope.[8]

Moses H. Segal may be right when he says that verse 9a "is a parenthesis breaking the context."[9] It is repeated in verse 17a and in 8.14, and is hardly an original part of the poem. But its very repetition should make one hesitant to delete it (in spite of Budde, Siegfried, Haupt, Dussaud, Staerck, Wittekindt, Haller). If, in parallel with 2.7 above, we are invited to shift from *ṣebî* to *ṣeba'ôt* and from *'ayalîm* to *'elohîm*, the word *'oper* in this verse stands out. It is found only in the Canticle (see 2.17; 4.5; 7.4; 8.14). By alliteration it evokes *'apar,* "dust," figuratively a derogatory term for idols, in parallel with the earlier mentions of "delight" and "dainties" in 2.3, 5. Perhaps, the lover's observation through windows is on the model of what is said in Psalm 33 of God, whose counsel "stands" (v. 11) and who "watches all the inhabitants of the earth" (v. 14; cf. also Ps 14.2, with another verb, however). In the psalm, YHWH "spoke" (v. 9), and he delivers from death (v. 19). In the Canticle, the shepherd also speaks (v. 10) and announces the end of winter and the coming of spring (vv. 11–13). As to the rare verb *ûds* II (always in the hifil form), it is used again only in another psalm (17.15), where the psalmist declares himself content with beholding the image of God. In the Canticle, the lover is beholding his beloved!

What the female lover says in verses 10–15 sounds strikingly close to texts already mentioned apropos verse 7 above, namely, Isa 51.17 and 52.1–2 (*qûmî šebî yerûšalayim,* preceded by the mention of *'apar!*). The formula *qûmî lekî* falls in parallel with the same order given by Amnon to his sister Tamar in the sordid story of the incestuous relations between the two (2 Sam 13.15). Another text with the

---

8. Pope, *Song of Songs,* p. 389.
9. Segal, "The Song of Songs," p. 473.

same formula, also in the feminine form, is the harsh 1 Kgs 14.12, an oracle of the prophet Ahijah to Jeroboam's wife: her son will die as a result of his father's infidelity to God, *we-'at qûmî lekî lebéytèk*. In 2 Kgs 8.1, Elisha tells the Shunammite, *qûmî ûlekî*, before a famine in the land. Once more the Canticle transforms highly negative texts into a positive one. The maiden may, at times, wish that her lover were her brother (8.1) and thus re-create, so to speak, the situation that transpired between Amnon and Tamar, but there is no outrageous incest here, and there is no danger that the lover ends up by hating his beloved one!

As to *lekî lak*, its kinship with the famous *lek leka* of Genesis 12 is too clear to be belabored here. *Lekî lak*, in the feminine form, appears only here in the Song (also 2.13), while the masculine in the story of Abraham remains without parallel. The raising up and the going away of the Shulammite is described in the very terms used by prophets for Israel's moving, at last, in the right direction and being restored after her deportation. She is about to know a glorious re-creation. A stake in the Song, however, is a vastly different program. It is now a question of another "restoration," the renewal of nature, the springing of springtime. The inclusio of verse 13b repeats the pressing invitational terms of verse 10 and emphasizes the parallel we saw earlier with Gen 12.1 by making the concluding formula of *lekî lak* an explication of the preceding *lekî* in the same verse. This renders the style somewhat awkward in verse 13b, but the author apparently considered that the stressing of the allusion to the call of Abraham was worth the encroachment on poetic beauty.

The shepherd is fond of saying "my dove" (see here in 2.14 and later on in 5.2 and 6.9), among other terms of endearment addressed to the beloved. Unexpectedly, however, she is described in terms used elsewhere to depict Edom hiding in "the clefts of the rock" (*behag^ewey hassela'*; Jer 49.16; see 48.28)! But there is a difference; Edom is an eagle, says Jeremiah (same verse), while the Shulammite is a dove. Besides, *sela'* and *séter* (rock and covert) are both metaphoric for YHWH (cf. Ps 18.3 for *sela'* and Ps 32.7 for *séter*; see also Ps 91.1; Isa 16.4). Edom thinks it can hide from God in crannies of the rock and is defied by God. If there is any defiance of the Shulammite by her lover, it is no invitation to make war but one to make love. She has nothing to fear from him, and she will come out with a fair form and a pleasant voice ("for your voice is sweet and your face comely"). In Jeremiah 49, Edom cannot hide from God (v. 16), but the Shulammite's hiddenness is from others than her lover, to whom she reserves her countenance (Cant 2.14). Her voice is sweet ('aréb), in contrasted parallel with the voice of God, which is heard thundering against Teman (Jer 49.14, 20). The latter falls with a fracas (49.21; qôl twice) that is heard afar.

Besides, the whole scene recalls Exod 33.18–23. Moses begged to see God's face but was allowed to see only God's back (see there v. 23). One notes the presence in Exodus 33 of words borrowed by Cant 2.14, such as "see," "face," "call aloud [the Name]," "rock," "cleft of the rock." The contrast between the texts of Exodus and the Canticle is evident. Moses wants to see God. The lover in the Song wants to see his belle. Moses sees only God's back. The lover sees her face. God's voice is thunder, and all people crawl on the ground (see Exod 19.16); her voice is sweet and pleasant to hear. God was the one hiding in the rocks, and Moses, the one requesting that he come out; she now is the hidden one, and he is begging for her presence. In the ears of religionists, all this no doubt sounded like borderline blasphemy.[10]

The foxes, little or not, of the following verse (v. 15) are somewhat mysterious.

> Catch us foxes, little foxes,
> spoilers of vineyards,
> for our vineyards are in blossom. (my translation)

The word for "foxes" is translated "jackals" by the New Revised Standard Version in Ezek 13.4, where it designates false prophets roaming "among ruins," and in Lam 5.18, where again jackals/foxes are prowling in a desolate Zion (see also Hos 2.15 and Ps 80.13 for the idea). The borrowing by the Canticle is thus clear, as is also the secularization of the discourse. Here, what is in danger is not Jerusalem, the city of God, but the lovers. The foxes/jackals are a metaphor, not for the Babylonians and other enemies of the covenantal people, but for those who are frowning at the free love of the

---

10. More on this verse below, in my discussion of Keel's commentary (p. 198).

couple in the Song.[11] Then, the adjective *little* can only refer to their pettiness. The whole verse may be a remote echo of Isa 13.2–5, where the themes of mountain(s) (vv. 2, 4), *qôl* ("voice," "noise"; vv. 2, 4a, 4b), and *ḥibbél* ("destroy"; v. 5) are combined as in this instance.

Canticle 2.16–17

In the introduction, I mentioned the evident parallel between "My beloved is mine and I am his" (Cant 2.16a; cf. 6.3) and Lev 26.12 (as well as many other passages; see p. 64, n. 153). See also a text that is by now familiar to us, namely, Hos 2.23 [25], " 'You are my people,' and he shall say, 'You are my God.' " Furthermore, the shepherd, like YHWH in Psalm 23, takes the Shulammite into "green pastures," to the lilies of the fields (see above p. 74).

With 2.17, we move on to another *crux interpretum.* Two ways are open to modern criticism: either to see here a place name (Aq.; Sym.; Vg; Winandy), that is, a village southwest of Jerusalem, or by etymology the verb *to cut.* Applying our hermeneutical method will allow us, I believe, to get into the text more accurately than by any other way. It is spoken here of the "beloved, comparable to a gazelle or a young stag upon separate mountains (*'al harey-bater*)," and the language is daringly — dangerously, should we say — close to the one of Gen 15.10 and its ideological parallel in Jer 34.18–19. Only in these two texts do the verb and/or the noun appear: the sacrificial victim is cut in two.[12] The LXX combines the two readings and renders the text, *epi orē koilōmatōn* ("the mountains of

11. For Rudolph, Gordis, and others, "vineyards" means nubile girls (cf. 1.6; 8.12), and the little foxes are lustful youths. There are parallels to the use of jackals and wolf cubs in Egypt, and, according to Keel, the foxes in ancient Egyptian poetry designate womanizers (*The Song,* p. 110); the same is found in Theocritus (for both men and women; cf. *Ode* 1.48–50; 5.112: the theft of grapes represents sexual intercourse). See also Fox, *Ancient Egyptian Love Songs,* p. 114.

12. The Targum refers to Mount Moriah and to Gen 15.10. *Midrash Rabba* also refers to the same Genesis text. P. Joüon (*Le Cantique des Cantiques*) translates, "the mountains of the [victims] cut in two." Keel's elegant suggestion (*The Song,* p. 117) that the term means "cinnamon" (Greek, *malabatron*) does not detract from the allusive sense of this unexpected term in the Canticle (see also 4.6; 8.14). Salvaneschi (*Cantico dei cantici,* p. 108) evokes also *bitrôn,* the hapax in 2 Sam 2.29 that is interpreted sometimes as a toponym for a valley "that divides the area" and sometimes as a chronological indicator "that divides in two parts" the day. In both cases, adds Salvaneschi, the idea is

the ravines"; cf. Marcia Falk: "in the clefts of the hills"). However, we are probably dealing here again with the recurring irreverence of the poet. "The separate mountains" of Genesis have now by metaphor become the woman's breasts![13] On the other hand, we have seen above that "gazelle" and "young stag" are terms that allude to divine names. The group formed by the lover lying upon the breasts of his belle has replaced the complex of the God of the covenant with Abraham the patriarch.[14] Furthermore, as is clear from parallel texts in the Song concerning mountains (4.6; 8.14), "holy geography" is here radically demoralized and desacralized. We are at the antipode of spiritual allegory.

As we conclude this chapter of our inquiry, covering the text of Canticle 2, it becomes increasingly clear that the poet dared put on a par the discourse of human love with the one that described the interaction between Israel and God. Israel's theologians had considered this miraculous encounter of the divine as the worthiest cause for singing the praise of YHWH. Paradoxically and scandalously, the Canticle adopts a similar wording to celebrate the coming together of the male and the female. In 2.12, for example, we read the words *'ét hazzamîr higgiya'*, "the time of singing has come,"[15] an expression rendered familiar by hymns and oracles in the spiritual literature of Israel (cf. Pss 27.6; 30.13; 57.10; Isa 24.16; 26.1; Jer 33.11). There is praise here and there but addressed to different praiseworthy persons: God there, the Shulammite here (in other contexts, the shepherd). Clearly, this constant parallelism between vastly different objects emphasizes the point that they are indeed comparable — not the characters themselves, however, but the types of relationship they

---

of a symmetrical division, the idea of duality being very present in the Canticle; see, e.g., *mahanayîm.*

13. In Cant 8.14, *bater* is replaced by *besamîm* (the word of the Pesh here = Th: *Thumiamatōn;* so, "mountain of spices" NRSV), and it is clear that in both texts the "mountains" in question represent the girl herself (so Siegfried; Haller). Krinetzki thinks of the "mons veneris" (*Das Hohelied*, pp. 214–15), following Haupt (*The Book of Canticles*). The same reading of 8.14 is proposed by Wittekindt (*Das Hohelied*). See also the following note.

14. For Haupt (see also preceding note), the "mountains of spice" are the vulva; cf. "The Book of Canticles," *AJSL* 18 (1902): p. 233. But Fox objects, why "mounts" in the plural if the *mons veneris* is meant? (p. 116). That is why for Lys (*Le plus beau chant,* pp. 134–35), the mounts of separation refer to the girl's breasts.

15. I will not follow the lead of the Versions here; they understand "pruning" (so LXX; Vg; Tg; cf. Isa 5.6); elsewhere in the Hebrew Scripture, the term designates songs of a ritual character.

initiate. What is similar between the relation of God with Israel (according to Psalms and the Prophets) and the relation of male with female (according to the Canticle) is *love*. This lesson of the Song of Songs has been particularly well rendered by Daniel Lys's commentary (*Le plus beau chant de la création*), a summary of which is given by Pope in these terms:

> The one who chose and loves Israel in spite of everything, at the same time that he has liberated Eros from its utilitarianism, has reclothed Eros with gratuity and liberty. It is thus...that the love of man for his neighbor and above all for his mate is none other than the love by which man responds to God's love.[16]

---

16. Pope, *Song of Songs*, p. 204.

Chapter Three

CANTICLE 3

Canticle 3.1–5

The next section, 3.1–5, contains at least four subversive elements: (*a*) a reference in verse 1 to premarital sexuality, that is, the girl's searching for her lover while in her bed; (*b*) in verse 2 the girl's roaming at night in the streets and squares of the city; (*c*) the mention in verse 4 of *beyt-'immî*, "my mother's house...the chamber of her that conceived me"; (*d*) *biṣ*ᵉ*ba'ôt 'ô be'ay*ᵉ*lôt hassadeh* in verse 5, an expression already encountered and commented upon above (see pp. 63–64). I shall not return here to this theme. The reader may remember that the terminology used by the poet is irreverently close to the religious oath formula by YHWH Tsebaoth and by El Shadday.

Along the same line, the motif of the quest — here at the service of Eros — is traditionally marked for the religious search for God. Isa 26.9 (that lies also in the background of other passages of the Canticle and hence was clearly well known by the poet) reads, "My soul (*nap*ᵉ*šî*) strives to you by night (*ballay*ᵉ*lâ*), yea my spirit inside of me is anticipating you (*'ašaḥareka*)" (cf. Pss 63.2; 77.3; on *šaḥar*, see above p. 72).

Speaking of night, it is noteworthy that, for Daniel Lys — following Franz Delitzsch, Karl Budde, Ernst Würthwein, and Robert Gordis — 3.1 to 5.1 as a unit reports a dream of love. The verbs are now in a tense (perfect) different from before. We are in the evening, the normal time for a tryst. The dream anticipates the reality.[1] The maiden looks for the shepherd almost frantically everywhere after

---

1. "[E]lle exprime à haute voix sa rêverie" (Lys, *Le plus beau chant,* p. 140).

discovering that he is not in her bed.[2] The structure itself of the unit emphasizes the swiftness of the quest, as well as its broad compass. The number *four* is central here, reminding one of the four cardinal points. The Shulammite uses the verb *to seek* four times; she looks for "him whom [her] soul loves" four times as well. At first, she finds him not (two times), while she is found by the guards and finally finds him (two more times). Verse 4 *in fine* ("into the room of her who conceived me") forms an inclusio with verse 1 ("by night on my bed"). One starts with the lovers' alcove, and one finishes with reminiscing about the begetting of the speaker. Meanwhile, the fourfold mention of "him whom my soul loves" amounts to an invocation and charges the poem with passion and desire.

Medieval Jewish and Christian mystics came to use such erotic language to describe the *unio mystica* of the individual soul with God. But to read the Canticle as if it were a mystical piece of the European Middle Ages is clearly an anachronism. Besides, a Saint Teresa of Ávila might conceivably advert to her genitrix, but if we have to see in the Shulammite the people of Israel, it becomes difficult to identify "her who conceived me." The allegorical interpretation finds solace in evoking the risqué language used metaphorically by Hosea to describe God's love. Even the theme of seeking-without-finding is common to both texts (Hos 2.9; Cant 3.2–4; 5.6–7). But one must concede that the prophet speaks of Israel as a prostitute and that such is her condition only when she abandons her God, not as she comes near to him! Furthermore, the one who deserts the "conjugal" bed is not she but he! The obvious sense of the text is that the Shulammite braves all conventions and is disapproved for it; the guards in 5.7, and probably already here in 3.4, mistake her for a prostitute. She must justify her suspect presence in the streets by night, "Have you seen him whom my soul loves?" As Lys pointedly says, "Comprendre que la profonde et incroyable sagesse de cette fille c'est d'oser prendre l'allure d'une prostituée par amour pour celui qu'elle aime."[3]

---

2. Note that it is her couch, not their wedlock bed!

3. "Understand that the girl's profound and incredible wisdom consists in the daring adoption of a prostitute's deportment, through infatuation for the one she loves" (Lys, *Le plus beau chant,* p. 144). A woman strolling in the streets can be propositioned, as is shown in Tamar's story: she is sitting on the side of the roadway (Genesis 38). Note the irony (or perhaps great wisdom) of classifying the Song of Songs as sapiential literature!

The guards who patrol the town bring to mind the sentinels upon the walls of Jerusalem who keep guard day and night tirelessly (Isa 62.6). The theme of searching and finding (or not finding) YHWH is familiar to the prophets (cf. Isa 51.1; 65.1; Jer 29.13; and once again chap. 3 of Hosea, already influential on the Song earlier; see Hos 3.5; 5.6, 15). The object of the quest, this time, is the young shepherd. The Shulammite cannot find her lover, but the watchmen found her all right! The problem, by then, is to know whether they were as vigilant to spot "the one whom my soul loves" — which apparently they were not, although he was not very far away. She says, "Scarcely had I passed them [the watchmen], when I found him." In other words, the lookout men do not see what they should, and they see what they should decently overlook. The town would be better off without them. They are found wanting! They do not tirelessly remind the Lord to care for Jerusalem, his beloved city, but rather spend their time playing the role of keepers of morality. There is no plot in the Song of Songs, but this does not mean that there is no progression from beginning to end. For instance, the scene with the guardians on the wall is repeated later with increased dramatic effects in 5.7.

The mention in 3.4 of the "mother's house" is striking by its unexpectedness. According to biblical (and Near Eastern) mores, females have male guardians all their life. First they are in their father's house, then in their husband's.[4] Part of the wedding ceremony consists in conducting in a procession the new bride to the groom's house.[5] Exceptionally, Isaac takes Rebekah in his mother's tent to wed her (Gen 24.67).[6] In the Canticle, however, the situation is different as the Shulammite takes her lover into *her* mother's house (see

---

4. See de Vaux, *Ancient Israel,* p. 26.

5. Ibid., p. 59.

6. Trible refers to Gen 2.24 with its statement about the man's cleaving to the woman: "This entry into the mother's house for intercourse suggests its opposite in Genesis 2.24" (*God and the Rhetoric,* p. 158). "The significance of the verse," says Westermann, "lies in this that in contrast to the established institutions and partly in opposition to them, it points to the basic power of love between man and woman.... This does not mean a social state, but a situation of very personal concern, fidelity and involvement" (*Genesis 1–11,* pp. 233–34). Meyers astutely adds, "Verse 24 declares, in a world not yet witness to childbirth or parenthood, that a couple's union supersedes the parent-child relationship." Then, the same author has a point when she says that "the Song of Songs is indeed a midrash, or exposition, of the Eden story" (*Discovering Eve,* pp. 86, 110).

also 8.2)! There might be a foreign parallel to this in the Egyptian song that Michael Fox calls "The Stroll";[7] there the girl identifies her home as "my mother's house." It is to be noted, though, that neither in Cant 3.4 nor in 8.2 does the mother play any active role. She is mentioned for the sole purpose of insisting on the pervasive female character of the poem.[8] The gist of the matter is that here we have an indication of the *non*marital status of the heroine (see also 8.2). If we had, as expected, "father's house" in the text, the reader could infer a situation in which "law and order" eventually prevailed. Here, however, the woman is free of all bonds, and her house is not *beyt-'ab,* "the father's house," as it "should" be for an unmarried woman (cf. Gen 24.28; Ruth 1.8).[9]

By the end of this section, it is evident that the poet goes deeper and deeper into the scandalous and presents the heroine with questionable traits from the point of view of social proprieties. Her taking over the initiative in amorous behavior invited the inevitable accusation of immorality.

Canticle 3.6–11

Moses H. Segal says,

> The nightly experience of the damsel led to the interpolation of a description of the watch over King Solomon's bed against "the terrors by night" (7–8; *balléylôt* v. 8, as in v. 1).... This whole material must be derived from a popular epic of the glory of the great king.[10]

Cant 3.6 asks a question: "Who is she that is coming up from the desert, like pillars of smoke, perfumed with myrrh and incense, and all the powders of the perfume merchant?" According to Chaim Rabin, "she" refers to *šayyârâ* (caravan), which is unexpressed.[11] He

---

7. No. 32; *Ancient Egyptian Love Songs,* p. 119.
8. See the Book of Ruth, where the same situation obtains (see 1.8). I send the reader to my *The Feminine Unconventional,* where I discuss the point. Let us note that the "father's house" would generally include more than one wife as well as concubines.
9. More on this section below, in my discussion of Keel's commentary (p. 199).
10. Segal, "The Song of Songs," p. 474.
11. Rabin, "Song of Songs and Tamil Poetry," pp. 214, 219 n. 29.

says, "The dust raised by the caravan rises like smoke from a fire, but the sight of the smoke is also in concurrence with the scent a caravan spreads around it as it halts in the market and unpacks its wares."[12] This is not the only possibility, however, as regards the antecedent of the interrogative pronoun *mî*. As writes Peter B. Dirksen, many translations render *mî* here as "what?" for there is no mention of a person in the text following.[13] Then the antecedent is *mittâ*, "bed" (v. 7; cf. in v. 9 *'appir*ᵉ*yôn*, "palanquin").[14] As a matter of fact, *mî* means "what?" in several texts, for instance, in Gen 33.8 (it is true that *maḥ*ᵃ*neh*, "camp," refers to people, not to a thing); Judg 13.17 (*mî šemeka*); Mic 1.5 (*mî peša* *ya*ᶜᵃ*kob*...*û-mî bamôt*). If, in spite of this, *mî* means "who?" as it often does, then as Marvin Pope suggests *mittatô šeliš*ᵉ*lomoh* is the answer: the entourage says *who* is in the litter, and they mean Solomon's bride.[15] Pope sees no conflict with verse 11 ("look upon King Solomon"), for it is a new beginning; verse 10 closes the description.

Be that as it may, the old commentary of Ibn Ezra makes a lot of sense (although I shall suggest below another possibility that I find more convincing). He reads Cant 3.6–4.1 as a discourse in the mouth of the youth, who sees her coming and running after him. The young man exclaims, "Who is this one coming from the desert?...Even Solomon needed guards, how could she come by herself from the desert....Solomon would build a magnificent baldachin wherein he would be himself, 'hot' for one of the girls of Jerusalem. But you are more beautiful than the one Solomon desired, and I don't need building an *'appir*ᵉ*yôn*." The belle is like a mirage in the desert or like a caravan whose vision is still blurred in the reflection of the sun on the desert sand, something unreal, as a column of light and smoke of which no distinctive traits and features can be fathomed yet. So is she within the aura of her blinding comeliness.

---

12. Ibid., p. 219.

13. Dirksen, "Song of Songs III 6–7."

14. Incidentally, Shalom Paul traces the origin of the word to the Persian or Sanskrit, not to the Greek ("Shir ha-shirim," col. 651); indeed, he denies the presence of a single Greek word in the Canticle (col. 652). Furthermore, as there is in the Canticle a medley of early and late linguistic elements, the phenomenon can be explained if the Canticle is the result of songs from different periods put together (cf. col. 651); however, "clearly the literary composition is late" (col. 652).

15. Pope, *Song of Songs*, pp. 423–24.

The image could be seen as self-contained in its aesthetic beauty. But tradition sees in the whole scene some reminiscence of the march in the desert under the lead of the column of smoke (cf. Exod 13.21–22; 14.19–20; Isa 52.12) and that it discovers, through the description of the mist of myrrh and frankincense, the smoke of incense ascending from the temple's altar (cf. Lev 16.13; on the incense in the ritual, see Exod 30.34; Lev 2.1–2, 15–16). For in the background of the composition, the inspirational material appears strangely familiar as it evokes what Paul Joüon identifies as the ascent of the ark of the covenant to Jerusalem. If so, the motif is congruent with the whole context of the Song of Songs, for we already know that the Canticle substitutes the Shulammite for sacred objects, and we will again meet such substitution below (cf. Cant 6.12). With the supposition that the scene is reminiscent of the ark, the ambiguity of the interrogative pronoun *mî* becomes ambivalence: its antecedent is concomitantly the maiden *and* the bed, for she is described in terms that become the ark of the covenant. The uneasiness of the reader with the words *mî zo't 'olah* comes from the close context that would rather demand *mî hû' 'oleh* in the masculine, namely, God. Thus, not only is the theological vocabulary exploited by the author for describing relations of Eros, but traditional formulas in the masculine are feminized.

The same sort of parallel is provided by 1 Kings 7 with the description of Solomon's building of the temple in Jerusalem. Ariel Bloch insists on kinship between the two texts. About Cant 3.7–10, he writes, "[T]he comparison text [is] in 1 Kgs 7.6–8 [also, 7.2–6, 15–16]. . . . The second comparison text . . . is Qoh 2.4–8. . . . [T]heir generic similarity does suggest some kinship."[16]

Furthermore, another element must be highlighted at this point. Hans-Josef Heinevetter emphasizes there is constant opposition in the Canticle between the lively woman and the place from where she comes — the arid mountains (4.8) or the desert (3.6; 8.5) — and the season of her encounter with the lover is contrasted with winter (2.11).[17] Especially striking is the contrast with the desert. Not only does it play a major role at different places, but it summa-

---

16. Bloch and Bloch, *The Song of Songs,* p. 161.
17. Heinevetter, *"Komm nun, mein Liebster,"* p. 175.

rizes in the best possible way *Thanatos*, against which Eros must fight. The desert is here in the company of Death, Sheol, many waters, forbidding mountains, lions, and panthers. In our reading of the Song of Songs, the theme's traditional investment is fully recognized. The *amatta* emerges from the desert as Israel emerged from it and entered the Promised Land as a new Eden. The Shulammite claims for herself a *typos* that seemed for all practical purposes to belong so intimately to Israel's *Heilsgeschichte* as to be absolutely unavailable for any other use, especially a private, erotic use as we find in the Song of Songs. The coming up from the desert motif is demythicized from its vertical axis (which made the numinous unreachable and nonrepeatable) and is horizontally "democratized," humanized, made habitual! By ricochet, intertextuality reinterprets the exodus from Egypt as driven by love. Only love was a moving force capable of overcoming the deadly and infernal desert. The Promised Land is the land of love, or else it is the land of the Canaanites, the Perizzites, and Hivites.... The Promise is the engagement oath; the Land is the nuptial chamber, that is, King Solomon's palanquin in our text.

Along that line, the presence of "Solomon" as a motif in the Canticle provides a hermeneutical key. The mention of the great king embraces also the temple that he built in Jerusalem, a trope that is still reinforced by the mention in verse 9 of "the wood of Lebanon" as the material of construction (Cant 3.9–10; *'asah*, "he made"; the verb appears often in descriptions of the construction of the tabernacle, as in Exodus 25–27). Right after this, however, the stage is set in the Canticle for Solomon's enthronement ("his crown") and wedding, a complex that reminds one of the Babylonian Akitu festival, which combines the two motifs. Now, if the *mittâ* is also a throne, the inspiration of the poet comes from another text, one in 1 Kgs 10.18–20, which credits Solomon with the fabrication of the throne (*'asah*)! In 1 Kings, it is true, the throne is said to be of ivory, but repeating the information about the ivory material would not have served the poet's purpose, which is to allude to the complex palace-temple.

The scene as a whole evokes still another setting in life, as described, for instance, in Judg 5.28–30 or in Psalm 45. In Judges, Sisera's mother expects her son's chariot (*rekeb*; cf. *merkab* in Cant

3.10) to come back from the battlefield, but she waits in vain, for he is dead. But in Canticle 3, the events are presented as if Solomon's chariot is coming back in triumph from the war, like Sisera in his mother's eyes, with a "girl or two for every man; spoil of dyed stuffs for Sisera, spoil of dyed stuffs embroidered, two pieces of dyed work embroidered for my neck as spoil" (Judg 5:30 NRSV). Solomon, however, is not coming back from war, and his sixty mighty men are not heroes of war; they guard the king against the terrors of the night! As to the overwhelming female presence around him, the motif is the pendant of a "girl or two for every man" in the dream of Sisera's mother. For there is here also a mother, like in Judges 5. Furthermore, as a king, generally speaking, cannot reign during his father's life, "mother" here indicates that, indeed, the father is dead, and she makes her son the successor of her husband, a role that is, however, unusual in tradition. Let us note in passing the embarrassment felt by the Targum, which does not read "mother" but "people" (*ʿamô* instead of *ʾimmô*).

Psalm 45, called a *maskîl* and "a love song," is an ode for a royal wedding. It refers to the king's handsomeness, to his chariot, to the fragrance of his perfumes, to his divinity(!), and also to a foreign "princess" (v. 13) in a palanquin (v. 14). There is an unmistakable parallel drawn here by the Canticle.

All this indicates that the focus is not on Solomon as such, who serves only as a reference. Strikingly, Solomon is so little an acting character in the Canticle that the text uses his name as a topic, at times setting him in contrast to the youth, as a foil, and at other times likening them both.[18] But, in any case, he is but a figure. We shall, therefore, savor the bitter irony in verses 7b–8: the great king is not exempt from "alarms by night," and he needs bodyguards, three scores of them, twice as many as had Samson (Judg 14.10–20) or David, his father (2 Sam 23.18–19). At another level of understanding, of course, one thinks of the throngs of Levites watching over the ark by night in the temple (see, e.g., 1 Chr 15.2; 16.4, 37, 39). If this point is accurate, it becomes highly ironic that the Levites of old are here replaced by Asmodeus-like demons (the "alarms of the night") that are lusting for the bride-to-be and

---

18. Cf. Fox, *Ancient Egyptian Love Songs*, p. 122.

must be defeated by the sword before the honeymoon (cf. Tob 3.17; 6.14–18).

In the subsequent description of the royal bed are the words *silver, gold,* and *purple* (Cant 3.10). These materials are only too natural when speaking of kingship, but they also recall P texts in the Pentateuch that describe the tabernacle, the vestments of the high priest, or his ephod (Exod 26.1, 36; 27.16; 28.6–43; 39.3; 2 Chr 3.14 says that the temple curtain was made with purple fabrics). Thus the uniformity of the epithalamium's backdrop is striking: smoke pillars, fragrant myrrh and frankincense, silver, gold, purple. In this paean to Eros, the parallel with the temple liturgy (cf. Exod 30.34; Lev 2.1–2, 15–16; cf. 1 Chr 9.20; Neh 13.5, 9; Jer 6.20; Isa 43.23) does not lack trenchancy, that is, trenchancy and irony! For while the Shulammite is magnified, the Solomonic constructions present at times disconcerting aspects. First, Solomon is in need of an army against the terrors of the night (vv. 7–8); then his glory is given him by his mother and for the exclusive admiration of women. The contrast is stark with the sixty heroes of the bodyguard. Again, the concurrence of enthronement and sacred marriage seems to lie in the background.

In conclusion to this unit, it may be said that the temple has been used as a symbol of a shrine dedicated to love (see v. 10). King Solomon belongs naturally to such a metaphor; he is not only the builder of the sanctuary (vv. 9–10), but he is metaphorically either the Shulammite's lover inside the shrine, now made into a tryst, or his foil (vv. 10b–11). King Solomon is protected by sixty bodyguards, but his real entourage is made of women (v. 11). As he is the paragon of love, this is not unexpected. The feminization of the scene, however, is so total that it cannot but reflect upon the male royal character inside the palanquin. Solomon is surrounded (drowned?) not only by females everywhere but also by their work ("decked in love by the daughters of Jerusalem"; v. 10b). Although it may be that women were employed in the temple for some specific works, their mention at this point by the Canticle enhances the feeling of voluptuousness and of decadence created by the whole description. A surprising detail, the crown put on the king's head by his mother is puzzling. André Robert, Raymond Tournay, and André Feuillet see in this precision one more prompting for allegorizing, for "we cannot find in texts that a King has ever been crowned by his mother on his wedding day."[19] Wilhelm Wittekindt, however, refers to Ishtar, the spouse and mother of Tammuz; she puts a crown on his head.[20] The parallel is striking as it transports us once again to the region of the Akitu festival. The poet may have turned her glance in that direction because of the central role played by women during the Babylonian New Year celebration. To recall, the earliest love song comes to us from within the framework of the sacred marriage between the king and the fertility goddess in the person of a priestess. Of particular interest to us, at any rate, is the radical democratization of the temple and palace operated by the Canticle. What used to be aloof and spoken about only in an awestricken whisper is now part of the quotidian discourse in reference to love as a "many splendored thing."

19. RTF, *Le Cantique des Cantiques*, p. 155.
20. Wittekindt, *Das Hohelied*.

Chapter Four

CANTICLE 4

෯෧ ෯෧ ෯෧ ෯෧ ෯෧ ෯෧ ෯෧ ෯෧ ෯෧ ෯෧ ෯෧ ෯෧ ෯෧ ෯෧

Canticle 4.1–7

Basically a repeat of Cant 1.15, 4.1a resumes the theme of the eyes
like doves. A new element is provided by the mention of Gilead
in verse 1b, a geographical name fitting the context, for, as Num
32.1, 4 say of Gilead, it is "a good place / a land for cattle" (cf. Jer
50.19; Mic 7.14). No need to look for a more sophisticated allusion
here, it would seem. But the following context forces us to linger a
bit longer on the motif. Beside a possible adverting to Gen 31.22–
23 (Laban's pursuit of Jacob in the hill country of Gilead), within
the ravishing description of the beauty of the Shulammite we come
across verse 3, an unmistakable double allusion to Tamar in Genesis
38. First, "Your lips are a crimson thread" echoes the crimson thread
that a midwife put on the hand of Zerah, son of Tamar, the twin of
Peretz (who eventually came out first against all expectation). Second, the veil, here hiding the maiden's temples, is made notorious
in the same risqué Genesis story.[1] There are remarkable parallels between Genesis 38 and our text. Tamar sits *be-petaḥ 'eynayim* (in an
open space; literally, "in the opening of the eyes"), and the *waṣf* of
Canticle 4 also starts with a description of the belle's eyes (v. 1). Second, Tamar is not recognized by Judah "because she had covered
her face" (Gen 38.15 NRSV); in Canticle 4, the veil is so transparent

---

1. A. Bloch insists that it is not a question of veil but of hair thicket, as in Isa 47.2–
3 — the only other passage where the term is found (*The Song,* pp. 166–68). Note that
tallying Cant 1.3 with the Isaiah passage is also glaringly suggestive.

103

that it hides nothing. To Tamar, Judah promises a *gedî* (*'izzîm*; Gen
38.17, 20, 23); the maiden in the Canticle has her hair streaming
down like a flock of *'izzîm,* "goats."[2] The Song's innocent *waṣf*
is also a veil thrown upon a less-than-innocuous double-entendre
speech (see below the conclusion to this section).

There is also a crimson thread in the story of Rahab — another
prostitute (Joshua 2)![3] And then, according to the Mishnah, there is
the scarlet ribbon that the high priest attached, part on the scapegoat
and part on the rock from which the goat was thrown. Let us note
here again the association of the themes of "thread of scarlet" and
"goat(s)." When the thread turned white (cf. Isa 1.18), it was a sign
that Israel's sins were forgiven.[4] Comparing the belle's hair to a flock
of goats streaming down the mountain is not made without reminiscing about the scapegoat thrown down the rock. Wherever a red band
is mentioned, the context is one of prostitution or sinfulness; thus, it
is difficult not to conclude that the Song's idiom is here deliberately
provocative. Such a dimension of the text did not escape Othmar
Keel's reading. He writes, "Comparing the hair of the beloved to the
impudent black goats in the wilds of Gilead reveals her vitality and
her own wild, almost demonic, lust for life."[5]

Another allusive text follows in verse 4, which speaks of "the
tower of David" where "hang a thousand bucklers, all of them
shields of warriors"! The referent of the image is not easy to identify. The first thing to note with Carol Meyers is that the female
imagery in the Canticle is often of a military kind: 7.4, "tower of
Lebanon"; the pools and reservoirs are also for military purposes;
8.10, a wall system; in 8.9, the plank is "used in military operations
connected with siege." All those terms of the male world are "without exception . . . applied to the female. [It is] an unexpected reversal
of conventional imagery," she concludes. But, in spite of that diction,
the Shulammite brings about peace (see 8.10): "The one to whom all

---

2. Incidentally, let us also note the threefold mention in Genesis 38 of the fact that
Judah could not *find* the harlot (vv. 20, 22, 23). We met the same theme of the quest
without/with finding above in regard to Cant 3.1–4.

3. The comparison with Rahab is also drawn by Keel, *The Song,* p. 143: "Like Rahab's scarlet cord, the bright red lips of the beloved are an invitation to love (cf. Prov
24.26)."

4. See *mShabb* 9.3; *mYoma* 4.2; 6.8.

5. Keel, *The Song,* p. 142.

the military allusions have been made secures the opposite of what they represent."[6]

All the same, the image of shields hanging in a tower resists interpretation. Enrica Salvaneschi calls attention to the term *dawid* of which a *scriptio defectiva* is found in the Canticle for the lover (*dwd*). She then points out the vocabulary of love between David and Jonathan in 1 Sam 20.17, for example. As the Shulammite and her lover are both "fair," so in 2 Sam 1.23, Saul and Jonathan are called *hanne'ehabîm we-hanne'îmîm*, and in verse 26, David tells of the late Jonathan, *na'amtâ lî me'od ... 'ahabatka lî me'ahabat našîm.*[7]

For the image as a whole in Cant 4.4, however, a model text may be found in 2 Sam 8.7 (also, 1 Chr 18.7), "David took the gold shields that were carried by the servants of Hadadezer, and brought them to Jerusalem," but the comparison between this text and the Canticle seems to lead nowhere. Thus, James Reese says that Cant 4.4 has been "never adequately explained." He quotes Keith R. Crim, for whom the meaning is that the woman is so beautiful that one thousand warriors would lay down their weapons at her feet in surrender.[8] The interpretation is attractive but partly misleading.

I suggest that the parallel to our text is provided by Ezek 27.10–11. It is a prophetic diatribe against Tyre with an evocation of her past glory: "they hung shield and helmet in you [Tyre]; they gave you splendor. Men of Arvad and Helech were on your walls all around; men of Gamad were at your towers. They hung their quivers all around your walls; they made perfect your beauty" (NRSV). The reader cannot but be impressed by the contrasting "day of your [Tyre's] ruin" in 27.27. To our surprise — mitigated by the frequency of such peripeteia — the Song reverses the Ezekielian sense. What was said of Tyre with derision by the prophet is now applied to the Shulammite with admiration! Let me add that it is not necessary to read this as an implicit criticism of Ezekiel, but it is certainly a barb against the fundamentalists in the author's time.[9]

---

6. Meyers, "Gender Imagery," p. 215. Let us note, however, that the "banner" in 2.4 belongs to the male partner; it also is converted from military to peaceful use.

7. Salvaneschi, *Cantico dei cantici,* pp. 86–87.

8. Reese, *The Book of Wisdom.* The reference is to Crim, " 'Your Neck Is Like the Tower of David,' " pp. 70–74.

9. "L'idée de la tour de David, avec la garde qui stationne au sommet et les boucliers accrochés aux créneaux, donne vraiment l'impression, par comparaison avec Ez 27.10–

The image of verse 5 ("Your two breasts are like two fawns, twins of a gazelle, that feed among the lilies") would be sufficient by itself to thwart any allegorizing interpretation of the Canticle. It makes clear that the poem is impressionistic. What the author tries to create is atmospheric; any term-by-term substitution of an alleged veiled reality kills the poetry, to say nothing of the message of the ensemble. No other image would better evoke harmonious similarity, firm softness, and peaceful provocation than to compare the maiden's breasts to two fawns, caught in their twin leap by the camera of imagination. Let us note that the perfect equality between the genders is again stressed here. The male lover "pastures...among the lilies" (2.16 and 6.3). The breasts of the belle also pasture "among the lilies." When it is remembered that the "shepherd(ing)" in the Bible is a recurring royal metaphor, it is clear that if the male rules over his environment, so does also the female. Besides, "fawns," to which the breasts are compared, are an emblem of the male elsewhere in the Song![10]

Our next stop is at verse 6. Its first verset is a repetition of 2.17a. The second part of the verse recalls 2.17c, which introduced the "cleft mountains" or "separate mountains" (*harey-bater*). These now become "the mountain of myrrh and the hill of frankincense." Above, at 2.17, I emphasized the shift from the covenant with Abraham in Genesis 15 to the breasts of the belle. There is reason to see again in the twin peaks of 4.6 the same metaphor for the feminine figure, especially as the maiden's breasts have just been admired in verse 5. The idiomatic referent, however, without leaving Abraham behind, has shifted to the temple once again. The *har hammôr* alludes to Mount Moriah (2 Chr 3.1), and the *gibeʿat hallebônâ*, to Mount Zion.[11] The irreverence is of course of the same cloth as in the whole context.

Verse 7 follows suit. The absence of *mûm* (flaw) in the damsel recalls the ritual laws in Leviticus (e.g., 21.16–24; 22.20) about the

---

11, d'une force au repos, et en même temps d'une beauté austère, faite de prospérité et de puissance" (Robert, in RTF, *Le Cantique des Cantiques*, p. 334). See more on verse 4 below, in my discussion of Keel's commentary (p. 200).

10. Landy (*Paradoxes of Paradise*, p. 80) calls attention to the reverse situation transpiring in 5.12f., where the description of the male's eyes, cheeks, and lips are "all feminine images." See more on this verse below (pp. 128, 154).

11. As already indicated above (see p. 98), frankincense is exclusively liturgical in the Bible: "[L]a Bible ne connaît que l'usage liturgique de l'encens" (RTF, *Le Cantique des Cantiques*).

offerings to God. True, there is a personal precedent to the Shu-lammite's flawlessness. On that score, 2 Sam 14.25 builds also an interesting parallel. Absalom is said to be without *mûm*. In view of the pitiful end of the lad, comparing the Shulammite with him builds not only a parallel between the two but also a stark contrast. Such a rapprochement of Cant 4.6 with the 2 Samuel text would be sufficient without calling on Leviticus, were it not for the Canticle's context that evokes Mount Moriah and Mount Zion. The allusions in the Song of Songs are seldom exclusive; the plurivocity of the background material is remarkable.[12]

At the close of this section on 4.1–7, a question arises. Why choose Genesis 38, inter alia, as a source of inspiration for a *waṣf* on feminine beauty? It is simply for the same reasons as before — the reversal of meaning of a well-known tradition. The Shulammite is daringly put on a par with Tamar, who played harlot. The Shulam-mite may look like one, but, like Tamar, she is not. Retrospectively, the story of Genesis 38 is read critically by the poet. Tamar's guile was based on her feminine attractiveness. Judah took advantage of it — and Tamar almost lost her life in the adventure. Within that context, the Shulammite is Tamar's vindication. Her beauty is cele-brated without restraint or mental restriction. Yes, it is possible with the Canticle to sing the curvy body of a woman without falling into vulgarity and without transforming the object of the song into a har-lot. For Judah before his "conversion," like for the contemporary right-thinking ones (mentioned anonymously in the impersonal form *wa-yuggad*, "and it was told," in Genesis 38), there is from love to fornication only one short step. But in the eyes of true lovers and poets, love between mutually committed adults is blameless, pure; it is a celebration of life and, ultimately, of God.[13]

Canticle 4.8–16

Expectedly, after the mention of Lebanon in wordplay with *lebônâ*, "frankincense," the last phrase of verse 8 evokes the Anti-Lebanon

---

12. See above, the introduction, on intertextuality (p. 24).
13. Regarding "committed," consenting is not enough. Commitment is the rock-bottom foundation of love as celebrated by the Song of Songs.

peaks. The Lebanon is, of course, the highest mountain in Hebrew experience (Deut 3.25) and hence a mountain of the gods or "the garden of God" (Ezek 31.8). It is thus understandable that the author turns her gaze toward the majestic northern mountains, but it is not self-evident why they are selected on the ground that they shelter lions and leopards. The combination of those two prey animals, sometimes with the addition of a third species, the bear, appears in different prophetic texts with always the same symbolism: they represent foreign nations that God takes as instruments of his wrath against his own people (Hos 13.7–8; Jer 5.6; Hab 1.8). Again here, the Canticle changes the prophetic oracle of doom into an idyllic image, not far from the scene sketched by Isaiah 11. The frail maiden of the Song comes down from a country where swarm bloodthirsty wild animals, but she is unharmed and fearless. Her name is Shulammite. She spreads peace all around her.

If we turn our attention to a nonprophetic text, namely, Genesis 2–3, as we have done above and will do again, we note in the Canticle, with Francis Landy for example, a restored relationship with the animals. Gazelles and does contrast with the notorious wicked snake by their genteelness. In spite of their congenital timidity, they show no fear in the vicinity of the lovers (cf. 3.5). As to lions and leopards (so often associated with goddesses), they are at peace with the woman.

It is significant that the maiden be called *kallâ* six times between 4.8 and 5.1 and only here in the book! The word designates a bride-to-be (Gen 38.24; Hos 4.13–14) and, more generally, a lover. Although the term is flexible and can refer to a married woman (in several texts, *kallâ* means "daughter-in-law"; cf. Ruth), it need not be so. In the Song, "legal affairs generally play no role," says Keel.[14] Here, as in many other contexts, it emphasizes that the belle is yet unmarried.[15]

In 4.9, the *kallâ* becomes *'aḥotî*, "my sister," and Daniel Lys wavers between three possibilities. First, the expression could have been borrowed from Egyptian love poetry. Although marriages between brother and sister were forbidden in Egypt as elsewhere, the pha-

---

14. Keel, *The Song*, p. 155.
15. Cf. Isa 49.18; 61.10; 62.5; Jer 2.32; 7.34; 16.9; see KB, s.v. *kallâ*.

raohs were above the law. Under the Lagides, they practiced this type of union to keep the dynastic purity. Later, under the Romans, such incestuous weddings became also widespread among the Egyptian populace. The term *sister* is thus a term of affection in Egypt; interestingly, it is used in Prov 7.4 and addressed to Wisdom personified (cf. also Tob 5.22; 7.12, 15). Second, the expression could be considered against a mythological background. Tammuz is fetched from the netherworld by his sister-wife Ishtar. In Ugarit, Anath declares to her consort, Baal, "You are my brother and I am your sister" (*Aqht* 3 verso, line 24). The god and his female companion are customarily called "husband and wife," "groom and bride," "brother and sister," or "mother and son." Third, according to Hurrian legal contracts, when a woman has no brother to protect her, she may be adopted by another male, who can also marry her. The status of "sister" supersedes the one of "wife." This might have served as a basis for the stories of the patriarchs presenting their wives as sisters in Genesis.[16] So much for Lys's understandable hesitation.

The last-mentioned point, however, although the Hurrian parallel has lost today much of its scholarly support, is heuristic in its focussing upon the patriarchal precedent to the Canticle text under consideration. In reaction to the mendacity at the root of the repeated patriarchal story of real/fake kinship between spouses (Genesis 12; 20; 26), there is in the Song an unabashed and joyful claim that love indeed creates intimate kinship. The idea is again stressed in 8.1–2: the woman brings her lover to her mother's house, for "the maternal nest replaces kinship ties in the scurrilous world," says Landy.[17]

With verses 9–16, the *waṣf* continues to extol the beauty of the Shulammite to the skies. We will consider a few details that, I believe, confirm further the validity of my hermeneutical approach. Verse 11, in particular, deserves attention. "Your lips distill nectar" (*nopet tittop^enah siptôtayik*) falls in evident parallel with Prov 5.3, "the lips of the loose woman drip honey [and her speech is smoother than oil]"

16. See Speiser, *Genesis*, pp. 91–92; Lys, *Le plus beau chant*, pp. 181–82. At any rate, adds Pope, it is difficult to see why God would call Israel his sister! (cf. Pope, *Song of Songs*, p. 484). One will not retain the "explanation" of Cook (*The Root of the Thing*), that the poet imagined the violation of the prohibition of incest as an expression of freedom.

17. Landy, *Paradoxes of Paradise*, p. 100.

(NRSV, *nopet tittop^enah siptey zarâ*).[18] The borrowing produces a pastiche. City-wall sentinels and other diehards tend to mistake the maiden for a loose woman? So be it, seems to agree the lad, if this means that honey drips from her lips. Insolence? Listen to what follows! "Honey and milk (*debaš we-ḥalab*) are under your tongue." It is impossible here not to think of the classic formula "a land that flows with milk and honey" (*'ereṣ zabat ḥalab û-d^ebaš*) of Exod 3.8, 17 and so many other texts.[19] The praise due to the Promised Land is here mobilized in the girl's honor. It is paradisiacal food (Deut 32.13–14; see Isa 7.15; Job 20.17), and the point in the Canticle is that the lover finds it under the beloved's tongue! We can imagine that not every religionist was pleased to hear that.

The maiden's garments smell like the scent of Lebanon (v. 11c). Gen 27.27 spoke of the scent of another's clothes (*begadîm*), namely, Jacob's, and Hos 14.7–8 promised that Israel's "fragrance shall be like that of Lebanon...their fragrance shall be like the wine of Lebanon" (NRSV; note the process of metaphorization in prophetic oracles). The Hosean text especially shows in what way the author of the Canticle consistently borrows from other Scriptures and gives the appearance of trivializing the religious idiom. Note also in retrospect the reason why she combines "fragrance" and "wine" in verse 10b.

The same text of Hosea inspired Cant 4.12, "a garden locked...a fountain sealed" (see also Hos 13.15b), an image that is not without evoking paradisiacal bliss. Landy rightly says, "What the Song does is very simply to substitute the Beloved for the garden of Eden through the metaphor: 'A locked garden is my sister, my bride.'...In her, Paradise can be reexperienced, through the arts of culture, poetry, perfumery, etc."[20] In this respect, it is not indifferent that paradise be described here as springing from the woman's sex as, indeed, the land has a flux (*zûb*) of milk and honey. (Jewish liturgy has understood "locked garden" as meaning "locked against promiscuity" and, specifically, against having intercourse during the woman's menses.) The word *canals* means "vagina"; so also does *fountain*. The whole creation is said to emanate from her, especially those aro-

---

18. Note here and there the assonance with the sound *ph*.
19. Cf. my "The Land in D and P."
20. Landy, *Paradoxes of Paradise*, p. 205.

matic items (Exod 30.23–24; 1 Kgs 10.10; Jer 6.20) that signify the cultic function of creation.

In the background of Hosea's and Canticle's texts, there is doubtlessly once again some reminiscence of the cult in the temple. On Cant 4.11b, the Gaon of Vilna (Rabbi Elijah, eighteenth century) comments, " 'the scent of Lebanon,' that is, the scent of the sacrifices offered in the temple, for 'Lebanon' alludes to the temple that whitens the sins of Israel."[21] If any confirmation in the Canticle is needed, verse 14 provides it: "nard and saffron, calamus and cinnamon, with all trees of frankincense, myrrh and aloes, with all chief spices" (NRSV). From Exod 30.23, we know that most of the perfumes and spices mentioned here entered the composition of the anointment oil. In the same Exodus text is found the expression *besamîm r'oš*, which is echoed in Cant 4.14 by *kol r'ašey besamîm*.

The song of praise comes to its culmination with verse 15; the lass is "a garden fountain, a well of living water, and flowing streams from Lebanon" (NRSV). Once again, the simile finds its parallel in Egyptian poetry: "woman is a well" says the so-called "Pessimistic Dialogue between Master and Servant."[22] Prov 5.15 also compares woman with well and water. But the whole expression *be'er mayîm ḥayîm* is found in Gen 26.19. Still more impressive is its prophetic metaphorization in Jer 2.13; 17.13; and Zech 14.8 (cf. Ezekiel 47). In Jeremiah in particular, the "living water" is God himself! Besides, for the Midrash, there is no living water in Scripture but adverting to Torah (cf. *CantR* 1 par. 2–3 on Cant 1.2, fol. 6a; *Tan de b El*, p. 105; *Ta'an* 7a). The recurring combination with "Lebanon" leaves no doubt about the iconoclastic intention of the poet.

The maiden is said to be a "fountain sealed" in verse 12. We can hardly avoid contrasting her with the leaking cisterns evoked by Jer 2.13. It may be that here, and in 8.8–10, we find the only references to moral qualities of the girl and, more specifically, to her sexual abstinence. But in reality, the virtue alluded to here is chastity rather than virginity, as the text-reference Prov 5.17 shows.[23] This is con-

---

21. Scherman and Zlotowitz, *Shir haShirim*, p. 140.
22. See *ANET*, p. 438.
23. Or potential fecundity. Salvaneschi (*Cantico dei cantici*, p. 73) translates *gal na'ûl* by "rock containing water" and sees in this a reference to Exod 17.6 and Judg 15.19, where we find a rock like a sponge full of water. The Canticle uses this as a metaphor for excellence.

firmed by the use of the verb *pataḥ* (open) in Cant 5.2. In Palestinian Arabic and in the language of the Talmud, this can be said only of a nonvirgin, even of an immodest girl.[24]

In Cant 4.13, the meaning of *šelaḥîm* is uncertain. It may mean "arid areas" (cf. Rashi and *mMoed Qat* 1.1) or "offshoots." The New Revised Standard Version has "channel"! Be that as it may, there is probably here an ironic pun with *šilluḥîm*, that is, the dowry in Canaan (cf. Exod 28.2; 1 Kgs 9.16; Mic 1.14). Along the same line, *megadîm* in the same verse (NRSV, "choicest") evokes *migdanot*, that is, the presents offered by the fiancé to his in-laws (see Gen 24.53).[25] These allusions to custom short-circuit its usefulness. Within herself, the maiden embodies her dowry and her "price." She comes with both to the one who is fortunate enough to get her as his mate.

One may wonder in 4.16 whether the matter is of perfumes or of personal female scent? The latter is found in Sir 24.15 (personified Wisdom is speaking of herself), a text that can be considered as the earliest partial allegorization of the Song (it is here applied selectively in this summarizing of the Canticle text). Interestingly enough, according to the pseudepigraph *Life of Adam and Eve*, Adam expelled from Paradise receives four of the scents of Cant 4.13 as remedies for life on earth.[26] So those plants were seen as heavenly. Here, those fragrances are spread all over by the north wind and the south wind. Keel comments, "The winds are to turn the slumbering garden into one that wafts abroad its fragrance";[27] he connects this verse in the Canticle with Ezek 37.9 (cf. also Ps 104.30) and the resurrection of the dead. The association of wind, garden, eating a fruit, and breathing (the hifil of *pûaḥ* means "to cause to breathe," "to bring to life," says Ariel Bloch) brings to mind not only Ezek 37.9 but also Gen 2.7.[28] In both texts, the verb *npḥ* is a cognate of *pûaḥ*.

In conclusion, the response of the woman to the ravished wonderment of her lover is an invitation to enjoy her delights. They are

---

24. Cf. Lys, *Le plus beau chant*, pp. 188–89. More on this verse below (pp. 189, 201).
25. These texts are suggested by Lys, who consequently understands the Hebrew as meaning, "Ta dot, ce sont tes surgeons délicieux" (p. 190).
26. *Life of Adam and Eve* 29.6 in Greek.
27. Keel, *The Song*, p. 181.
28. Bloch and Bloch, *The Song of Songs*, p. 178.

meant for him. They are not to be kept as a "garden locked up and a sealed fountain" (see 4.12). Her fragrance, her perfumes, her nectar, milk and honey, her fruits, her wine and oil and spices, mean nothing if he does not "come to *his* garden."[29] The exclusivity of the relationship between God and his people, so strongly emphasized by the Law and Prophets, is now transformed into the delightful encounter of man and woman. True, "les amoureux sont seuls au monde," but this *solitude à deux* is the most marvelous thing in the world, which only "the most beautiful song" is worthy of putting in words.

---

29. Let us note at this point the movement towards the center. Landy, who, as it is well known, compares and contrasts the Canticle and Genesis 2–3, writes, "The centripetal attraction of the winds...inverts the centrifugal divergence of the four rivers in Genesis" (*Paradoxes of Paradise*, p. 198). He also says (p. 209) that while woman in Genesis is taken secondarily from man's side, in the Song she is the garden into which man reenters.

Chapter Five

CANTICLE 5

☙ ☙ ☙ ☙ ☙ ☙ ☙ ☙ ☙ ☙ ☙ ☙ ☙ ☙

Canticle 5.1

The next section (of only one verse) is put in the mouth of the lad. These "merisms" (honeycomb/honey; wine/milk) sound strange. One does not eat the honeycomb, and one does not mix wine and milk. The term correspondence is not horizontal but vertical, so to speak: honeycomb and wine, honey and milk. While the latter pair has already been met above (Cant 4.11), the other pair clearly alludes to 1 Samuel 14, the only other text where is found an amalgam of such keywords as "come" (surprisingly emphasized in the Samuel text), "honeycomb," and "eating" (a forbidden food, a forbidden mix; 1 Sam 14.10, 12 [x 2], 25, 27, 32–35). Let us note incidentally that 1 Sam 14.25 and Cant 5.1 are the sole texts in the Bible pointing to a tree as the locus of honey.

The Canticle's vocabulary is borrowed from 1 Sam 14.25–27 (the story of Jonathan, son of the king, who ate *debaš* and *ya'ar*, not knowing about Saul's vow). After Jonathan ate, his "eyes were enlightened" (*wa-taro'enah 'eynayw*), as in Gen 3.7 we had *wa-tipaqaḥ enah 'eyney š^eneyhem* (the eyes of both were opened) after eating the "forbidden fruit." In both texts (1 Samuel and Genesis) are the violation of a taboo and an impending punishment by death. The Song of Songs here daringly challenges the taboo. The groom finds delightful the honey eaten in the garden revisited with the woman glorified. Note here again the identification of the Shulammite with the land through the association of honey and milk. In the lover's eyes, the maiden is fulfillment of the promise included in the expression "a land that flows [has her menses] with milk and honey [instead of an impure bloodstream]."[1]

Another literary parallel is drawn with the combination of wine and milk in Isa 55.1; they represent abundance in the produce of agriculture and nomadism.[2] In the texts of Isaiah and the Canticle, the evocation is heavenly. Everyone is invited to enjoy fully and without restriction this new "Eden" (cf. Isa 55.2), even to the point of drunkenness.[3]

Adrianus van Selms finds another parallel in Hos 2.5 [7]: "my bread and my water, my wool and my flax, my oil and my drink." He writes,

> Probably in this text [of the Canticle] the gifts are mentioned as metaphorical indications of erotic pleasure, but even so it is evident that the imagery has been borrowed from the lovers' custom of exchanging presents.... It is remarkable that in both passages [Hosea and the Canticle] six gifts are enumerated; that in both instances the gifts are paired; that all the gifts carry the suffix of the first person singular. And that the background in reality is always the exchanging of gifts among lovers.[4]

What needs further to be emphasized, however, is that in Hosea the woman receives gifts from her illegitimate lovers; in the Song, the woman *gives* gifts to her *singular* lover. In the former case, there is a reflection of the societal custom, according to which the female is supported by the male in charge, father, brother, or lover.[5] In the Song, the woman demonstrates her independence by reversing the order of giving-receiving. Furthermore, the first person singular possessive pronoun is used by the adulterous woman in Hosea in her description of the salary of her prostitution. To such arrogant complacency, God responds by claiming "my grain...my wine...my

---

1. See my "Une Terre qui découle" and now "The Land in D and P." See above p. 110 and below pp. 153ff.

2. So Lys, *Le plus beau chant*, p. 202. About the text of Isa 55.1, Westermann speaks of a "crescendo from the things essential to life, water and bread...to what is superfluous, wine and milk" (*Isaiah 40–66*, p. 282).

3. This latter characteristic has become a customary feature during the festival of Purim, probably on the basis of a text like Isa 55.2.

4. van Selms, "Hosea and Canticles," p. 88.

5. Hence the predicament of the widow is particularly pitiful as is shown by the examples of Naomi and Ruth.

wool and my flax" (Hos 2.9 [11] in contrast to 2.5 [7]). In the following prophetic context, the woman has strikingly lost her assertive speech in the first person singular: there are in verses 10–15 [9–17] a multiplication of third person singular forms to speak of "her" and all that belongs to "her." The transformation in the Canticle could not be more complete!

On the last part of verse 1, it may be said that the lover's call to his companions is as bantering as was Jonathan's in 1 Samuel 14. The New Revised Standard Version renders *dôdîm* by "with love" in spite of the parallelism with the preceding term! Indeed, *dôd* designates exclusively the male character in the Canticle. In an elegant variation, David A. Dorsey thinks that the exhortation *'ikᵉlû re῾îm* is the poet's "own words addressed to both lovers."[6] *Re῾îm* (friends) and *dôdîm* (beloved ones) would designate the girl and her lover together. That may well be, as it may also be that Gomer's opening up to all lovers is here redeemed by the opening of the woman, "locked garden" and "sealed spring," to her lover. This latter solution has the preference of Francis Landy; he writes, "Self-fulfillment, then, is achieved through self-surrender." Let us note also, in passing, that Cant 5.1 for Landy constitutes the Song's "emotional center."[7] The main point is that the "friends" and "beloved ones" are now described as roaming the new Eden. As it were, the first human couple are now invited to drink the cup to the last drop and to be merry. "Once again, life snatches itself from Tehom," says Hans-Josef Heinevetter.[8] The human guilt, if any, does not belong to the sexual order, in spite of a perennial interpretation of the Genesis myth by moralists of all times.

Canticle 5.2–8

"The shift from scene I to scene II was a shift in space; the one from II to III, a change in time; between III and IV, the change is in attitudes (sleep/waking, or dream/reality)," says Daniel Lys.[9] The new

---

6. Dorsey, "Literary Structuring," p. 95.
7. Landy, "The Song of Songs," pp. 313, 317.
8. Heinevetter, "*Komm nun, mein Liebster,*" p. 197.
9. For Lys, the new section is "Chant IV. 5.2–6.3" (*Le plus beau chant,* p. 205).

section — scene IV according to Lys — runs from 5.2 to 5.8 and is put in the woman's mouth. Let us note, in passing, the incongruity, from an allegorical viewpoint, of God's being the one long expected instead of Israel, as the allegory requires. Similarly, she is called by her lover "perfect," not perfected; she is pure, not purified (v. 2). Furthermore, the metaphor of the land or countryside, which had been applied to her above, is now claimed by him in verse 2b. It is one more way for the Canticle to show its consistency, for there is throughout the poem a perfect equilibrium between the genders and the particular metaphors that characterize them. They are for the most part interchangeable.[10] That is why Michael Fox states, "The equality of the lovers and the equality of their love, rather than the Song's earthly sensuality are what makes their union an inappropriate analogy for the bond between God and Israel."[11]

The complaint of the shepherd before the closed door may well imitate Egyptian love songs, as affirmed by Fox. At any rate, the eroticism of the description is unmistakable. I know that Paul Haupt sins by exaggeration in his almost obscene interpretation, but when Wilhelm Wittekindt and Max Haller see, behind the "hole"[12] and the "hand" in 5.4, the "vagina" and "phallus" (figuratively, *hand* means "penis," in Ugarit, Egypt, Israel; cf. Isa 57.8, 10, with which the Canticle here is in kinship), the only mistake they make is in their mythological reading of the Song, not in seeing the obvious. Even if one takes the scene at face value, it remains that the sexual connotation is so crystal clear that it is not required from any reader to have read Freud beforehand. When eroticism is so evident in "serious" literature, its defiant character is, to say the least, probable. To insist on that point with a detailed analysis would be unbecoming. I shall only raise here a few possible ironical connections of the author's discourse with ambient traditions.

---

10. On that score as well the Canticle sets a model that should not pass unnoticed in the contemporary debate about "patriarchal" metaphors in the Bible. The Song of Songs shows that it is indeed biblically possible to use "androgynous" metaphors (see above p. 70, n. 5).

11. Fox, *Ancient Egyptian Love Songs*, p. 237.

12. Harper tells us that this is not a keyhole but a hole in the door "through which women could look out upon and speak with men without being unduly exposed to observation themselves" (*The Song of Solomon*, p. 36). At any rate, says Frymer-Kensky, "to open the door" in Sumerian myth means performing a formal act of marriage (*In the Wake of the Goddesses*, p. 22).

As discussed above in the introduction, the Song of Songs reverses the scene of Genesis 2–3. We are thus not surprised when we find in the Canticle allusions to clothing and disrobing. In 5.3, the woman declares that she has removed her clothes; in chapter 7 also, she is naked and described as such; 5.7 says that the watchmen take away her veil, thus exposing her to shame, "the great enemy of the two lovers," as says Landy.[13] Earlier in 4.11, the text celebrated the fragrance of her garment. On this score as well, the contrast with Genesis is remarkable. While in this latter document, clothing is a sign of embarrassment, of estrangement between the genders, and of alienation from the animal world, in the Song nakedness and clothing are uncannily the two faces of the same thing. Again in this part of the Canticle, the contrast with Hosea is stark. Hos 2.5, 12, 13 (in English, vv. 3, 9, 10) know in the Song their very reversal. She is beautiful, clothed or bare; her garments do not hide her but enhance her comeliness and attractiveness, like jewels with which her dress is associated (cf. Cant 1.10–11; 4.9).

Cant 5.4b is almost verbatim Jer 31.20 (*ḥamû me'ay lô*), but in Jeremiah, God expresses his sentiments for Ephraim! The kinship of Cant 5.6 with the same text of Jer (31.22) goes in the same direction (see here below).

Verse 5 says, "[M]y hands dripped with myrrh, my fingers with liquid myrrh, upon the handles of the bolt." The liquid myrrh is a liturgical fluid mentioned in a text that, by now, is familiar to us, namely, Exod 30.23 (on the anointing oil in the tabernacle/temple to undulate the tent of meeting, the ark of the covenant, the altar of burnt offering, etc.). All comments on this verse in the Canticle, therefore, seem superfluous here.[14]

The New Revised Standard Version's translation of verse 6b reduces the erotic impact of the verb. The beloved has not just "turned"; he has "slipped away" (cf. Jer 31.22), after she opened to him. Above, we saw what to think about this "opening" (see p. 117). Now, he is gone. Understandably, she is dismayed ("My soul failed me" or, figuratively, "I died"; cf. Gen 35.18). The slipping away of

---

13. Landy, *Paradoxes of Paradise*, p. 224; cf. Ezekiel 16; 23.
14. Perhaps it is even permitted to see at this point a bold image reversing the empirical idea that the human is born from a "stinking drop," as says *P.A.* 3.1 ("Whence thou comest, — from a fetid drop"; Herford, *Pirke Aboth: The Ethics of the Talmud*, p. 63).

the lover is compounded by the reason given by the maiden for her "dying," namely, *bedabberô*, meaning not "when he spoke" (NRSV) but "when he escaped, when he fled" by changing only the vocalization with Ferdinand Hitzig (*bedoberô*; cf. the hifil in Pss 18.48; 47.4: "to push behind").[15]

The following two formulas in verse 6 ("I sought him / I called him" vs. "I did not find him / he gave no answer") are "des clichés de la littérature prophétique," say André Robert, Raymond Tournay, and André Feuillet.[16] The referent is above all Hosea (2.9; 3.4–5; particularly 5.6, 15). Jeremiah echoes this in 29.13 (see also Isa 51.1; 65.1; Zech 8.21–22). Once again in the idiom of the Canticle, the shepherd becomes the substitute of God. (More on these verses below; see pp. 198, 200.)

After the suggestive scene of verses 2–6, we are not surprised that the guards consider the Shulammite as a lewd woman and treat her with disrespect. Besides, in the preceding verses, the situation described of a young woman living in her house by herself, with no family around, totally free of her movements, was not short of being scandalous in the ancient Near East (it would still be today in Islamic countries, for example). A very strict rule, which is illustrated in Deut 22.20–21, was that a girl was to remain chaste until her marriage. Now the woman of the Canticle leaves home at night and is alone in the streets, helpless and vulnerable, and the guards, either through contempt or wantonness, abuse her as a prostitute — the disrobing is part of the humiliation inflicted upon a prostitute (cf. Isa 3.18–24) — when she is only intoxicated with love.[17] One could see here an "imitation" by the Shulammite of the behavior of Wisdom according to Prov 8.1–4 (cf. Prov 7.9–12). But, a closer parallel is, I think, provided by Hannah in 1 Sam 1.13. She also, she first, had already been confused with a drunken woman when she was only absorbed in her prayer! Here, however, the ill-treatment goes a

---

15. Hitzig, *Das Holelied erklärt.* As Tournay says, "This reading is confirmed by the semantics of the root *dbr,* whose original meaning is 'to be behind,' hence 'to follow, to push behind, to push back, to put in flight' (cf. Ps 18.48; 47.4). Those meanings are found again in Arabic, in Akkadian, and in Aramaic" (in RTF, *Le Cantique des Cantiques,* p. 445).

16. RTF, *Le Cantique des Cantiques,* p. 205.

17. The term translated by "veil" appears only in our Canticle text and in Isa 3.23, which speaks of a wanton woman, that is, Jerusalem personified.

great deal further. The loving maiden is subjected to outrage at the hands of brutes. In that respect, it is highly striking that in verse 8 (as well as in the similarly worded expression of 2.5), the LXX has *tetrōmenē,* which presupposes the verb *ḥll* in Hebrew, that is, "to pierce through" (the Shulammite has been wounded by the guards, according to v. 7) instead of *ḥlh* of MT (NRSV: "I am faint"). In a prophecy of doom against Babylon, Jeremiah says, "They shall fall down slain (*ḥalalîm*) in the land of the Chaldeans, and wounded (*meduqqarîm*) in her streets" (Jer 51.4).[18]

As indicated by one of my students, Carol Koskelovski, the issue here is one of women's boundaries. According to traditional views, the woman must be chaste; she is even a property to be protected. In the Canticle, the woman radically redefines her boundaries and, as a result, is assaulted by the guards assuming that she is promiscuous or a prostitute. Within this perspective, I call attention to the surrounding context. There is a real clash between verses 2–6a (part A) and verses 6b–7 (part B): in B she is mistaken for a prostitute or at least a wanton woman; in A she presents herself as modest. Through that literary device, the author barred the way to a wrong understanding of B: she may *appear* as a whore to the guards, but the reader already knows in the light of a recent example that she is not.[19] A similar situation is obtained in the subsequent context (v. 8). The transition from the guards to the "daughters of Jerusalem" is a stroke of genius. In the eyes of a woman, they only can understand to which extremes takes female infatuation. The negative judgment of Lys upon those "daughters of Jerusalem" in the book (they are mentioned some six times) should not blind us to the fact that, at times, they seem to be a prolongation of sorts of the Shulammite, as the "companions" are of the shepherd.

Hannah had been humiliated by the priest Eli; the Shulammite is "wounded" by "sentinels of the walls"! How could anyone miss the

---

18. *Meduqqarîm* is not the same word as in Cant 5.7 (root *pṣʿ*), but, interestingly enough, it is the term used by the famous Zech 12.10 text (*daqarû*).

19. Allegory changes the modesty of the girl (who would not open) into sin, the contrary of the plain sense, says Lys (*Le plus beau chant,* p. 207). In reality, the issue between the maiden and the guards is social. The "Vase of the Cairo Museum," a large ostracon at the Cairo Museum (IFAO 1266+Cairo Mus. 25218) studied by Derchain, provides an interesting comparative development. The female lover declares that even if she were flogged through Syria or down to Nubia, "she could not bow to their projects nor give her own decision up" (quoted by Derchain, "Le lotus, la mandragore et le perséa," p. 79).

allusion to the prophetic saying, "Upon your walls, O Jerusalem, I have posted sentinels" (Isa 62.6 NRSV)? Now, the least one can say of those sentinels is that they are not particularly softhearted. It is not the first time that we find in the Song a derisive allusion to the prophets as a corporation. Texts of Hosea, Jeremiah, and Ezekiel have been ironically used so far. Now, the poet takes aim at sayings in the Book of Isaiah. Indeed, another Isaianic passage comes to mind: "In that day the Lord will take away the finery of the anklets, the headbands, and the crescents; . . . the festal robes, the mantles, . . . and the veils (*redîdîm*)" (Isa 3.18–23 NRSV). The term *redîdîm* appears only in this text and in Cant 5.7. The Isaiah text adds (v. 24) the following, which will serve as an introduction to the next section, "Instead of perfume there will be a stench; and instead of a sash, a rope; and instead of well-set hair, baldness; and instead of a rich robe, a binding of sackcloth; instead of beauty, shame" (NRSV). The Canticle is the total reverse of the Isaianic text.

Canticle 5.9–16

The lyric glorification of the male lover (5.10–16) distances itself from Isaiah 3, while its wording is reminiscent of Lam 4.7 (within a literary unit that comprises 4.1–8). The text in Lamentations describes the terrible transformation of Zion from gold and jewels, as she previously was, to earthen pots and refuse after her destruction. Robert, Tournay, and Feuillet saw that parallel with our text but rejected it because, according to their prejudicial interpretation, God cannot "porter sur son visage la trace des souffrances de l'exil" ("bear on his face traces of the suffering of exile [*sic*]").[20] Beside the fact that Jewish thinking would not shrink from attributing pathos to God,[21] the parallel with Lamentations 4 is incontrovertible. One finds *ṣaḥ* and *'adôm* of Cant 5.10 also in Lam 4.7;[22] so is *ḥalab* of Cant 5.12. Here and there whiteness contrasts with blackness (cf.

---

20. RTF, *Le Cantiques des Cantique*, p. 211.

21. Cf. Heschel, *The Prophets*, passim (The divine pathos).

22. David also had been called *'admônî* in 1 Sam 16.12 and 17.42, which insist on his handsomeness (hence the text is messianic for Tournay; see RTF, *Le Cantique des Cantiques*, p. 445). In 1 Sam 16.12, in particular, one has a rare description of male beauty, with the mention of his eyes, as in Cant 5.12. This text may have been a model for the

šeḥôr in Cant 5.11 and Lam 4.8; albeit in the Canticle the opposition is purely aesthetic); in Lam 4.1–2 are found *r'oš, ketem, paz,* as
in Cant 5.11. In fact, the parallel between the two texts is so evident
that versions of the Canticle read "stone of gold" instead of "finest
gold" (*'eben* instead of *ketem*), influenced as they were by Lam 4.1
(*'abeney* and *ketem*.)[23] It is, however, evident that the Canticle reverses the sense of the imagery of Lamentations. The time of love
has replaced the time of mourning. Strikingly, the Canticle takes exception with the tears of Lamentations, as it did with the curses of
Genesis 3! (see the introduction, p. 37). Love in the Song of Songs
is redemptive; it is able to change guilt into innocence and weeping
into laughter.[24]

    With consistency, the poet speaks in verse 11 of "his wavy locks
[of hair]," a trait inspired by Lam 4.7's mention of the Nazirites
(NRSV: "princes") and again by the Isa 3.24 text ("well-set hair").
The locks continue the metaphor conjured up by Lamentations 4.
The root of *tal'talîm* (wavy) is *tll* I (from which comes the word *tell*)
and makes one think of Jerusalem in ruin, reduced to a tell (cf. Jer
30.18). It is not so under the pen of the poet. Here, the hair locks of
the beloved inspire wonder, not distress.

    The terms of the metaphor, at this point, shed a precious light
upon the way the author uses her similes, for the lad is not blond,
as the vehicle "finest gold" would infer. The following verse makes
clear, on the contrary, that his hair is "black as a raven"! We are led
to conclude that, like the other metaphors in the Song, this one is
relevant only by indirection. The impression made by his hair is to
be compared with the impression that *ketem paz* (finest gold) would
make. It may even happen that the artist was thinking of Baal statues
with a gold-plated head.[25] Be that as it may, on the level of surface
meaning, distance is maintained between the referent and the referee,

---

poet, but to conclude that she had messianism in mind is unwarranted. After all, the same
term, *'admônî,* designates Esau in Gen 25.25!

    23. Aquila also has *lithea tou chrusiou.* Syriac: *k'apha' dedahaba';* Symmachus: *hôs
lithos timios* (like a stone a great worth).

    24. See what I said in the introduction (p. 31) about the poet's "theology." Heinevet-
ter also sees in this Canticle text "heilsgeschichtliche Dimensionen" (*"Komm nun, mein
Liebster,"* p. 186) and speaks of "theological world-view" (cf. pp. 189–92).

    25. Keel writes, "descriptions of the statues of gods" (*The Song,* p. 198). Incidentally,
Keel also cites Lam 4.7 in this context. A. Bloch refers rather to Daniel 2, the idol erected
by Nebuchadnezzar (Bloch and Bloch, *The Song of Songs,* p. 185).

the vehicle and the tenor.[26] In fact, the poet takes advantage of that literary device of distancing to risk another "slip"; she introduces the raven, an unclean animal in the rest of biblical literature but here a positive term of comparison![27] The model text for 5.10–11, Lam 4.7 (see also v. 2), presents the same assemblage of contrasting colors. Jerusalem's princes, it says, used to be "purer than snow, whiter than milk; . . . [whose] bodies were more ruddy than coral," and "their hair [was] like sapphire" (NRSV)!

What we just saw about metaphors applies to the next simile. In verse 12, the man's eyes are, like the woman's were in 1.15 and 4.1, "like doves." That is, the eyes shine as "the wings of a dove covered with silver, its pinions with green gold," in the words of Ps 68.13 NRSV.[28] They shine all the more so as these "doves" are "beside springs of water" ('al 'apîqey mayîm), although the "water" happens to be milky or to look like milk. Among the different texts where the term 'apîq or 'apîqîm occurs, two stand out: Joel 1.20 and Ps 42.1 [2]. Both are about crying to God for help. In Joel, we read, "The beasts of the field cry unto you, because the springs of water are dried up." And in Ps 42.1 [2], we find the clause "as a deer longs for brooks of water." Again, the situation of distress and want is transformed in the Canticle into one of "plenty" (mille't);[29] the brooks are flowing abundantly; the doves can bathe in them. Since the water is "milk," the doves come out of it still whiter. Milk and whiteness were important ingredients in Lamentations 4, which we read earlier (cf. vv. 7–8). In the Canticle, the blackness of famine has all but disappeared. Love is the great provider.

In verse 13, the cheeks of the lover are "yielding fragrance" (NRSV), literally "towers of fragrance." This latter expression makes

---

26. Distance is maintained unless the description in the Canticle be seen as bawdy. On the basis of the Deir Alla "Inscription of Bileam," where the term dodu means "penis," Baruch Margalit understands zeh dôdî in Cant 5.16b that way. He also reads verse 11, ketem paz, as "red gold" (that is, mixed with copper) and as designating the color of the male member, surrounded by a black mons pubis, "black as a raven"; see in 4.6, har hammôr, gibe'at hallebônâ (personal communication with author).

27. Cf. Keel, "the black raven belongs to the realm of the hairy goat-spirits and the wild demons (Isa 34.11; Zeph 2.14) . . . it depicts the mysterious and uncanny side of the beloved" (The Song, p. 199). Note the stark contrast with the white doves in the following verse.

28. See above p. 80.

29. The LXX has epi plērōmata hudatōn; Vg, "iuxta fluenta plenissima"; the Pesh, 'al salmutha, "on perfection."

one think of Exodus 30 (quoted earlier several times), where the root *rqḥ* (to mix) appears no less than six times.[30] In Exodus 30, to recall, it is a question of the oil for anointment that must be used strictly in an appropriate manner, on pain of exclusion from the community. The preparation of the holy oil necessitates a great number of ingredients, including *besamîm* and *mor* (Exod 30.23–24), as we have *bosem* and *môr* in our Song text. The Canticle here summarizes the Exodus list with the word *migdelôt*, to be probably understood colloquially, something like "tons of." But now, it is not to anoint the tabernacle, the ark of the testimony, the utensils of the temple, the altar, etc. In spite of the threats against any misuse of the oil, the beloved shepherd is to be anointed with it for, as says Othmar Keel, these "fantastic hyperboles and superlatives ... imply that the woman's beloved evokes notions of divinity"![31]

With the remainder of verse 13, we do not leave the adverting to the temple. The sentence "His lips are lilies, distilling liquid myrrh" not only repeats in its last words an expression already encountered in 5.5, but a comparison with 1 Kgs 7.23–26 regarding the "molten sea" shows that the Song's author had that object in mind when describing the lips of the lover. Also the "lips" of the bronze basin were shaped like "lilies" (or lotuses; 1 Kgs 7.26). We are led to suspect that the descriptions in verse 14 were also inspired by details in the temple (see, e.g., 1 Kgs 7.20, which also speaks of "belly").

Still in the same vein, verse 15 comes with a comparison between the shepherd's legs and the temple columns, set upon "sockets of fine gold." The word *'adanîm* is a technical term for the sockets in the temple supporting the boards of the tabernacle and the columns on which are hooked the curtains of the court (see P; Exod 26.18–25; 27.11–18). The mention of cedars that follows orients in the same direction, for every temple piece of furniture was made of cedar (1 Kgs 6.9–10, 15–16, 18).[32]

The author shifts to a proximate referent in the last verse of chapter 5: "His speech is most sweet" (NRSV). The Syriac adds "like

---

30. See also below, Cant 8.2, p. 162.
31. Keel, *The Song*, pp. 201–2.
32. In the Gilgamesh epic, the cedar trees belong to the gods, who set the monster Huwawa (or, Humbaba) as their guardian (III.iv.136). The mountain of the cedar is "the dwelling place of the gods" (IV.v.6).

sweet combs of honey." *Maḥᵃmad,* "delight," directs once again
to the temple, as is shown by texts like Isa 64.10; Lam 1.10; and
2 Chr 36.19 (cf. Job 4.5).[33] Now, ironically, the author specifies
that she is not, in spite of appearances, praising the temple but "my
beloved...my friend/lover" (cf. Jer 3.20)! The Midrash at this point
pushed intertextuality so far as to tally "This is my beloved, this
is my friend" with both "This is my God, I will beautify Him"
(Exod 15.2) and "This is God, our God, He will lead us unto death"
(Ps 48.14 [15]). This way, the Midrash tied up together Eros and
Thanatos, a complex that "took flesh" in the martyrdom of Rabbi
Aqiba.[34]

   This *waṣf* about the shepherd is the only one in the lass's mouth.
Formally, it may have been influenced by the polychromia of Egyptian statues.[35] Some scholars think that a divine character (the god
Dôd?) provided the model, but the proposition of Jacques Winandy,
who calls forth the description of the high priest in Sir 50.5–12,
is more felicitous. It corresponds better to the general slant of the
poem. But whether influenced by a divine or by a pontifical model,
the *Beschreibungslied* displays a blown-up extravagance, both in the
similes and in the abrupt shift of moods from mourning to exultation. Perhaps the extravagance is made still starker by the very
borrowing of the literary genre of the *waṣf* at the benefit of a man.[36]
Generally, the *waṣf* is about the woman.[37]

   In conclusion to this section, two points need to be stressed. First,
faithful to her principle of using the same metaphors for both genders, the poet in this textual unit presents a *waṣf* comparing the
young lad with the temple in Jerusalem. The same equation had ear-

---

33. Texts suggested by Tournay in RTF, *Le Cantique des Cantiques,* p. 447.

34. To recall, according to Rabbi Aqiba's legend, he came to the Torah through the
love of a woman, and leaving behind his shepherding, he went to school at the age of
forty. It is also in the name of love (of God) that he lost his life as a martyr. Cf. p. 67,
n. 161. "All through the Middle Ages, Jews went enthusiastically to a martyr's death with
R. Akiva's words on their lips," says Boyarin (*Intertextuality and the Reading of Midrash,*
p. 128). On the martyrdom of Rabbi Aqiba as the only way to fulfill the commandment
of love, see Boyarin, pp. 125–26 and p. 39.

35. Dubarle, "L'amour humain dans le Cantique des Cantiques."

36. The Canticle's *waṣf* praising the shepherd's handsomeness may have served as a
literary prototype of the male physique. Cf. Dan 2.31–35 (difference: the decreasing values
of the statue parts).

37. Let us also note in passing the peculiarities of vocabulary (many words are special
to the Song of Songs); see below p. 176, n. 46

lier been drawn between the lass and the Solomonic shrine. Second, there is no room in the Song of Songs for laments and breast-beating. (Even when she is mistreated and wounded by the sentinels on the walls [5.7], the maiden sheds no tears). Traditional texts about guilt feelings and mourning see their message reversed by the author of the Canticle, who borrows them for the sake of showing love triumphant and properly redemptive. Love is the golden key to Paradise Retrieved, a paradise that is not projected into another space and another time (even eschatological) but is found in the *hic et nunc* of the gender encounter.

Chapter Six

CANTICLE 6

ৰ্জ ৰ্জ ৰ্জ ৰ্জ ৰ্জ ৰ্জ ৰ্জ ৰ্জ ৰ্জ ৰ্জ ৰ্জ ৰ্জ ৰ্জ ৰ্জ

Canticle 6.1–3

Canticle 6 opens up with a question by the chorus, "Where has your beloved gone?" (NRSV). This is one of the occasions when the chorus plays an ambiguous role in the book. Its female members are called sometimes to witness occurrences and sometimes to empathize with the Shulammite. But they also represent "propriety" in the eyes of contemporary society. Then their questions betray irritation, even bitterness. Here is a case in point. "Where is your beloved?" means something like, "Mr. Wonderful seems to have just dropped you! Shall we look after him for you?" Moreover, behind the seemingly "innocent" questioning, ancient Near Eastern ears would perceive familiar reminiscences of mythological origin: the disappearance of Baal, the ritual questions of Anath to the Sun-goddess, and the promise of the latter that she will be looking for him.[1]

The term of endearment "fairest among women" (*hayyapâ bannašîm),* addressed to the maiden and already met in 5.9, should not deceive us. At least, it does not deceive her. It may be, with James Reese, that the title is linked to the Sumerian goddess Inanna, as in one of the *hieros gamos* poems. But even so, it should be kept in perspective, for it is not the first time that we see the poet's use of existing love songs from various provenances (especially from Egypt, but also from Sumer and Akkad). Her alchemy, however, changes everything in sight. In any case, we are a far cry from the allegorical reading, for which the expression "daughters of Jerusalem" refers to

---

1. Ug. "Baal and Moth" 6.3.10ff.

the prophets, who offer their help to find God, lost on account of Israel's sin.

The "fairest among women" answers the chorus that it is not worth their while to look after her beloved: he freely comes to her (v. 2); he and she belong to each other (v. 3); there is no need for a third party, and certainly not for mediation. Rather than letting himself be convinced by the daughters of Jerusalem, he keeps his distance from the chorus, which represents the nonlove (cf. 2.17; 8.14). The daughters of Jerusalem would not understand the sort of relationship that exists between her and him, which is expressed in terms that conservative diehards find objectionable. Again in this reply of the Shulammite, she says — on the model of "I am your God and you are my people" — "I am my beloved's and my beloved is mine" (v. 3 NRSV), as in 2.16.[2]

The recurrent use of the word *šôšannîm*, "lilies" or "lotuses," in this short section emphasizes still more the author's predilection for that metaphor. It appears in Cant 2.1–2, 16; 4.5; 5.13; 6.2–3; 7.3. Most of the commentators pass it by, seeing in it a charming poetic term to be classified among the numerous natural metaphors of the booklet. But, already above, regarding Cant 2.1 and 5.13, we have seen that the *šôšannâ* is a large flower and that it may be a trope for a female's genitals. But there is more to this metaphor. The word *lily/lilies* is not frequent in the Hebrew Bible, where it is used in the description of the temple's column capitals (see a text already cited in the same connection, 1 Kgs 7.19, 22) and its bronze basin's brim, whose shape is said to have been "like the flower of a lily" (1 Kgs 7.26 NRSV=2 Chr 4.5). In Hos 14.6, the term is a figure for Israel. Thus, once again, the Song's author shows her irreverence by uttering her claim for the primacy of love — a primacy on the fringe of transcendence. The heroine is compared to lilies, as the temple's column capitals and the "molten sea" are shaped like lilies. In the process, the woman of the Canticle is "sacralized," and the temple of Jerusalem is eroticized!

Before we leave this section, it is time to reflect upon the surprisingly recurrent motif of the shepherd's pasturing among the lilies. As in 2.1, the *šôšannâ* is the beloved maiden; it is clear that the word in

---

2. See above, Cant 2.16, p. 90.

the plural designates females (including the Shulammite) and that the male seems to be described as in promiscuous company on several occasions. This is all the more unexpected as the declaration about his shepherding comes to cap the formula of exclusivity, "I am my lover's and my lover is mine"! The fact of the matter is that the Song of Songs sees the man as epitomizing all the lovers; he is *the* lover. As to the woman, she also is all women, the whole of womanhood; their mutual love summarizes and surpasses all other loves. Therefore, all women around the woman praise her beauty, in which they recognize the paradigm of their own; all the males participate in the lover's quest, desire, and wonder. He has become all his companions (cf. 5.1b; 8.13); she, all her cohorts (cf. 6.8–9); their love includes the totality of love in the whole world; and the poem of their encounter is the song of all songs. The idea is the same when Francis Landy notes that "each act of intercourse repeats that of one's parents, and so all parents,... each act of conception takes us back to our birth, and so history is confounded by a series of identical moments."[3]

Canticle 6.4–11

The next section in chapter 6 is another *waṣf* in the shepherd's mouth praising the beauty of the Shulammite. It starts with verse 4 and runs to verse 11, after which she speaks in verse 12. He first likens her with Tirzah in the north and Jerusalem in the south. Consistent with the use of metaphors in the Song, this "geographical" comparison must be understood the way Michael Fox, for example, indicates. The Shulammite does not look like these cities, but

> The degree of her proud beauty equals theirs.... *Tirṣah* was probably half-legendary by the time the Song was composed. ...[Cf.] the resemblance of its name to the verb *rṣh*, "want," "take pleasure in"; thus LXX *eudokia*, "pleasing one," Pesh *ṣbyn'*, "delight," and Vg *suavis et decora*, "pleasing and graceful." ...[T]he interpretation of the word in this way in the

---

3. Landy, *Paradoxes of Paradise*, p. 208.

Versions shows that a pun could easily be heard in the name
Tirzah.[4]

The choice of Jerusalem as a norm of beauty is not surprising (cf. Jer
6.2; Isa 33.20; Psalm 48; Dan 11.41), but why Tirzah rather than
Samaria, for instance? André Robert, Raymond Tournay, and André
Feuillet are probably in the right when they see here a polemical slant
against the Samaritans at the time the poem was composed.[5] The
bypassing of Samaria and the preference for the hoary place name
of Tirzah, first a Canaanite city before becoming an Israelite one
(Josh 12.24), is a sign of the late date of the poem, when animosities
increased between Judeans and Samaritans, says also Reese.

The young person is compared to cities whose antiqued handsomeness is thus reflected in her heraldic beauty. She is, like the name
Tirzah indicates, pleasant and desirable (the root *rṣh* means also "to
love" or, as preferred by the Targum here, "to desire"). What then
does the name *Jerusalem* say in parallel to Tirzah? It says, no doubt,
that she is the "Shulammite," the peacemaker. Jerusalem and peace
are associated in texts of great poetic beauty (Isa 33.20; 60.17 [cf.
v. 18]; 66.12; Ps 122.6 [cf. verses 7–8]). The damsel joins north
and south as the depiction of her beauty transgresses all limits and
displays dimensions of universality.

Also consistent with the rest of the poem, "the description of the
heroine is made after the history and the geography of the Holy
Land" — says Daniel Lys — "and this is the reverse of the process
of allegory."[6] Speaking of which, I do not resist the urge to quote,
with Marvin Pope, the marvelous insight of Athanasius, who used
the Greek rendering of the Hebrew *trṣh* with the sense of "approval"
(see our pointing to LXX above). He applied this to the assimilation
of Jews and Christians,

Those who come from the Gentiles ought not to be unlike Jerusalem, that there may be but one people, for this is so when we
honor the Law and believe in Christ. For the God of the Law

---

4. Fox, *Ancient Egyptian Love Songs,* p. 151.
5. RTF, *Le Cantique des Cantiques,* p. 233.
6. Lys, *Le plus beau chant,* p. 235.

and Gospels is One, and whoever is not made like Jerusalem does not become the Bridegroom's friend.[7]

More difficult to understand, even for the allegorical school,[8] is the remainder of verse 4: "terrible as an army with banners" (NRSV), a simile that is repeated in verse 10. The phrase 'ayumâ kannid*e*galôt is diversely understood, as evidenced by the Versions and the ancient commentators. The LXX has *tetagmenai,* "ranked"; Symmachus, *hōs tagmata parembolōn,* "like ranked troops of the camps"; Pesh, "like elected"; Ibn Ezra, "camps with banners"; Christian Ginsburg, "bannered hosts." Andrew Harper analyzes the form as a participle nifal of a denominative, from *degel,* "banner," that is, "companies of soldiers about a flag" (cf. LXX). The metaphor would describe the girl as conquering, overcoming as an army, or as inaccessible. Harper judiciously adds, "It is a marked peculiarity of the Song to repeat similes and epithets. They are introduced first for some special reason, then immediately they seem to crystallize into standing epithets."[9] We could add that such similes, as we pointed to earlier, are often taken from the military (cf. 4.1–8, above p. 104). In fact, the thinking in this latter text (verse 4) is comparable and has been already dealt with; it need not be further developed here. Furthermore, verse 5 prolongs the same line: the woman is so "terrible" that a look of her eyes overwhelms or, in military terms, repels, pushes off, or even "assaults," as the parallel texts of Isa 3.5 and Prov 6.3 explicate.

Verses 4–5 are not the only time in the Song when notions coming from religious horizons other than the Yahwistic are in their turn parodied and secularized. Here the Canticle may couple beauty and terror, as these features were commonly combined in ancient Near Eastern goddesses. They are now applied to the Shulammite, the little shepherdess idealized by her lover. But, closer to home, the biblical use of the term *terrible,* as in Hab 1.7; Gen 15.12; Jer 50.38; and Job 20.25, builds with the Canticle a contrast that Enrica Salvaneschi

---

7. In Pope, *Song of Songs,* p. 563; see also there the commentary of Gregory the Great.

8. RTF simply do not translate the expression! In a note, RTF state, "A la fin, on omet: 'redoutable comme des bataillons'" (*Le Cantique des Cantiques,* p. 233). In the commentary, they explain that these words of verse 4 are probably a gloss based on verse 10.

9. Cf. "feeding among the lilies" in Harper, *The Song of Solomon,* p. 46.

qualifies as a "kind of *coincidentia oppositorum:* what is said in a Yahwistic reference is transformed into a panegyric of the loved one, and her praise is molded within a [formerly] negative reality."[10]

The end of verse 5 repeats 4.1, verse 6 is a simpler rewording of 4.2, and verse 7 is the literal repetition of 4.3b. Note the striking repetitions that occur in the Song. In general, critics and commentators are content with noting the fact: "les répétitions sont dans le style du Cantique," say Robert, Tournay, and Feuillet.[11] But, in reality, it suffices not to treat the phenomenon as a simple peculiarity of the poem. I shall examine the matter at the end of this book in a section titled "Ritornello" (p. 190).

Canticle 6.8–10: Verses 8–9 draw a stark contrasting parallel between the great number of the king's mates ("sixty queens and eighty concubines, and maidens without number"; NRSV) and the uniqueness (*'aḥat*) of the girlfriend. What is at the basis of the authorial selection of the numbers *sixty* and *eighty* is hard to know. The text falls in parallel with 1 Kgs 11.1–3, where the numbers given are, however, considerably higher: seven hundred and three hundred, for a total of one thousand. No doubt, in the Song, the number *one thousand* is not retained because it would indicate the fullness of love, whereas only the shepherd and the maiden of the Canticle enjoy that fullness. But the text of 1 Kings invites us here also to add the different numbers, that is, $60+80=140$ ($=70\times2$). The number 140 means something like "numberless," whose imprecision is stressed in the latter part of the same verse. This computation obtains also when the difference between 1,000 and 140 is made ($=860$), for, by a "gematria" of sorts, 860 represents $8+6\times10=140$ (again).[12] In other words, the text insists, as expected by the context, on the very great number of queens, concubines, and maidens.

The numbers are ostensibly in praise of Solomon's grandeur, but the truth of the matter is that the poem derides the great king. To him be the "thousand" and the "two hundred," 8.11–12 says with a biting irony, for the shepherd's vineyard is incomparable and is worth all the concubines of the world. To him, the maiden is *'aḥat!* The

---

10. Salvaneschi, *Cantico dei cantici*, p. 53.
11. RTF, *Le Cantique des Cantiques*, p. 236.
12. If need be, the computation indicates how firmly this text of the Canticle presupposes and depends upon the text of 1 Kings.

term is put in evidence; it is predicated in an emphatic form. It has the meaning of "unique," which, as Ariel Bloch reminds us, is expressed elsewhere by the word *yaḥîd* except when the text wants to insist on a religious connotation, as in 2 Sam 7.23, "a unique nation on earth" (JPS). Furthermore, *'aḥat* is repeated a second time, which is a way to stress its importance but which also raises the reader's expectation that it will be repeated a third time. Instead, it is replaced by the substitute epithet *barâ*, which stresses not only the proximity with Deut 6.4, where God is proclaimed in his uniqueness, but also, for instance, with Ps 19.9 or Ps 2.12 (*našᵉqu bar*), where God's anointed is the preferred one, as the maiden here is the preferred child of her mother.[13] In other words, a whole complex theological pronouncement about God and his elect is here feminized and demythicized! (Or perhaps, because of the margin of interpretation left open by the poem, are we allowed to understand that, among the seven hundred and three hundred candidates to divinity, or the sixty and eighty and numberless pretenders to lordship, the uniqueness of God is mirrored in the uniqueness of the beloved one? Love does not deal in numbers or in quantity, any more than does God enthroned in the midst of a pantheon). Let us note with Othmar Keel the parallel with Nathan's parable contrasting the "many flocks" to the "one lamb," that is, the royal harem to Uriah's one wife (2 Sam 12.2–3).[14]

Ezekiel also comes to mind. He opposed the uniqueness of Abraham to the multiplicity of people in the land (Ezek 33.24: *'eḥad hayah Abraham . . . wa-'anaḥᵉnû rabbîm*). But while there is no trace of irreverence in the Ezekiel text, the poet's tone is unmistakably taunting some "orthodox" ears accustomed to the affirmation that only God is "the unique," a benchmark in the proclamation of the *šemaʿ* in Deut 6.4. If there is any doubt in the reader's mind, the rest of verse 9 in the Canticle leaves no room for hesitation: "The maidens saw her and called her happy (*wa-yeʾašᵉrûha*); the queens and concubines also did praise her (*wa-yehalᵉlûha*)." The two verbs *beatify* and *praise* are found together again in Prov 31.28, also com-

13. On the motif of the mother in the Song, see below p. 162. Note that *'eḥad* can have either a numerical or a qualitative meaning: "one" (vs. many) or "unique" (*unice delecta*; vs. common, ordinary). Both meanings are present in the Cant 6.9: "Only *one* is my dove perfect, she is *unique* to her mother, flawless to her that bore her" (my emphasis).

14. Keel, *The Song*, p. 219.

bined as here with the *waw* conversive; note that this form appears here in the Canticle for the first and last time. In Proverbs, the subjects are in the masculine (sons and husband), while here, on the contrary, the subjects are maidens, queens, and concubines, that is, persons whose femininity is strongly stressed. The verbs in the Song are thus expected to be in the third person feminine plural, while they in fact are in the masculine. Through that bias, they stay closer to the Proverbs model and also are purposely in homophony with Genesis 30.13 (*'iššᵉrûnî banôt*) and the psalmic *halᵉlûyah*.[15]

The verb *hll* is clearly cultic. It is, however, used by Egyptian princes to praise Sarah's beauty before Pharaoh, who takes her into his harem (Gen 12.15).[16] Thus, we have one more text speaking of a royal harem versus a uniquely beautiful woman, Sarah, who cannot just be added as another unit to a mass of queens, concubines, and maidens, for her incognito creates an impossible confusion. The same situation would obtain in the Canticle, but even her own mother recognized the heroine's uniqueness. She is indeed like the moon and the sun, as Abraham's people would sometime be like the stars in the sky or even *the* star, as says Balaam, insisting in his turn on the uniqueness of God's nation (Num 24.17), for it is "a people living apart and which does not mix with [other] nations" (Num 23.9).

About *wa-yeʾašᵉrûha* in verse 9, something must be said in consonance with what we saw above regarding *barâ*. In Psalm 2, for instance, God and his "preferred one" were envisaged. Here, similarly, the background remains one of praising God and His blessing of the king, as in Ps 72.17, or of the land, as in Mal 3.12. The Shulammite has taken the place of the one and the other.

In the following verse (6.10), the description the shepherd gives of the maiden goes one step further. She is not only superior to queens, but she is like a goddess.[17] Roland Murphy quotes a beautiful Sumerian parallel from ca. 1950 B.C.E. that is addressed to Inanna, who is identified with the morning and evening star:

---

15. The shift from -*yah* (YHWH) to -*ha* (personal pronoun in the third person feminine singular; "her") encapsulates the whole message of the Song of Songs.

16. See the similarities in vocabulary between Cant 6.9 and Gen 12.14–15 (verbs *praise* and *see*, adjective *beautiful*).

17. The *TOB* capitalizes "Dawn" and understands it to be the name of a goddess.

> [T]he one come forth on high,
> I will hail!
>
> . . . .
>
> The great [queen] of heaven,
>   Inanna,
> I will hail!
>
> . . . .
>
> of her brilliant coming forth
>   in the evening sky,
> of her lighting up in the sky
>   like Moon and Sun,
>
> . . . .
>
> . . . I will sing![18]

In the Canticle, verse 10 begins with the oft-repeated question *mî zo't* (cf. 3.6; 8.5) but does not continue with the customary verb *'olah.* The verb here is *nišqepah,* a third person singular feminine nifal perfect that is found again only in two other texts: Judg 5.28, already cited, where it characterizes Sisera's mother's expectation of the return of her son, while weeping with the premonition of bad news; and (especially) Jer 6.1, *kî ra'â nišq^{e}pah miṣṣapôn,* "evil looms out of the north" (NRSV). See also the following verse, Jer 6.2, about the "daughter of Zion" whose comeliness is lost. The shift from *'olah* in Cant 3.6 to *nišqepah* has been caused by the imitation of these Judges and Jeremiah texts, which, as usual, the author transforms into their opposite. The Shulammite brings *šalôm* where there was devastation. She is not the *ra'â* seen by Jeremiah, nor is she like the stupid young man of Prov 7.6 whom Wisdom watched (*niš^{e}qaptî*). The Shulammite comes like light itself (*šaḥar, lebanâ, ḥammâ*) in contrast with *be-nešep-be-'ereb yôm be-'îšôn lay^{e}lâ wa-'apelâ,* "in the twilight, in the evening, in the dark and black night," of Prov 7.9, and with Jer 6.4, *qûmû we-na'aleh baṣṣohorayim . . . panah hayyôm kî yinnatû ṣileley 'ereb qûmû we-na'aleh ballay^{e}lâ,* "Up and let us attack at noon! . . . the day declines, the shadows of evening lengthen! Up and let us attack by night" (NRSV). Not for

---

18. Hymn attributed to Iddin-Dagan, cited in Murphy, *The Song of Songs,* p. 51.

the first time we see the poet take a stance that runs counter to the prophecies of doom, as if the ambient milieu around her had been morbidly harping on those predictions of cataclysm.

The end of verse 10 repeats part of verse 4 above, "terrible as an army with banners," and by now, the repetition does not surprise us as it is a familiar phenomenon in the book. Our puzzlement originates elsewhere, namely, in the fact that the phrase seems to replace an expected simile about stars. Earlier, the moon paralleled the dawn; the sun in the second verset begs for a similar correspondent. Inconspicuous as it may appear, the parallel is to be found in the phrase "army with banners," which alludes to the heavenly "army" as in the phrase, *YHWH ṣeba'ôt*.[19]

Before leaving this verse, let us note the expression "bright as the sun"; it uses the same participle *barâ* that we found in verse 9 above, where it had the meaning of "preferred." Pointing back to 1.5 where the heroine was complaining about the burning sun, Landy notes here the image of full integration and adds that the planet "has met its match!"[20]

Canticle 6.11: Cant 6.11 offers less interest for us, barring a couple of elements that deserve mention. It is unclear who is now speaking, but chances are that the maiden is responding to the *waṣf*.[21] The following verse (v. 12) is put in her mouth, and furthermore, it is clear that the visit to the nut orchard is the feat of the woman meeting with her lover. It is also the way the LXX has understood the text, for it adds, perhaps on the model of 7.13b, "There, I will offer you my breasts." Strikingly, the garden is here called *ginnâ*, in the feminine form when it designates the male partner, while the regular form in the Canticle is *gan*, in the masculine when it designates the female partner. One cannot be more equitable or gender inclusive! No decisive conclusion can be drawn from the use here of *'ibbey*, from the root *'bb*, which is frequent in Aramaic with the meaning of "to grow," "to mature." Metaphorically, it can be ap-

---

19. More on this verse below, in my discussion of Keel's commentary (p. 201). A. Bloch rejects the interpretation of banners here and suggests "daunting as the stars" (Bloch and Bloch, *The Song of Songs*, p. 191).

20. Landy, *Paradoxes of Paradise*, p. 151.

21. Pace RTF, *Le Cantiques des Cantiques*, p. 242 (but cf. Tournay, "Les chariots d'Aminadab [Cant 6.12]," p. 292: she is speaking).

plied to the man's or the woman's charming features, said Tournay.[22] Another metaphor in verse 11, *paraḥ* (to bud) is used as a simile in Isa 27.6 and Hos 14.6 for Israel's restoration after the exile in Babylon.

"To come down and look" in verse 11 may be a tongue-in-cheek play of words with 6.2, which said that the shepherd *yarad ... lirᵉ'ôt*, while we have here in the mouth of woman, *yaradᵉtî lirᵉ'ôt!* As to this latter wording, it evidently echoes Gen 11.5, where God comes down to look at the tower that people were building in the plain of Shinar. Again a negative text is turned into a positive one in the Canticle.[23]

Canticle 6.12–13a[7.1a]

Cant 6.12 is a downright *crux interpretum*.[24] Numerous theories have been advanced to resolve the problem posed by this text, and I cannot review them all here. The MT reads as follows: *lo' yadaᵉtî napᵉšî samatᵉnî marᵉkebôt 'ammî nadîb*. The French translation in the *TOB* thinks that it is uttered by the Shulammite who says, "Je ne reconnais pas mon propre moi: il me rend timide, bien que fille de nobles gens!" ("I do not recognize my own self: he makes me shy, although I am the daughter of noblemen!"). The text is difficult right from the first words of the verse, and when we continue reading, things do not become any easier. The LXX betrays its embarrassment, "My soul did not know it had made me the chariots of Aminadab" (also, VLat, Arabic, etc.). A score of Hebrew MSS would shore up this understanding, but the LXX translation is as problematic as it is literal.[25] The Vg binds *napᵉšî* with *samatᵉnî* and understands the verb from the root *šmm*, "to be astounded";

---

22. In RTF, *Le Cantique des Cantiques*, p. 448, quoting M. Held, "A Faithful Lover," p. 20.

23. More on verse 11 below, p. 201.

24. Echoing the frustration of commentators, Landy gives up on translating the verse, which he calls "the most notoriously obscure in the Song." He is of the opinion that the man is speaking (*Paradoxes of Paradise*, p. 333 n. 34).

25. Let us note that there is nothing conclusive to draw from the extant 4QCant a col. 2 that "covers" our text. The fragment, whose photograph has been graciously communicated to me by my colleague Emmanuel Tov, is too minute. Tov is presently preparing the publication of several 4QCant fragments.

the initial *m* of *mar^ekebôt* is the partitive *min;* and *'ammî nadîb* is the proper name *Amminadab:* "Nescivi; anima mea conturbavit me propter quadrigas Aminadab."

Let us start with the last word, in Hebrew *'ammî nadîb,* which is understood by the Greek, and often since, as the proper name elsewhere spelled Amminadab. The name *Amminadab* is well attested (Exod 6.23 [father-in-law of Aaron]; Num 1.7; 2.3; 7.12, 17; 10.14 [in Numbers, it is always the father of Naḥšon]; Ruth 4.19–20 [Amminadab is the great-grandfather of Boaz]; 1 Chr 2.10 [father of Naḥšon]; 6.22; 15.10–11 [the name of a Levite]). In biblical Hebrew it resembles closely another name, Abinadab; hence a certain confusion arises in texts and readers alike. In fact, in the LXX (as is attested by 1 Sam 7.1; 2 Sam 6.3–4; 1 Chr 13.7) we always have Aminadab, with an *m,* and not Abinadab, with a *b* as sometimes in the MT.

What is this Abinadab/Amminadab/Ammî-nadîb doing in the Song? First of all, honoring the spelling of the MT, one may invoke the biblical connection often made between *'am,* "people," and *nadîb,* "noble" (see Judg 5.9; Num 21.18; Pss 47.10; 113.8; 1 Chr 29.9; = Aq, Sym, Quinta, Pesh). One can follow, I would suggest, the lead of the LXX and consider the combination *'ammî-nadîb* as a proper name, similar to Amminadab (hence, in all probability, to Abinadab). Such a suggestion has an old tradition in its favor, and besides, it does not seem unreasonable to see the words *'ammî* and *nadîb/nadab* purposely associated by allusion to the well-known names Amminadab and Abinadab. Now, we have reviewed above the evidence regarding Amminadab, and the conclusion is that this track is not the most promising as far as the Canticle is concerned. If we turn to *Abinadab,* however, among the different people called by that name, one distinguishes (*a*) a son of Jesse (1 Sam 16.8; 17.13; 1 Chr 2.13); (*b*) a son of Saul (1 Sam 31.2; 1 Chr 8.33; 9.39; 10.2); (*c*) the one who housed the ark before David transferred it to Jerusalem (1 Sam 7.1; 2 Sam 6.3–4; 1 Chr 13.7).

From such a perspective, we can make several points regarding our text. Their cumulative impact will help decipher it. First, verse 12 (like v. 11) is from the lips of the Shulammite (cf. LXX, "There, I shall offer you my breasts," as we saw above; furthermore, the response to the lover began in v. 11, and the same verbal construction is found in both vv. 11 and 12). Second, with Salvaneschi, let us note the "configuratione idolatrica" of all contexts when it is a question of "not knowing" (see Isa 1.3; 45.20; 56.10; Ps 14.4). Not knowing expresses "a state of passivity and stupor before an incomprehensible or unanticipated occurrence."[26] Job compares himself to mountains without knowledge as regards the action of God (9.5), so when God passes him by, *lo' 'eda' nap^ešî* (9.21). But in the Canticle, it is not God who provokes that loss of self-consciousness but the "impulso passionale"![27] Third, the terms *chariots* and *Ammî-nadîb* (so close to Amminadab/Abinadab) refer, in the mischievous mood of Canticle that is felt all along, to the Books of Samuel. In 1 Samuel 6, the ark of the covenant is put on a chariot and sent away by the Philistines. It came to be housed by Abinadab (7.1). Later on, according to 2 Samuel 6, the ark is brought on a chariot from Abinadab's house to Zion. Note in 1 Samuel 6 the presence of the verb *sîm* (put) three times (vv. 8, 11, 15); the verb *yada'* (know) is also present three times (vv. 1, 3, 9); and especially the verb *šûb* (return) appears seven times, with a double form in v. 3 (see vv. 4, 7, 8, 16, 17, 21)! Thus, in this text, which serves as one of the references for Cant 6.12d, the central word is clearly "return." Now, we should note that in the verse that follows our text (Cant 6.13 [7.1]: "Return, return, O Shulammite! Return, return, that we may look upon you"; NRSV), the verb *return* appears four times — a possible allusion to the compass and, beyond, to prophetic visions of the return of exiles from all corners, like in Ezekiel 37.

Regarding the structure of that unusual quadruple feminine imperative, one thinks of the powerful prophetic exhortation to Zion in Isa 52.1, *'ûrî 'ûrî*, itself echoing, within the same song, 51.17 and further 51.9, *'ûrî 'ûrî!* As to the restored city of his vision, the prophet speaks of "beautiful garments" (52.1); the poet speaks of the nice-looking aspect of the Shulammite (7.1). Besides, her feet are beautiful, like those of the messenger of good tidings in Isa 52.7; her neck is haughty, as Zion's neck is free of bonds in Isa 52.2. As a marriageable girl, she cannot be bought by money (Cant 8.7), as Jerusalem is "redeemed without money" (Isa 52.3; cf. 55.1).

---

26. Salvaneschi, *Cantico dei cantici*, p. 101.
27. Ibid.

Furthermore our text strikingly parallels 1 Sam 7.3 ("If you are returning to the LORD with all your heart"; NRSV), which comes immediately after the mention of the ark's transfer into the house of Abinadab! One should also draw a comparison with a prophetic text in which both themes of the ark and the return to YHWH appear, namely, Jer 3.14–16: "Return, O faithless children,... they shall no longer say, 'The ark of the covenant of the LORD.' It shall not come to mind, or be remembered, or missed" (NRSV). In Jer 31.17–19, there is no mention of the ark, but the return is strongly emphasized (four times in the text). Here the theme is conjugated with the one of self-knowledge (v. 19b) as in the Canticle![28] In this Jeremian text, however, as in the other possible parallels to our Canticle verse, the accent is set on repentance, and the mood is somber, a far cry from the jubilant note in the Canticle.

At this stage, we can make the following points about Cant 6:12–13a. First, texts of 1 and 2 Samuel, Job, Isaiah, Jeremiah, and Ezekiel served the author of the Song as literary models. Second, the "return" mentioned in these texts is charged with a theological meaning. It is a matter of repentance and change of life. In the Song, however — this must be emphasized — the "return" of the Shulammite has totally lost any direct spiritual dimension. Third, the "chariots," in Hebrew *mar*^e*kebôt*, recall the famous *mer*^e*kabâ* (sing.) of Ezekiel (1 and 10) or again those (*rekeb*, collective sing.) of Elijah and Elisha (2 Kgs 2.12; 13.14). In these latter narratives, the two prophets are so imposing and terrible that each one individually is worth all the chariots of Israel.[29] Elijah, of course, "goes up to heaven" in a *rekeb 'eš* ("chariot of fire"; 2 Kgs 2.11–12). In the anthological text as reshaped by the Song, however, we no longer soar to such summits. The ninth-century prophetic inspiration used to lift up men and mountains; now, it is Eros that transports the Shulammite. True, she does not, as did her models, become a "guru" of sorts, but

---

28. *aḥarey hiwwade*ʿî (*TOB*: "sitôt que je me vois sous mon vrai jour").

29. Salvaneschi (*Cantico dei cantici*, p. 55) emphasizes this military aspect of the motif. "The coach belongs to Yhwh's panoply," she says. "It designates in a syncretistic anthropomorphism [God]'s majesty (Ps 68.18) and anger...(Isa 66.15...see Hab 3.8)." It can also point to the violence of invaders in opposition to YHWH (Isa 4.13; 2 Kgs 23.11). Psalm 20 is especially close to the Canticle here (v. 6 mentions banners; v. 7, we read, ʿattah yadaʿtî). She concludes — as she did about 6.4, 10 above — that formerly negative elements are now used in similes about the loved one.

she can declare, as it were in their wake, "I no longer know my-self" (lo' yada'etî nap'šî) — for the phrase conveys a certain sense of intoxication, prophetic or erotic![30]

A first conclusion imposes itself regarding the text of Cant 6.12. It was simply impossible for anyone in Israel to miss the allusion to the ark of the covenant or to the spirit of prophecy, both associ-ated, as in the evocation of King Solomon in his palanquin,[31] with a chariot (rekeb or mer'kabâ), veritable jewel case for the "high-priced pearl." True, we are not dealing with a pure citation from Samuel or Ezekiel, but this makes the manner in which the Canticle reflects those traditional sources all the more significant. On the bedrock of the universal image of the lover being possessed by what the French call "les grands transports de l'amour" (the great rapture of love), the Song of Songs describes the elating effects of being loved by the shepherd-lover. This feeling is expressed, as usual in the Song, by using Israel's sacred repertoire.

In fact, Cant 6.12 touches on two chords at the same time; let us call them "metaphorical" and "rhetorical." Metaphorically, the Shu-lammite is compared with the chariot that carried the ark of YHWH or with those prophets of old who were identified with the whole chariotry of Israel. The shepherd's love transforms the Shulammite into the (sacred) chariot that transported the ark of the covenant to and from the house of Abinadab.[32] The name of the latter is occasion for the author to use the other chord, a rhetorical one. Abinadab/ Amminadab is spelled by her as Ammî-nadîb, thereby changing the meaning of the name, as Abram became Abraham. Abinadab, who housed the ark at the time of Saul and David, is 'ammî nadîb, "my noble people." Thus, the Shulammite appears to her lover as princely and awesome as was the chariot of the ark, the most famous chariot in the history of Israel, the mer'kabâ or YHWH's throne. To this, he

---

30. M. Deckers ("Structure of the Song of Songs," p. 195) quotes Catullus's complaint, "Odi et amo, quare id faciam, fortasse requiris. Nescio, sed fieri sentio et excrurior" ("I hate and I love, why should I do that, you might ask. I don't know, but I feel it happening and I hurt").

31. Translated "chariot" in King James Version of Cant 3.9!

32. The metaphor of the "chariot" for a woman is hoary. The Sumerian text Lu-dingir-ra reads, "My mother is a palm-tree with a very sweet smell, A chariot of pinewood, a litter of boxwood" (text cited by Holman in his communication to the IOSOT Conference in Cambridge, England, in July 1995, under the title, "A Fresh Attempt at Understanding the Imagery of Canticles 3:6–11").

glosses ʿammî and *nadîb,* that is, Israel, the noble people. Further-more, the vocabulary here evokes the Jeremian *bat ʿammî* (6.26; 8.11, 21–23; 14.17), that is, Zion, a term that in Jeremiah is never used in punitive passages. It is set in parallel with *bat ṣîôn,* "lovely and delicate"(6.2 Heb.) that "faints before the killers" (4.31). Note that all of this arises out of an erotic evocation![33]

If this complex metaphor looks to us extreme, suffice it here to recall striking Egyptian parallels. Philippe Derchain, for instance, in an article already mentioned above, studies an erotic song in which the female lover calls her friend "my god, my lotus!"[34] Their union is described as "la création elle-même, comme le moment le plus sublime du monde, comme un équivalent de sa naissance" (p. 72). It is doubtful, however, whether Derchain is right to state that "le chant d'amour n'en prend pas pour autant un caractère religieux, mais au contraire aide à concevoir dans quelle mesure les thèmes de la mythologie et de la symbolique sacrée étaient familiers et intégrés à la vie quotidienne" (ibid.). Even if he were right in the Egyptian case,[35] a similar declaration would be impossible as regards the Song of Songs, not only because of the character of biblical traditions but also because of the subversive nature of the poem.[36]

Pursuing our investigation, we now turn to the transformation of *nadab* into *nadîb,* which opens the door to another wordplay. We have seen that the following verse summons four times the Shulammite to "return." The text continues in 7.1 [7.2] with a

---

33. Herbert, "The Song of Songs," p. 473 (par. 410b) has seen the parallel between Cant 6.12 and 2 Sam 6.3, but he cannot believe his own eyes! He adds, "But to suggest that the betrothed one be identified with God's Ark is hardly probable."

34. Derchain, "Le lotus, la mandragore et le perséa."

35. But even here one is skeptical. Krinetzki says that from Egyptian love songs them-selves we learn that some of them were called "proverbs" or "wisdom songs" with the purpose of teaching practical ways on the basis of religious principles. He writes, *"Pro-fane Liebeslieder in unserem heutigen Sinn gab es in diesem Kulturbereich nicht"* (*Das Hohelied,* p. 43, his emphasis).

36. As Müller writes, "Es wäre nicht das einzige Mal, dass das Schöne, nachdem es das Heilige abgelöst, nun seinerseits dem Heiligen aufhilft." And further, "so ist in lyrischer Reproduktion ein Stück religiöser Ursprache wiedergewonnen" ("Poesie und Magie in Cant 4:12–15," pp. 157, 161). Rather than contemplating with Derchain a divorce of sorts between religion and the "daily life," thus projecting on the ancient world a mod-ern dualistic conception, I suggest that it is preferable to apply to erotic literature of the ancient Near East what Bakhtin, for instance, says of carnival (see above, esp. p. 64). Carnival satirizes kings and bishops and all authority. Similarly, I think that the erotic lit-erature, in Egypt(?) as in Israel, is subversive; it is therefore related to the religious world it parodies.

new designation for the belle, namely, *bat-nadîb* ("fille de noble" [a nobleman's daughter], says the *TOB*). With respect to this, one should evaluate the theological weight of the stem *ndb* in Scripture. The Chronicler, in particular, insists strongly upon this verbal root.[37] In the hitpael (reflexive mode), it can signify a voluntary commitment to God; see especially 1 Chronicles 29, where incidentally we find both *'ammî* and *hit^enaddeb* in verses 17–18, while verse 24 emphasizes the importance of the root *šlm* (at the basis of the name *Shulammite*). Indeed, for Chronicles, the Israelites are *nadîb*, "noble," and are committed to God (*hit^enaddeb*) because they are a "theophoric" people, to cite Tournay.[38] This is the reason why the chariots mentioned in the Canticle and elsewhere are fearsome; they belong to the sacral and sometimes become instruments of death for those who handle them improperly (in 1 Samuel 6, seventy men die; in 2 Samuel 6, the victim is Uzza). The Shulammite also can signify ambivalence. In Cant 6.4 and 10, the Shulammite is "terrible as an army with banners."[39]

The association of the "return" motif with the nobility of personages brings to mind Ps 113.8, where "[the Lord elevates the poor] that He may set them with princes, with the princes of His people." On the basis of this striking parallel, the Blochs "restore" the order of words in the Canticle as *nadîb 'ammî*. But this hypothetical inversion is, I believe, unnecessary, although I see it as a further emphasis on the poet's surprising but purposeful order of words, in conformity with *bat nadîb*.

The development inaugurated in 6.12 does not stop there, but with verse 13 is a rebound of sorts with new motifs. We now turn to that new outgrowth of the general theme.

Canticle 6.13b[7.1b]

The text continues on its own impetus. After the "return" motif (brought about by the metaphor of the chariot), and before the desig-

---

37. So does also 1 Maccabees, which prolongs here the line initiated by Chronicles. In 1 Macc 2.42, the Hasidim are called "the dedicated to the Torah" (*hammidnaddebîm*).

38. See above p. 136, n. 21.

39. See above Meyers's remark about the military metaphors used in the Canticle to describe the Shulammite (p. 104).

nation of the lass as a "nobleman's daughter" (an expression created by association with the name Amminadab/Abinadab), comes the motif of a dance (or a quadrille, according to the *TOB*) in 6.13b[7.1b]. It occurs most unexpectedly in this context. Not surprisingly, it has been diversely interpreted and has given rise at times to more or less far-fetched scholarly reconstructions. One of the least exaggerated suggestions is to see it adverting to a war dance or a saber dance. The merit of this reading lies in the parallel it draws with the Books of Samuel wherein King David is readily associated with songs and dances celebrating his military exploits. But according to this interpretation, the allusion to David is at best vague and indirect, whereas, as we shall see, it should be explicit.

Our leading hermeneutical principle again offers the advantage of simplifying the matter. When the ark was transferred to Zion, we are told, David led the procession while "swirling with all his might" (2 Sam 6.14). Several texts in Samuel must be cited along the same line: 1 Sam 18.6; 21.11 [12]; 29.5 (cf. Jer 31.4).[40] With Cant 6.13b[7.1b] being built against that background of Davidic traditions in the Books of Samuel, the theme of dance imposed itself here also. True, *meḥolâ* is absent in 2 Samuel 6, but "the term would have been quite appropriate to the [Davidic] celebration," says Marvin Pope.[41] As already seen above, the author does not borrow servilely her references. Her rule is to transform her sources although never beyond recognition.

With the mention of *maḥᵃnayim* — probably the place called "Mahanayim" or a wordplay on it — the textual reference shifts to 1 Kgs 4.14. There, one of the twelve prefects of Solomon, named Ahinadab (the author of the Canticle probably confused him with Abinadab, who is mentioned precisely a few sentences before in 1 Kgs 4.11), is given official functions by the king at Mahanayim. The confusion in Canticle is understandable, but perhaps it is conscious and on purpose.

As a final point, I want to stress that in Cant 6.13 [7.1] the maiden is called "the Shulammite" (twice) for the first and only time. This designation deserves attention, especially as it has no parallel else-

---

40. All those texts spring forth from Exod 15.20.
41. Pope, *Song of Songs*, p. 603.

where. We know one Abishag the *Shunammite* (that is, a person coming from Shonem or Shunem) in 1 Kings 1.[42] We remember this "extremely beautiful" young girl brought to King David (him again!) to share his bed and warm him up in his old days (or rather, nights). We are also told that the unfortunate maiden remained a virgin in this sordid affair. We find her once again in 1 Kgs 2.22 as a stake in court intrigue, where as usual no one asks for her opinion.[43]

It would seem that the construct *Shulammite* in the Song of Songs is in wordplay with the "gentilic" designation *Shunammite* in the Davidic saga.[44] Several MSS of the LXX and Vg have *Sounam(e)itis*; the VLat has *Sunamitis*. Besides, there is in the poem a constant pointing to the story of King David and, more specifically, to the beginning and the end of his reign in Jerusalem. The young David "swirls with all his might" (2 Sam 6.14); by contrast, the old David is senile and impotent. Similarly, in the episode of the transfer of the ark on Abinadab's chariot, the young maidens play an active role (so active that Michal takes umbrage at her husband's indulgence with them; see 2 Sam 6.20–22). But, in contradistinction to such dynamism, in the sad latter days of the great king, the "extremely beautiful" Abishag of Shunem is unable to arouse him. Such a flamboyant start and such a pitiful end! The story of Israel's "messianic" king, and of God's indwelling in Zion, cannot forever end on that note that sounds like a knell.[45] Just as Abinadab ("my noble father") becomes Amminadab/Ammî-nadîb ("my people are noble and generous") in the Canticle, so does the Shunammite become the Shulammite.[46] But what a find! The Shulammite is the anti-

---

42. As the confusion earlier in the text between Amminadab and Abinadab was made, it seems, on purpose, there is presently a second such alliteration between the Shunammite and the Shulammite. The two phenomena in mutual proximity are so closely related that they render it impossible to consider them as coincidental. Goitein has also seen the correspondence between the Shulammite and the Shunammite, but he explains that Shunem was later called Shulem; he adds that *Shunammite* became a generic byword for feminine beauty ("The Song of Songs").

43. The Shunammite also could have said, *lo' yada'etî nap^e šî*. Pope, *Song of Songs*, p. 598, rightly suggests that Solomon in his turn did not remain indifferent to the charms of Abishag. This is probably not foreign to his violent reaction to Adonyah's request in 1 Kings 2 (although there were also assuredly strong *raisons d'état*).

44. First suggested by Budde and Siegfried, this connection has been rejected by Rowley in "The Meaning of the Shulammite" but accepted lately by Keel, *The Song*, p. 228.

45. A parallel can be found in the redeeming of 1 Samuel 15's events as retold in the Book of Esther. See my *The Feminine Unconventional*, pp. 49–83.

46. See Tournay, "Les chariots d'Aminadab (Cant 6.12)."

Shunammite! While the latter was a passive and reified woman, the former is quicksilver, an active subject whose first person pronoun dominates the poem from start to finish. And she spells out "peace/contentment" for her lover.

The Shunammite Abishag served as a link between the reign of David and the one of Solomon, his son (1 Kings 1–2). Her presence does, so to speak, unify the two kings, but not in the best of ways. She is used and abused by both; there is with young Solomon no improvement to her uncouth situation (1 Kgs 2.13–25). Indeed, one may reach the conclusion that as David's pitiful end was mirrored in the sad figure of the Shunammite, so the same feminine presence constitutes an ominous beginning in Solomon's reign.

In the so-called Succession Narrative, the role of Abishag during David's final and Solomon's initial days is described in dispassionate terms. The Song of Songs, however, shuns such objectivity. In the poet's opinion, something so wrong must be righted; someone must redeem the unforgivable manipulations by father and son of the woman-object. Such is the role of the Shulammite; she is the transfigured Shunammite. She is also the anti-Solomon, not only in her refusal to be manipulated by him, as was her ancient foil, but in sharing contrastingly a name similar to hers and to his. *Shulammite* and *Shelomoh* are united within a common verbal root.[47] The specific intent of this rapprochement is emphasized in Cant 8.10, where the belle is "the one who encounters peace (*šalôm*)."[48]

Now, there is a biting irony in calling her "pacified." This form

---

47. There is a great deal of irony in feminizing the great king! (So in Mesopotamia, Ninlil is the feminine form of Enlil.) Like Ahasuerus in the Book of Esther, Solomon readily personifies the universe of the phallus. Speaking of Esther, one should cautiously envisage the theory that sees in the name Shulammite in the Canticle a Hebrew form of the Akkadian goddess Shulmànitu (as Mordecai recalls Marduk; and Esther, Astarte); see here below. By contrast, it is interesting (and possibly coming originally from the Song of Songs) that the maiden who requested from Herod Antipas the head of John the Baptist received from tradition the name of Salome, that is, Solomon in the feminine! Rowley ("The Meaning of 'the Shulammite'") went in that direction as regards the Canticle and rendered Shulammite as "the Solomoness," that is, as a title for Solomon's consort. Pope (*Song of Songs*, p. 597) sees a confirmation of this in a text of Ugarit that speaks of Dan'el's wife as Lady Dantay (*mitt dnty*); the article before the title, he says, serves here as equivalent to the vocative particle.

48. This parallel is strongly emphasized by Harper (*The Song of Solomon*, p. 60), who thinks of an ironical reference in Cant 8.10 to Solomon's raising the siege from the "city" he could not invest. According to 4QShirShabb frgs. 1.20–22 also, "Shulammit" comes from *shalom* (see below p. 184).

is, however, shored up by the versions of Aquila and the Quinta: *eirēneuousa,* the "Pacified," corresponding to a form *qutal* in Hebrew. We would rather have expected something like "the fiery one" in such a dynamic context (see Cant 6.10c), all the more so if we see in the background, with William Albright, Shulmànitu, goddess of love and war in Babylon.[49] But, to recall, in 1 Sam 7.1, 13–14 it is said that peace was restored after the victory over the Philistines and the transfer of the ark to the house of Abinadab. Once again, the poet plays on several strings at the same time and with the same brilliance. (I shall return to the meanings of the maiden's name below, p. 184.)

The conclusion to the analysis of this discrete section is also valid for the whole of the poem. We are again in full irreverence. By using a language that is "sacred" within a Yahwistic context, the singer reverses the prophetic process of metaphorization. A prophet or a historiographer could speak of the ark as a living person (see, e.g., 2 Sam 7.2); here the poet speaks of a living person as the ark of the covenant. The belle says either that the shepherd has put her on the very chariot of Abinadab that transferred the ark of the covenant to Jerusalem in the time of David or that he transformed her into that very chariot. The idea is the same in both cases. She says that she has been brought by him to sit on or even to become the most prestigious chariot of Israel's history. Hence, the call to "come back" in Cant 6:13 [7.1] is in a feminine imperative form, *šûbî* (in contradistinction with 1 Samuel 6 generally, where the verb appears six times in the masculine, but in parallel with v. 3, where the verb is in the feminine), as it fits not only the gender of the addressee but also of the ark (the *'agalâ* [*hadašâ*] that came [back] in 1 Samuel 6 and 2 Samuel 6).

From the Shulammite as the ark of the covenant or its chariot, the metaphor shifts to a description of her as the people dancing around the carriage; she is the "virgin Israel, taking her tambourines, and going forth *bim^eḥôl m^esaḥaqîm*" (in the dance of merrymakers), as says Jer 31.4 (a text already mentioned as a model for Cant

---

49. Albright, *Yhwh and the Gods of Canaan,* p. 150. Then, one must see here a process of demythologization of the warrior goddess into the "Pacified"; this "Jerusalemite" par excellence, as fair as the Shunammite Abishag, has found her own "Solomon" (see Lys, *Le plus beau chant,* pp. 251–52).

1.4). *Meholat* in the Canticle or *maḥôl* in Jeremiah might come from *ḥûl*, "to dance," or from *ḥll*, "to celebrate," "to sing." Jeremiah's *bimᵉḥôl mᵉšaḥaqîm*, however, is changed in the Canticle into *kimᵉḥolat hammaḥᵃnayim* to fulfill three purposes. First, the allusion is to Jer 31.13: "Then shall the virgins rejoice in the *maḥôl*, and the young men and old together." The virgin maidens are ranging in one group, and the *baḥurîm* and the *zeqénîm* in another, thus forming two camps (an idea that the Song expressed by the dual form of *maḥᵃneh*). A second purpose is expressed in the guise of an echo to another text utilized here by the Canticle, namely, Gen 32.1–2[2–3]. On his way back to his father's from Mesopotamia, Jacob sees angels of God and exclaims, "This is God's *maḥᵃneh!* And he called that place *Maḥᵃnayim,*" (v. 2; literally, "the two camps"). Jacob, we are further told, divided also his party into two camps (*li-šᵉney maḥᵃnôt*, Gen 32.7–8, 10) [8–9, 11]. A third reference is brought about by Athalya Brenner. She recalls the skirmish between Joab and Abner at Gibeon in 2 Sam 2.12–16. Abner has come there from Maḥanayim (vv. 8–9), and the fight occurs between two rows of twelve representatives for each camp.[50] The poet brought together the three texts — of Jeremiah 31, Genesis 32, and 2 Samuel 2 — on the basis of the presence in all three of a duality of camps. This theme appears to assume a particular importance in the Canticle text. Here is why: those who are addressed by the shepherd in the terms of Jacob's story are primarily the chorus of maidens; they are supposed to constitute one of the two choirs, the other being implicitly constituted by the cohort of shepherds around the lover. The Shulammite is surrounded by two choruses that responsively praise her. Jack M. Sasson, on the basis of an Akkadian cognate of *maḥôl* (*melultu*), says that the word designates an antiphonal singing, thus a double group of performers (cf. the verb *'anah*, "respond," in Exod 32.18; 1 Sam 21.12b; 39.5; perhaps Ps 88.1).[51]

The cause for joy and gladness is described in "scriptural" terms. The religious vocabulary is mobilized for the sake of celebrating Eros. The same sacred vocabulary also allows the dancing girl to identify herself with the "two camps" that Jacob saw, formed either

---

50. Brenner, *A Feminist Companion*, p. 245 n. 3. (Note, however, that the term *camp* does not appear in this Samuel text.)

51. Sasson, "The Worship of the Golden Calf."

with two clusters of angels or with Jacob and his kin facing the angelic army. It is also the reason why the poet turned for her own composition to the Jeremian text, which speaks of the changing of sorrow into joy, of mourning into dance, but then the occasion was provided by the return of the exiles to Zion. Both scenes — Jacob's and Esau's reunion and the return from exile — are reinterpreted, or rather reused, within a different context. The Shulammite is now the centerfold in the process of peacemaking (between the two brothers or between the divine and the human "camps") and of "resurrection" (through Israel's restoration). I claim once more that no one in the singer's audience could have missed the allusion to these "biblical" traditions.

We must, however, proceed further as regards the borrowing from the Genesis episode, for still another element of that particular text was felt important by the author, namely, the motif of the return of Jacob (Gen 32.9; "Return [šûb] to your country"). As we have seen above, the theme of homecoming is central in Canticle 6. With this new allusion to a previous tradition, the "return" of Jacob, the range of borrowing is complete. The Canticle brought together and daringly equated four returns — of Jacob, of the ark, of the exiles, and of the Shulammite (four times repeated in Cant 6.13 [7.1]). The latter return, however, does not take us to the Alpine theological levels the theme had reached in the Pentateuch and the Prophets! But, what was lost in the process is perhaps compensated by an easier breathing. The point is debatable. What is beyond doubt, however, is that for the poet, love is the key that opens all doors. The loves between the man and the woman of the Song are put on a par with *Heilsgeschichte* in all its aspects and thrusts. The couple relive the whole of revelation in their mutual relationship. When the Shulammite returns after an absence so brief, so long, they experience the return of the exiles to Jerusalem in their very flesh; they experience the frantic dance of "restoration" when she is again present to her lover; the reunion of the awesome estranged brothers enters their familiar universe when she is again in her lover's embrace; the glorious entrance of the ark in the city of David, the city of God, is their "daily bread" when she comes in and he sees her as if she were the *merᵉkabâ* itself! The poet describes Eros as epiphany.

Postscriptum

At the end of this development that started in Cant 6.12, some hindsight reflection is appropriate. There is no way for us to know what kind of familiarity people in the ancient world had with what constitutes today's biblical traditions. I tend to believe that these were at least as well known then as they are today. What we have gained through their collection in "Scriptures" is counterbalanced by the flood of other information and traditions with which they conflict in our modern minds. Before such a flood broke its dikes, however, I imagine that the ancestral traditions in all their details and nuances occupied a large place in popular memory. Besides, if I am too optimistic on that point, little of my argumentation above is jeopardized. For one did not need to have a cross-referential proficiency in "biblical" literature to be aware, at least in part, of the allusive character of the author's poetry (which by nature is referential). Above, I have reviewed several angles from which to identify the allusiveness of terms like *chariot* and *Ammî-nadîb*. It was sufficient that the original audience be aware of one or two of them.

Chapter Seven

CANTICLE 7

Ɔ⊂ Ɔ⊂ Ɔ⊂ Ɔ⊂ Ɔ⊂ Ɔ⊂ Ɔ⊂ Ɔ⊂ Ɔ⊂ Ɔ⊂ Ɔ⊂ Ɔ⊂ Ɔ⊂ Ɔ⊂

Canticle 7.1–9 [7.2–10]

In what immediately follows, the lass's deportment is described with delight, and nothing of what has just been said is lost for all practical purposes. She is now called in 7.1 [2] *bat nadîb*, echoing *'ammî nadîb* of 6.12. Andrew Harper comments, " 'a born lady' as we say" (p. 49). The LXX A and VLat read "daughter of Aminadab"! Be that as it may, she is seen dancing in attire reduced to the strict minimum, leaving little to imagination, it seems.[1] The whole scene might conjure up a Gypsy girl giving herself in spectacle. The preceding statement that she is "a born lady" was thus not superfluous. It is not the first time that we encounter that inner contradiction in the social status of the lady. Already in Canticle 1 she described herself as blackened by the sun (in contrast with the fairness of city-dwelling belles carefully protecting their skin against sunburn) while her lover thinks of her in princely or royal terms. If she is contemptible, it is in the eyes of some only. If here she appears as a Gypsy, it is not through vulgarity but through the great rapture of love, as we said above (p. 141).

All the same, the Shulammite, it must be admitted, repeatedly puts herself in questionable situations. Here, she dances in a circle, and her swirling flights inspire the author with an image in which her curving thighs compare with swinging necklaces. On another occasion, another *nadîb* person, indeed a king, swirled "with all his

---

1. Let us note, however, Keel's refusal here to see a dance. He says that battles were preceded "by all kinds of crude games, fights, and jokes between the two hostile armies (cf. 2 Sam 2.14–16)" (*The Song*, p. 229).

might" and did not keep a proper composure in the eyes of some (2 Sam 6.14, 20). That textual rapprochement is certainly not foreign to the authorial intent in the Canticle, as we have seen. But, still another comparison imposes itself, this time with a prophetic text that has become familiar to us from earlier contexts. Jeremiah 31 was in the background of Cant 6.13 [7.1]; here again, in verse 2, the same Jeremian chapter is used by the author. In conformity with Jer 31.22 is found the root *ḥmq*, "to withdraw" (cf. above, Cant 5.6, p. 118), hence in Jeremiah's context the meaning "to waver" and in the Canticle text the sense of "to swing." See also in both texts the term *bat*, "daughter." Jeremiah describes a female's hemming movement (*šbb* and *sbb*). Likewise, the curves of the Shulammite here are described in terms such as *šûb* (three times), which is a cognate of the preceding roots; *ḥmq*, "curving" (common to both texts); *ḥala'îm*, "necklaces," which is probably from *hûl* (pilpel *ḥôlél*, "to dance in a circle");[2] *'gn*, "bowl," "basin"; and so on. This sheds light on the poet's interpretation of the Jeremian crux ("How long will you *waver*, O faithless daughter? For the LORD has created a new thing on earth: a woman *encompasses* a man" [Jer 31.22 NRSV; my emphasis]): the prophecy is now realized in the movement of the Shulammite, barring that the latter is not *šôbebâ* in the sense of "backsliding." So, in a certain way, André Robert, Raymond Tournay, and André Feuillet are correct to read the Song's text as "eschatological," for the day announced by Jeremiah has now arrived and is manifested in Eros's embrace. But once this concession is made to them, we must qualify the term *eschatology*, which here can be understood, not the way they do, but in an ironic sense! It is also with irony that the female curves are said to be "the work of a craftsman," for the text echoes Prov 8.30 — speaking of Wisdom!

The swirling of the Shulammite is a rare spectacle. People around encourage her to turn and turn, faster and faster. But what they actually say is rather arresting. They use the verb *ḥzh* in *neḥezeh-bak!* This evokes vision rather than view, theophany rather than play. Suffice it to turn to Gen 15.1; 2 Sam 7.17; Isa 21.2. In this particular instance, we may perhaps not speak of borrowing on the part of

---

2. Delitzsch, at this point, says that her moves imitate the swinging of a necklace (*Commentary on the Song of Songs*, p. 121).

the Canticle, but, like her heroine, the poet is daringly teasing her hearers/readers.

About 7.2 [3], Daniel Lys says that *šôrér*, generally translated by "umbilicus" (cf. Ezek 16.4), designates either "navel" or "valley" in Arabic, the root meaning "to be firm." Here, however, he continues, "[T]he comparison is better fitting for the pubis, the sex...[and], facing it, the pubic hair has the shape of a crescent" (*sahar* seems to mean "moon-shaped").[3] The author tells us that instead of circling the wheat with thorns to keep animals and people out, now thorns are replaced by lilies to entice.[4] Regarding the firmness of the vulva, Lys refers to Gilgamesh VI.ii.69.[5] Be that as it may,[6] the craftsman, of whom the preceding verse spoke, is not far. The belly of the female is not only geometrically, as it were, circle shaped, but it evokes crafted vessels from which there is no lack of mixed wine. "Rounded bowls" were part of the cultic vessels of the ancient shrines (see Exod 24.6, where Moses uses such basins for the blood of the covenant between God and people; in Isa 22.24, those vessels belong to priestly utensils). The erotization of the cultic objects needs no further comment. But we come dangerously close to blasphemy, all the more so if we see with Francis Landy in *ma'ªseh yedey 'aman* (7.1 [2]) a "disturbing echo of *ma'ªseh yedey 'adam* familiar from prophetic polemics against the production of idols."[7]

Excursus: The Shulammite and the Land of Israel

At this point, I wish to suggest a parallel between the "earthly" descriptions of the belle's body, on the one hand, and the famous

---

3. So Rashi; Kimhi; see *Sanh* 37a. Lys, *Le plus beau chant*, p. 258.

4. On lilies (in fact, lotuses), see Cant 6.1–3, above p. 128.

5. Gilgamesh blames Ishtar for her constant promiscuity with different males, even with her father's gardener, Ishullanu, to whom she went saying, "My Ishullanu, let us take pleasure in your strength. Reach out your hand and touch my vulva!" (see Gardner and Maier, *Gilgamesh*, p. 152). The reference to this text of Gilgamesh VI.ii.69 does not look decisive to me.

6. Whether *šôrér* means "navel" or "vulva," one can follow Krinetzki and see here the archetypal feminine symbol of the vessel containing the world. Each lover sees in the other the whole world (see Krinetzki, "Die erotische Psychologie des Hohenliedes," esp. p. 416). Landy (*Paradoxes of Paradise*, p. 89) says that the motif connotes the idea of bounty.

7. Landy, *Paradoxes of Paradise*, p. 259.

óde to the country of Israel, calling it "a land that flows with milk and honey," on the other. Elsewhere, I have called attention to the sexual meaning of the verb *flow,* which should better be rendered as "to have a flux," as is the meaning of the verb elsewhere. The land, personified as a woman, has her flux transformed from impure blood into "milk and honey," and the expression is thus transcendent and/or eschatological.[8] This would provide a further reason why the *waṣf*s praising the bride's beauty in the Song of Songs are so much inspired by topographical particularities of the land. As faith "sees" the land, so love "sees" the beloved: they both are sublime females, such as into themselves they are transfigured in the eyes of the beholder!

The following verse (7.3 [4]) is a repetition of 4.5, the context of which must be kept in mind while reading it. It is again the context of a tower here in 7.4. *Migᵉdal haššén,* "ivory tower," however, is substituted for *migᵉdal davîd,* "tower of David" in 4.4, and there are here no shields hanging by the thousands. Also the *berékôt beḥešᵉbôn,* "pools at Heshbon," parallel the doves standing by the basin in 5.12. Regarding Cant 4.4, we saw that the motif of the shields was coming from Ezek 27.10–11. In conformity with this latter text, 7.4 [5] conjures up an ivory tower spoken of in the text with the same demonstrative article as we have in Cant 4.4 regarding *the* shields. There is, therefore, real intuition in Hugo Winckler's suggestion — which I do not follow, however, see below — to replace Heshbon by *ḥelᵉbôn* as in Ezek 27.18 (the "wine of Helbon").[9] *Saḥar* (to trade) of Ezek 27.18 has become in the Song *saḥar* (round; 7.2 [3]); other terms common to both texts are *rab* and *maᶜᵃseh,* while *yayin* (wine) of Ezekiel has become *mezeg* (mixed wine; a *hapax legomenon*). The alteration of *ḥelᵉbôn* into *ḥešᵉbôn,* two topographical names, can be explained through contamination with *bat-rabbîm,* which evokes the idea of counting (*ḥešᵉbôn*). *Bat-rabbîm* is mysterious, but the parallel with the aforementioned text of Ezekiel sheds some light. In the Ezekiel text, there is emphasis on *rob* characteriz-

---

8. The Midrash on Gen 2.10–14 sees in the four rivers that water paradise, four streams flowing from the roots of the tree of life; they are rivers of wine, oil, milk, and honey (see Ginzberg, *The Legends of the Jews,* vol. 1, p. 20).

9. Winckler, *Altorientalische Forschungen,* vol. 1, p. 294, quoted by RTF, *Le Cantique des Cantiques,* p. 263. The French critics reject the emendation as arbitrary.

ing Tyre and the multitude of its artifacts, wares, riches, wine, wool, and so on. The prophetic idea was of variegated plenty (that was doomed to perish with the city); it is here adopted by the Song in terms of the girl's stature and prestige (at least in the eyes of the lover). Looking to the north, the prophet saw the fate of Tyre; gazing in the same direction, the poet sees (Mount) Lebanon and Damascus (v. 4; cf. Ezek 27.5) and its towers (cf. Ezek 27.11). She thus eclectically borrows Ezekiel's terms to describe the impression made by the belle's nose towering like Mount Lebanon. Several features of her body's upper part are compared with towers (cf. 8.10); so are her nose and her neck (v. 4). Its material is ivory, as is also mentioned in the Ezekiel text (27.6). Her head is like Mount Carmel (Cant 7.5), and as a whole she is "stately as a palm tree" (v. 7; NRSV). What is said, therefore, of her nose may be surprising aesthetically, but it simply means that she has a majestic head bearing (see next verse).

The shift to royalty in 7.5 [6] is smooth and expected. The curls of the belle are purple, that is, royal (Rashi, Pesh, Aq, Sym, and Vg have "like royal purple"). "A king is bound in the locks" of her hair alludes to the lover-speaker (see above, p. 19). The metaphor is a common one in love poetry in all languages. For example, Harper quotes Richard Lovelace's poem "To Althea, from Prison": "When I die tangled in her hair." Closer to the time of the Canticle is Chester Beatty Papyrus I C #43, as adverted to by Othmar Keel, "With her hair she lassoes me."[10]

The lover is king — he is Solomon — as also she is everything noble and princely as far as she is concerned (in 7.1 [2] she was called "a born lady"; NRSV has "queenly maiden"). That is why in 1.16 he returns to her the compliment she has been addressing to him and says, "How beautiful you are and how pleasant, love with sensuality." More important to us is the realization that the present development would be conceivable under the pen of a prophet sarcastically denouncing the sinful amours of Israel, prostituting herself to YHWH's rivals, as in Ezek 23.3, 21 (cf. Cant 7.8–9). The Song of Songs reverses the prophetic accusation. What is shameful is not to make love with false gods, but not to make love! Were it not anachronistic, one could believe that the Canticle reacts negatively to

---

10. Keel, *The Song*, p. 141.

any attempt on the part of theologians and moralists to have *agape* supplant *eros*. What is praised here is "love with sensuality," love incarnate, so to speak. One is invited to get intoxicated with "wine" (v. 9 [10]). The mention of mandrakes in verse 13 [14] goes in the same direction, as is shown by Gen 30.14–16.[11]

In conclusion, the most striking of this passage's features consists in putting the lass on a par with the beloved land of Israel. In the one as in the other, woman becomes "such as in herself eternity changes her," to paraphrase Mallarmé. A queen, she is encountered by a king, for love is an agent of metamorphosis (notwithstanding Ovid). Love is a font of surprises. The "king" acknowledges that he has been "encompassed" by the "queen," and this, indeed, is a "new thing," as Jeremiah foresaw. Such is the power of Eros. It fulfills the boldest visions of the prophets!

Canticle 7.10–13 [7.11–14]

The torpor after drinking wine (v. 9 [10]) recalls the scene depicted in Gen 9.20–24 with Noah's intoxication. Noah's nakedness is occasion for a sordid succession of events, while the Shulammite's unveiling (cf. v. 8 [9]) is, on the contrary, associated with a delightful erotic sleep.

With Roland Murphy, one must note that the shepherd's yearning for the Shulammite reverses Gen 3.16, where the woman is yearning for the man.[12] Wesley Fuerst concurs, "[T]his book has no message, except the implication that human and erotic love is a good and joyful part of God's creation.... [The Canticle] celebrates sexual love."[13] Cant 7.10 [11] builds up a counterpart to Gen 3.16 and 4.7, that is, the only two other texts where the term *tešûqâ*, "desire," appears![14] In both contexts, the term is "univocamente negativa," as says Enrica Salvaneschi, who, incidentally, sees this Canticle text as contrasting also with Isa 58.13, for the Shulammite is *batta'anûgîm*

---

11. More on this verse below, p. 201. See also there the development on verse 8.
12. Murphy, *Wisdom Literature and Psalms*, p. 99.
13. Fuerst, *The Books of Ruth*, p. 199.
14. A. Bloch also calls attention to a phenomenon common to those three texts: "the prepositional phrase marking the object of desire occurs before *tešuqah* for emphasis" (Bloch and Bloch, *The Song of Songs*, p. 207).

(7.6 [7]), perhaps to be read *bat taʿanûgîm*; the Isaianic text speaks of *šabbat* . . . *ʿoneg*, and verse 13 [14], of *titʿanag* in wordplay with Isa 57.3–4 (*beney ʿogenâ*, "sons of the sorceress").[15] Hans-Josef Heinevetter sees in the mention of "desire" a redactor's conscious alteration of Cant 2.16 and 6.3 ("my lover is mine and I am his"), thus making explicit the implicit theology of the author. For the term *desire* in any other biblical context is theological. It is bound with sin and death, while here "it becomes the vehicle to a return to the garden."[16]

In my introduction above, I mentioned the contrast between Genesis 2–3 and the Song of Songs. There is in this poem a total equality of genders; what is said of one is carefully repeated about the other. The term *tešûqâ*, "desire," while attributed to the woman in Gen 3.16, is said, in an egalitarian spirit, of the man in our text. As seen above, the Canticle sets itself in opposition to the text of Genesis, for the latter does not imply reciprocity of the woman's "fatal attraction" to the man. In our poem, however, the perfect balance between genders required, in parallel to the statement "I am my beloved's," that it be forthwith said, "his longing is upon me." Now, the equality of the sexes is formulated by the poet in the very terms that describe the mutual relationship between God and Israel in Lev 26.12, among other texts (Israel is God's people, and YHWH is Israel's God). Hence, by a ricochet of sorts, it becomes apparent that the perfect balance between the sexes here and now is grounded in divine-human mutuality, expressed in the famous formula of the Holiness Code. That leaves no room for the suzerain-vassal relationship emphasized elsewhere in Israel's tradition. The religious vocabulary of the H source is desacralized, but it is evident again that in the process there is no evacuation of all theological reflection. The egalitarian conception of the author is grounded, not on humanism or humanitarianism, and only indirectly on an ethical sense of justice. The genders are in perfect mutuality because they are mirroring the I-Thou relationship of God and people.

The religious vocabulary opens up to the poet an inexhaustible treasury from which to draw. This is clear again with the next scene,

---

15. Salvaneschi, *Cantico dei cantici*, ad loc.
16. Heinevetter, "*Komm nun, mein Liebster*," p. 192.

where the female tells the male, "Come,... let us go forth into the fields" (Cant 7.11 NRSV), an invitation in which one readily recognizes the echo of a textual filling of the gap left open by the MT of Gen 4.8 (for instance in the Samaritan and the other ancient Vss)! In Genesis also, the theme comes right after a mention of "desire" (in the preceding verse). The outcome of the proposition in the Canticle is, however, the reversal of the one in Genesis, for in the country villages the lovers will spend the night making love, not war! Again in the morning, she will offer him her love (or, with the ancient Vss, her breasts).

Clearly, we cannot take literally the mention of fruits (vv. 8–9), "both new and old," as says verse 13 [14]. Robert, Tournay, and Feuillet are most probably correct when they see in Hos 2.17–18 the "texte-source."[17] It is speaking of the time of Israel's youth, when she was in the desert, and of the oncoming day when, repeating what happened then, she will call again God her "husband." But, contrary to the prophetic pattern of Israel's idyllic youth, soon followed by blatant infidelity, until the time of repentance that will restore the days of yore, the Shulammite bridges the past and the future of her relations with the young man without hiatus or hurdle. She shall be his as she always has been. The old and the new are in a mutual embrace; love is both and neither.

By contrast to Hosea — or to Ezek 23.3, 21 — the shepherd intends to enjoy his girlfriend's breasts,[18] for he considers his enjoyment legitimate. Consequently, her invitation to do exactly that (vv. 11–13) conveys nothing impure, improper, or promiscuous. The enjoyment is mutual, and it is boundless. If only for this total lack of restraint, the Song of Songs is a "strange book" in wisdom literature!

The tryst is idyllic, but more importantly it provides a natural erotic rhythm to which the human couple will be attuned. The contrast with the rest of Scripture is here less verbal than conceptual. All throughout its existence, the community of Israel has been trained to be attentive to the message inscribed, as it were, within historical events. Prophecy is entirely based on that conviction that God speaks

---

17. RTF, *Le Cantique des Cantiques,* p. 282.

18. RTF invoke Middle Eastern representations with palm trees carrying two symmetrical hands of dates. They refer to Danthine, *Le palmier-dattier,* p. 52; and, for Palestine, to *DBV* vol. 3, col. 1389, 1394; vol. 4, col. 2062 (RTF, *Le Cantique des Cantiques,* p. 271).

a *dabar* within the occurrences (*debarîm*) of Israel's history so that the *dᵉbar YHWH* is echoed in the *dibᵉrey hayyamîm* of the nation.

Against that strikingly consistent background, no one in the audience of the poet could avoid being either incensed or thrilled when hearing her exhortation to watch vineyards, vines, pomegranates, mandrakes, and heed their invitation to make love. In a defiant mood, it is here again, as it was in Genesis 3, "Eve" who entices the man — and almost with the same bait! The in-depth meaning of all this is thrown into relief against the background of the Genesis myth, which conveys a stern divine caveat against nature. Nature must be trampled down under feet (cf. Gen 1.26). Thus, Eve's move becomes in the Canticle less Eve's temptation than Eve's revolt in the name of a pleasant nature, "delightful for the eyes," "good for food," and "desirable to convey intelligence." Yes, intelligence. Gen 3.7 adds that when the human couple "ate" the fruit, "the eyes of both were opened and they knew that they were naked" (NRSV). Intelligence, sensuality, and nudity are strangely concurrent. In a similar vein, the Legend of Gilgamesh had shown Enkidu as acquiring wisdom by having intercourse with a female prostitute (instead of mating with animals as before). In both myths, of Enkidu and of Adam, what is coveted is "to become like a god" (Gilg. I.iv.34) through sexual knowledge put on a par with wisdom.

The Canticle sets itself as an anti-Genesis. In hindsight, the poet judges the early human couple as too submissive, too diffident, too quickly convinced of the sadness of sexuality ("post coitum triste animal est"). "Let's go to the fields, my love" — let's go back to the garden where our ancestors blundered so badly, and let's start everything from the beginning—"There, I shall give you my love!"[19]

---

19. More on this section below, in my discussion of Keel's commentary (p. 202).

Chapter Eight

CANTICLE 8

ᏯᏜ ᏯᏜ ᏯᏜ ᏯᏜ ᏯᏜ ᏯᏜ ᏯᏜ ᏯᏜ ᏯᏜ ᏯᏜ ᏯᏜ ᏯᏜ ᏯᏜ ᏯᏜ

Canticle 8.1–5

With chapter 8 of the Canticle, we reach the climax of the poem. More than ever the recourse to an allegorical reading of the text is excluded. If the shepherd is a disguise for God, how could Israel ("she") wish that he be her brother "nursed at [her] mother's breasts"? It does not make any sense. True, the allegorical school skips the difficulty by seeing "him" as designating the messiah rather than God. "Born of the same mother," says André Robert, alludes to Israel of old! More consistent but displaying a daredevil type of courage, Rashi sees God himself in the shepherd; in the wish of Israel, the great commentator sees the desire to be comforted in her exile "as Joseph comforted his brothers who wronged him" (Rashi on Cant 8.1).The kisses she wants to lavish upon him are in fact for his prophets, who are speaking in his name in the streets. Before Rashi, *CantR* had interpreted God as the "sister" and Israel as the "brother" (103.1)! More daringly yet, the Midrash reads Cant 8.8–10 as referring to Abraham! He is the little sister of God and has no breasts; that is, he is too young yet to be submitted to religious duties (*CantR* 110.1). He was "spoken for" (8.8) means that Nimrod decreed that Abraham be thrown into the fiery furnace on account of his impiety, as he had burned his father Terach's idols, according to legend.

There are still other ways to dodge the impossibility. One can, for instance, have recourse to the Hurrian customs or legal contracts mentioned above (see "my sister, my lover" in Cant 4.9 expounded on p. 108) or to the Assyrian so-called *erebu*-marriage, perhaps whereby a boy was adopted with the idea of marrying him to a daughter of his adopted parents. One can also understand here the word *brother* as designating someone closely related (even a husband for that matter!), as in Egypt where, as we saw, it can be a term of endearment.[1] But it is certainly sounder, with Daniel Lys for example, to take the term literally. True, it is used here paradoxically, for if he actually were her brother, she would have little urge to kiss him in public![2] This last point suffices to discard James Reese's suggestion[3] that the verse reflects an old custom: only blood brother and sister (not even spouses) were allowed to display affection in public. Even if he were right, it remains that only a sexually frustrated couple would wish they were allowed to display their affection in any public place (and not only in private or even, as in this case, in secret!). The couple is clearly not married (and the song is no wedding song).[4] Furthermore, Reese's statement is probably incorrect as far as Israel's society is concerned, for public demonstrations between legitimate wedded people are accepted in Gen 26.8 (Isaac and Rebekah) and 29.11 (Jacob and Rachel; see also Esth 15.12–15). If there is a contrasting background to this text, we should turn to Prov 7.6–27 (esp. v. 13), which probably is the model text here. Verse 12 has the same term *ba-ḥûṣ* (outside) as here, and in verse 13 is the same verb *našaq*, "to kiss"; the idea of shame in the Canticle text is also found in this Proverbs passage ("she hardens her face," 7.13). In Proverbs, however, it is a matter of a lewd woman, whose demonstrations of "affection" are a disgrace (she has an "impudent face" [NRSV]), while the Canticle maiden expressly states that "no one would despise me" (8.1 NRSV). Thus, the Shulammite is running the risk of being taken for a prostitute. Such a fear is constantly on her mind, as can be expected from someone whose mores put her at the margin of her society.

---

1. There might be indeed an Egyptian parallel here, for the immediate context also sounds "Egyptian." On the vase of Cairo analyzed by Derchain, the male lover says, "I wish I were the Black woman at her service!" and the text continues with evoking the intimacy possible in that case. See Derchain, "Le lotus, la mandragore et le perséa," p. 77.

2. See Lys, *Le plus beau chant*, p. 278.

3. Reese, *The Book of Wisdom*, p. 247.

4. One will admire the candor of RTF (*Le Cantique des Cantiques*, p. 283) when they write, "We must confess that, until now, the maiden has given little sign of having any care for public opinion (3.1–4; 5.6–8; 7.12–13)." That's the least one can say!

Robert Gordis sees in the *ke* of *ke'ah* (literally, "like a brother") not a comparative but an asseverative: "Would thou wert indeed my brother" (p. 95). However, to be "like" her brother would not solve her problem, which is to kiss him unabashedly in public. But Ariel Bloch, for example, disagrees and recalls Gen 27.12 and Ps 126.1, where the preposition has the value of "as if."[5] Be that as it may, it is clear that in the ardor of her passion, she wishes she could caress him, even in public. Secrecy evokes no romanticism in the Canticle, only imposed limitations. To become public would be liberating, as the maiden and her lover would then be able to express the full measure of their mutual love. There is no attempt at magnifying the clandestinity of forbidden loves, which will reach its climax with the High Middle Ages' "courteous love." What the Shulammite wishes for is, not some kind of incestuous relations, but the absence of the obstacles set by society between her and him, as is made clear in the following verse.[6]

Verse 2 continues to erect a dam against allegoresis. The girl wishes she could lead her paramour into her mother's house. We have encountered the motif of the mother earlier, in Cant 6.9. After noting that both lovers identify themselves with the mother, Francis Landy adds,

> Mother love is the archetype of love, which all subsequent loves reconstitute; the lovers reenact this primordial relationship.... [I]n 4.5 the Lover imagines himself as an infant at the breast, and...in 8.1 the Beloved imagines him as a fellow suckling. The breasts coordinate adult erotic feelings with an infantile correlate.[7]

One may wonder why there is such insistence in the Song on the mother genitrix. In Cant 8.1, the mother's breasts are mentioned; in verses 2 and 5, the text lingers on the "chamber of the one who bore me" and on "your mother...in labor...she who bore you was in labor" (NRSV). By contrast, in Genesis 1–2, the creation of the

---

5. Bloch, *The Song of Songs*, p. 209.

6. Heinevetter insists on the public side of the proposition: the "city" would only tolerate a public kiss between siblings (*"Komm nun, mein Liebster,"* p. 187). Indeed, the fear of censorship is here transparent and reveals the societal background that the poem confronts from the beginning. More on this verse below (p. 202).

7. Landy, "The Song of Songs," p. 313.

human couple is independent of parents. When the natural birth is envisaged in Genesis 3, it is through pangs and pain and female submission. In the Canticle, human birth is endowed with beauty, and even the labor of birth is transcended by its outcome: a handsome couple of lovers. Future fertility, which plays a central role in wedding songs, here retrocedes to the past generation. The lovers regard themselves as more the effect than the cause of procreation; the fecundity they enjoy is the one that brought them to life and constitutes the backdrop of their sexual awakening (cf. 8.5). Robert Alter writes, "[T]his perfect consummation of union, for which fraternal incest serves as a surprisingly beautiful metaphor — shared life-source, shared nurturance, transmuted into the lovers' shared pleasuring..." etc.[8]

The verb *nahag* (to lead) in 8.2 is found in Isaiah, in connection with the people that God leads back to Zion (49.10; 63.14). In Ps 78.52, God led his people "like sheep" in the desert. *Nahag* (meaning also "to drive") is often used, as a matter of fact, with cattle as an object complement (Gen 31.18; Exod 3.1; Ps 80.2) or with animals in general (Isa 11.6; 2 Sam 6.3) or again, in a derogatory way, with prisoners (Isa 20.4; Lam 3.2). In its metaphorical sense, the verb, as we just saw, is used to describe YHWH's leading his people out of Egypt or out of Babylon, that is, out of captivity. In view of all this, it is inconceivable that God would become the object complement of *nahag*.

The lass would introduce her lover to her mother (the chamber is symbolic of the womb, the generous envelopment, and the nexus of life giving) and invite him there to teach her, *telam^edénî*. One has reason to be somewhat suspicious about the integrity of the text at this point, and it is not surprising that Karl Kuhn omits the *m* of *telam^edénî* and gets *têl^edénî* "[who] bore me."[9] But the very concepts of guidance (with other verbs than *nahag*, it is true) and teaching are associated elsewhere in some interesting ways, and this should not be overlooked (see Jer 31.33–34; Isa 48.17; Pss 25.5;

---

8. Alter, afterword to *The Song of Songs*, by Bloch and Bloch, p. 129. In the same book, C. Bloch has this striking sentence, "Though the history of the tribe is shaped by the fathers, the traditions of love, in the Song at least, are handed down by the mothers" (p. 6).

9. Kuhn, *Erklärung des Hohenliedes*, ad loc.

143.10). Besides, there is a striking relation between shepherding, on the one hand, and imparting wisdom and understanding, on the other, in Jer 3.15, for example! I thus suggest that *têl^{e}dênî* is what the audience expected at this point; it is the *lectio facilior*. But the poet surprises the reader with a twist in the language. She uses *lmd* in a sexual sense (cf. Jer 13.21), as it occurs sometimes in the usage of the verb *yada‘*, "to know" (cf. Gen 4.1). The mother in wisdom literature is symbolic of education (cf. Prov 1.8; 4.3; 6.20; 31.1; see also 2 Chr 22.3); here she is flanked by someone with another kind of instruction. Note again the breach with tradition. In fact, the lover's initiation of the girl substitutes itself not only for the mother's but, more subtly, for God's. God teaches his people according to Pss 25.5; 48.17; 143.10. Here, another icon is broken.

As a reward for his "teaching," she is ready to give him to drink "spiced wine, the juice of my pomegranate." The reader of the Hebrew text is sensitive to the wordplay of *'eššaq^{e}ka* (I would kiss you) in verse 1 and *'aš^{e}q^{e}ka* (I would let you drink) in verse 2. The pun emphasizes the erotic configuration of the text. Besides, the use of the first person possessive pronoun in "my pomegranate" leaves no doubt as to the sensual drift of the text.[10] The pomegranate was a symbol of fecundity; it is used here as an aphrodisiac. But this is not what "spiced wine" and "pomegranate" first evoke within Israel's tradition. Both words are associated with the temple, its ornamentation, its utensils, and its personnel. In Exodus 30, the word occurs six times, and its assortment with the roots *qdš* and *mšḥ* is striking. So, once again the erotic supplants the religious. Hence, Kuhn has a point when he concludes from such a parallel between our text and liturgical *didachēs*, that the Shulammite is ready to give her blood for the beloved.[11] Eros has displaced Thusia (sacrifice).

Verse 3 repeats verbatim Cant 2.6, but for the omission of the preposition *le* before *r'ošî* (the reader is thus sent back to chapter 2, p. 85). As to verse 4, it is the same refrain (with some variations) as found in 2.7, the first such adjuration, and in 3.5. Verse 5a is identi-

---

10. Unless we follow the *BH*[3] suggestion and read *rimônîm*, "pomegranates" (without the possessive pronoun). Landy writes, "The subversive desire, that he should be both lover and brother, can be expressed only through a fantasy of infantile regression, to a time before there were prohibitions and before society imposed secrecy on lovers" ("The Song of Songs," p. 312).

11. Kuhn, *Erklärung des Hohenliedes*.

cal with 3.6a. All this explains why Moses H. Segal views verses 3–6 as "stray verses. V. 3–4 are copied from 2.6–7."[12] My proposal to see in the Canticle a ritornello or rondeau spares us those scholarly insensitivities.

The mention of the desert in verse 5 is totally unexpected at this point, that is, after and before evocations of orchards. It led Andrew Harper to give a restricted definition of mid^{e}bar, "the uncultivated open pasture lands round the village." Such a pragmatic explanation of the presence of mid^{e}bar in this context is insufficient, for this verse's location just before the evocation of paradisiacal vegetation and the man's slumber from which state he must be awakened — not by God but by the woman! — speaks for itself. Furthermore, as we will see about the next verse, the concurrence in the Canticle of "desert" and "arousing" refers to several Second Isaiah texts in which Cyrus is aroused by YHWH (Isa 41.2, 25). According to this sixth-century prophet, the desert is transformed into paradise (Isa 40.3–4; 41.18–19; 42.16; 43.19–20; 44.3; 49.9b–12; 55.12–13). The desert here in the Canticle and in Second Isaiah is the midnight before dawn, the expectation before the gift, the interval that will be filled, and hence, through expected concurrence, the gestational desert of Exodus, the place of betrothal par excellence (Jer 2.2).[13] Rashi paraphrases the words "leaning on her beloved" in Cant 8.5a into "while she was still in exile in Egypt." Here, the one she leans upon, though, is not God but her lover.

After the desert the Promised Land comes with its (relative) fertility (v. 5b). The scene is now the bower of a particular apple tree. There, says the MT, the shepherd's mother bore him and was in travail. A first "difficulté insurmontable," as described by André Robert, Raymond Tournay, and André Feuillet,[14] namely, that of a birth under a tree as among Bedouins, is perfectly resolved by the remark of Michael Fox: "The story of Jacob and the sheep (Gen 30.31–43) shows the ancient and widespread idea that the setting of coitus affects the offspring."[15] A more imposing hurdle, of course,

---

12. Segal, "The Song of Songs, p. 476.
13. Its first mention is in Exod 3.1: Moses led (nahag) his father-in-law's flock "beyond [in] the wilderness," that is, beyond the area of domestication, hence into the wild.
14. RTF, Le Cantique des Cantiques, p. 297.
15. Fox, Ancient Egyptian Love Songs, p. 169.

is the mention here of the shepherd's mother, a very embarrassing detail for the allegorical school, which consistently has seen the person of God himself in the male lover. In order to keep up with their allegorical interpretation, the school must change the pronouns from the masculine to the feminine (he aroused her under the apple tree where her mother gave birth to her). Such violation of the text is evidently forbidden. The Jewish traditional reading does not fall into such snares; with derring-do it maintains the MT as it is but must have recourse to even more improbable devices and imagine that the arousing is of God's *love* and that the Shulammite/Israel becomes a mother *unto nations* (so Rashi here; cf. *Shabb* 89a).

In fact, *'ôrar°tîka* means "to arouse someone to some activity," especially war, work, or love. Since a similar root (*'ûr* II) means "to be naked" (*'rr='rh='ûr*), there may be here a play of words ("I [fem.] stripped you [masc.] naked"). Marvin Pope, who also mentions that latter possibility, calls attention to the "erotic and mythological associations of the apple (tree)," a theme illustrated in Cant 2.3, 5; 7.8. The word *ḥbl*, Pope adds, alludes to the labors of a parturient woman but also to the "pleasurable process of conception, as in Ps 7.14."[16] Like the pomegranate earlier, the apple is an aphrodisiac. The Shulammite arouses the young man to a new birth, the birth of love, says Lys.[17] That is why, the French exegete continues, the text speaks of the mother to whom he owes his first birth. The second birth, however, makes him more than just a man; he becomes a king (see Cant 3.11).

In religious vocabulary, of course, arousing is the action of God. He may arouse himself (Pss 80.3; 35.23: "Wake up! Bestir yourself for my defense" [NRSV]; Job 8.6: "He will rouse himself for you and restore" [NRSV]). God may also rouse up enemies against Israel, against Babylon, and so on. In Second Isaiah, he stirs up Cyrus the liberator (see Isa 45.13; see also 41.2, 25; Ezek 23.22).[18] It is not the first time, nor the last, that we see a traditionally divine action being

---

16. Pope, *Song of Songs*, p. 664.

17. Lys, *Le plus beau chant*, p. 284.

18. The "arousing," outside of the Song of Songs is always *against* some people. Beside the texts already mentioned, see Isa 13.17; Jer 50.9; 51.1, 11 (against Babylon); 1 Chr 5.26; 2 Chr 21.16 (against Israel). Westermann concludes, "In all these passages the meaning is practically the same: Yhwh rouses or stirs up a nation or a king destined to destroy Babylon" (*Isaiah 40–66*, p. 88). The exception set by the Canticle is striking.

attributed to the Shulammite rather than to the male hero. Consistent to a fault with her own style, the author retrieves for Eros a vocabulary "metaphorized" by prophets and psalmists for religious evocations.

In Cant 8.1–5 style and vocabulary concur to prohibit an allegorical interpretation. Once more, the Shulammite is the driving force in the relationship with the shepherd. As indeed "his desire is for her" (7.10 [11]), the whole of the Song can be seen as an explication of Gen 3.16 (her desire is for her man), barring the theme of male domination over the female. For she is rousing him under an apple tree! In Genesis 2, God was the one who, implicitly, awakened Adam, as he was also the one who caused him to sleep in the first place. Once more, in the Canticle the woman's role replaces God's. Incidentally, this Canticle text seems to have "contaminated" the identification of the tree in Eden (Gen 3.1–19) with an apple tree. At any rate, it is interesting that Jewish tradition explains the absence of Adam in Gen 3.1–5a as due to a nap after lovemaking. Then Eve must wake him up to share with him the "apple."[19]

The "house of my mother" (8.2) is fitting a context in which the image of the mother is amazingly strong. Such a theme cannot pass unnoticed. A motherly love is in the background of the amour of the lad and the lass. A feminine love has brought them together and has paved the way to their mutual love. Eros that binds them is a child of Maia. And this in turn colors their mutual devotion: it is an impassioned infatuation, but it burns without being consumed and without consuming the lovers. It is a love with a memory, a love with a past. If it is an untraditional affair, it is not, however, without genealogical credentials. When Othmar Keel states that in the Song of Songs the ties with the past and future are disregarded (see here p. 50, n. 119, and p. 51), he is right only to a point, for the relationship between the lovers has "depth" also on the chronological plane. Strikingly, however, the patrilinear continuity is replaced by the matrilinear. This is no sign of literary antiquity, needless to say, but constitutes an aspect of the poem's subversiveness. In no other book of the Bible is the female cause championed with more

---

19. More on this verse below (p. 202).

pep. Nowhere else in Israel's literature is the male dominion over the female (cf. Gen 3.16) rejected more decisively.

Canticle 8.6

To the allegorists' confusion, the MT continues to suggest the reading of the personal pronouns as referring to the "wrong" persons in verse 6: "Set me [fem.] as a seal upon your [masc.] heart" (NRSV). Robert, Tournay, and Feuillet unabashedly swap them, making the masculine into feminine, and conversely.[20] For the call to fidelity should not be addressed by the girl to the boy, that is, by Israel to God! In reality, there is no need for twisting the MT to make it confirm a biased preunderstanding. At a first level of understanding, one may emphasize the meaning of ownership that the apposing of a seal on an object represents. As *the* girlfriend is the seal, the stamp, on his arm/heart, she claims him as her very own and thus reverses the habitual relation between the male and the female.

On a deeper level, the imagery is heavily influenced by the religious world, whose vocabulary is redirected. An example of what this means is provided by the unexpected image that follows, which constitutes another crux in verse 6: the placing of the signet *upon the arm* (*'al zerô'eka* preceded by *'al libbeka*, "on your heart"). The signet ring is normally set on the finger, of course. The surprising mention of "on your arm" (for a seal!) led traditional Jewish interpretation, as well as some modern authors, to thinking of the phylacteries. In the *Midrash Rabba*, "Rabbi Berekiah applied the seal on the heart to the recitation of the *Shema'* (Deut 6.6) and the seal on the arm to the application of the phylacteries," says Pope.[21] All the same, the number and the nature of religious allusions in the Canticle are such that we are not surprised to find another one here. Even Pope concedes, "[T]he following lines [of the Song] which emphasize Love's power over against that of Death suggest that there may be a blending of the functions of the signet with the memento and the phylactery."[22] Deut 6.6–8 and 11.18, where we find the prescrip-

---

20. RTF, *Le Cantique des Cantiques*, p. 299.
21. Pope, *Song of Songs*, p. 671, although this reading does not convince him.
22. Ibid., p. 667.

tion regarding the phylactery, orders that the commandments be "on your heart" ('*al lebabeka*) and "bound on your hand (*yadeka*) to be to you as a sign"; 11.18 repeats *wesam*e*tem*... '*al-lebab*e*kem*...*le'ôt* '*al yed*e*kem* (as a sign on your hands).[23] Still more important are texts speaking of God's putting a "signet" upon himself, as in Jer 22.24, where King Jehoiachin is "a signet ring on My right hand (*ḥôtam 'al yad yemînî*)," or in Hag 2.23, where Zerubbabel will be made a "signet ring" to God (*sam*e*tîka kaḥôtam kî beka baḥar*e*tî*). We also remember that the high priest's ephod was "like a signet" on his breast/heart (Exod 28.21; 28.36; 39.6, 14, 30).

Let us note the process of demythologization in this central passage of Cant 8.6, a segment unique in the poem. It is "the only moment of objectivity, the only foundation," says Franz Rosenzweig.[24] It is also here that a trace of the divine name might be found; the last word of the verse is *šal*e*hebetyah*, which seems to be composed with the theophoric element -*yah*, for YHWH. Many commentators either follow the LXX (it read the suffix as the third person feminine singular pronoun, *phloges autēs*, "her flames"; along a similar line, it should be noted that the ancient commentators did not exploit the possible presence of the name of God here),[25] or else they emend the text. Yet as our reading will show, it is unnecessary either to emend the text or to turn to a non-Masoretic version. Here again the author displays irreverence, and in this context -*yah* is used in a "secular" way (something like our "by Jove!") — all the more so since there is in the immediate neighborhood of verse 6 an allusion to Canaanite divinities (Moth, Rešeph) and to the mythology of Yamm/Chaos (v. 7: "many waters"; cf. Genesis 1; Isa 51.9–10; Ps 76.12–14; Jonah 2.3, 5–6). This makes

---

23. Also Alter writes, "[I]t is reminiscent of the injunction in Deut 11:18" (afterword to *The Song of Songs*, by Bloch and Bloch, p. 131).

24. Rosenzweig, *The Star of Redemption*, loc. cit.

25. *šal*e*hebetyah*: "The alleged occurrence of the name of God was not exploited by early interpreters" (Pope, *Song of Songs*, p. 672). According to Cross, at least in later texts, the form -*yah* had nothing to do with the divine name but was a vocative particle like *y* in Ugaritic or *ya* in Arabic. See Cross, "The Cave Inscriptions," p. 306 n. 17. Cf. Fox (*Ancient Egyptian Love Songs*, p. 170): The lesson may be read, either in the Ben Asher text, i.e., one word with the affixed -*yah* indicating an intensive force; or in the Ben Naphtali text, i.e., two words with a *mappiq* in the *heh*="flame of Yah." The Vss show that the *Vorlage* was in one word, like the Ben Asher text (hence, no mention of YHWH). This is confirmed by A. Bloch, who reminds us of the use of such composite terms as *ma'*e*pelyah* in Jer 2.31 or *mer*e*ḥavyah* in Ps 118.5 (*The Song*, p. 213).

kammawet (death) the perfect equivalent of the "kingdom of the dead," that is Sheol, in verse 7. Moth (the same word as *mawet*) is the god of Sheol in Ugarit. There is even a Canaanite expression that says, "Moth is strong, Baal is strong." And from a private letter from Ugarit, called "Message from Iwarshar to Palsajdis," the following declaration is noteworthy: "The love of the gods is here like death, violent, terrible, powerful."[26] Such is the background of the Song development here. What is said with fear and trembling of the unpredictable gods of Canaan inspires the poet's artistic creativity about Eros. "Meanwhile [i.e., before the end comes], the only force to pit against Death is Love," as says Pope.[27]

From verse 6 to verse 7 there is progression: love is said to be as strong as death itself. In the meantime, so to speak, love resists Chaos; it keeps the power of destruction at bay; its strength matches the power of death! Even as love cannot be forced, neither can it be resisted once it has started between two people. Strangely, but characteristically, while with love we are at the antipode of a dynamism of power, the way the poet chooses to speak of love is power. Love is not passivity; it is a power of another kind; love has its own dynamism.[28] Besides, it is not a foregone conclusion that, in the Canticle, love is not even stronger than death. In fact, the text in verse 7 passes from a comparison of equality (strong as death) to one of superiority (stronger than the waters of chaos; the expression "many waters" appears twenty-eight times in the Hebrew Bible with the uniform meaning of "death")! Theologically speaking, love is that kind of power that God chooses also for himself, for he is the God of life and of love! Conversely, it is implied that when death does occur, it occupies a void of love.[29] Ultimately, love is the sole force capable of defeating death, for God is love.[30]

---

26. In Jirku, *Die Welt der Bibel,* chap. 3.4, "Spiritual Art and Culture in the Canaanite Era," p. 53.

27. Pope, *Song of Songs,* p. 669.

28. Cant 8.6, says Trible, reverses the tragedy of death according to Genesis 2–3, for here the poet "asserts triumphantly that not even the primeval waters of chaos can destroy Eros" (*God and the Rhetoric,* p. 163).

29. When, according to John, the Nazarene declares, "I give [my sheep] eternal life, and they will never perish" (10.28 NRSV), the same idea is expressed. Jesus' followers shall never fall into a void of love.

30. Rabbi Aqiba, recalls Landy, taught that "human love and divine love are united in Torah, with which, he said, the world was created (*P.A.* 2.18)." That is why, for Aqiba, what remains last when everything else is lost is the Song of Songs, that is to say, love/

Love is here compared to "a flame of Yah[weh]" (or to a flame of intensive force). The expression is ambiguous. It can indicate just a superlative (cf. Ps 29.3–4 [thunder]; Job 1.16 [lightning]), but in the subversive language of the author, one must undoubtedly perceive what Andrew Greeley calls "a reverse metaphor."[31] Besides, consistent with Roland Murphy's reaction against the idea that love in the Song is deified, the fact that it is described as "a flame of Yah" indicates precisely that human love can only be described with terms commonly used for divine love.[32] They are the only fitting terms of comparison. Human love is a "flame of Yah" in its consuming intensity, and its ardor is on a par with death swallowing up people, as says Prov 1.12. No one went as far as the author of the Song of Songs in her conception of love's powerful nature ('azzâ and qašâ).

The comparison between love and death is here made on the basis of the whole gamut of human feelings of love, from the most elated state of joy or fullness of life to the most desperate sadness of the one who feels she is in a valley of death. Hence, love and death in conjunction offer a powerful shortcut expressing the paradoxical amorous mix of deathlike self-abandonment and life-full self-achievement reached at the peak of the sexual act. Both partners are dealing to each other life and death. Ecstasy, rapture, and release are contiguous. Love is strong as death.

This, of course, did not escape ancient myth. The kinship of sexuality and death is expressed in ancient Mesopotamia by the sisterhood of Ishtar (goddess of love) and Ereshkigal (goddess of the netherworld), a kinship that threatens cosmic balance by improperly mixing cosmic realms. Insatiable is the netherworld according to myth, and the fact is recognized also by Prov 1.12 or 27.20, for instance. Now, to the extent that the Canticle contributes for its part to

poetry, for the latter "recreates the experience" (see Landy, *Paradoxes of Paradise*, pp. 14–15). On love stronger than death, see also Heinevetter, "*Komm nun, mein Liebster*," p. 196.

31. In Greeley and Neusner, *The Bible and Us*, p. 35.

32. For the Targum: "Strong as death is the love of Thy Divinity, and powerful as Gehinnom is the jealousy that the peoples harbor toward us. The enmity which they nurture toward us is like the coals of the fire of Gehinnom which YHWH created on the second day of the creation of the world to burn therewith the devotees of foreign worship." Murphy says here that human love is the mirror of divine love (*The Song of Songs*, p. 104). The same idea was already developed by Heinevetter. He sees here a redactor's intervention in the text, with his customary explication of the implicit theology of the Canticle metaphors (*"Komm nun, mein Liebster*," p. 193).

the Israelite rejection of the mythological, it may well be, as indicated above, that there is here a repudiation of the god Death (Moth), king of the underworld, entailing a cult of the dead. This possibility is also contemplated by Reese, who emphasizes the allusion to the grave, as in Hos 13.14. He writes, "Death shows its strength by its *'jealousy,'* which is not confined to sexual competition, but is better seen as the consuming zeal that will stop at nothing, and that ruthlessly eliminates any rivals seeking to challenge its domination over human existence."[33] This certainly is a correct explication of the word *qin'â* in our text. Not by chance, however, it applies also — it applies above all — to divine jealousy. The theme is well illustrated in biblical texts, one of which stands out in striking parallel with Canticle 8, namely, Deut 4.24 (NRSV), "For the LORD your God is a devouring fire (*'eš 'ok^elâ*), a jealous God (*'el qana'*)." In the same vein, see Deut 29.20 ("His jealousy shall smoke against"); Ps 79.5 ("How long... shall Your jealousy burn"); Ezek 36.5 ("in the fire of My jealousy"; cf. Exod 34.14; Isa 42.13; 59.17; Zech 8.2; Zeph 1.18; 3.8). It is particularly idolatry that stirs YHWH's jealousy (cf. Ezek 8.3, 5 [Astarte]). As for the term *šal^ehebet*, it appears elsewhere only in Job 15.30 and in Ezek 20.47. The Ezekiel text says that the fire that God will kindle against the Negeb is a "blazing flame [that] shall not be quenched" (NRSV).[34]

One does not generally pay enough attention to the stark contrast, in the wording of verse 6, with other biblical traditions. Neither the sexual realm (here, *'ahabâ*) nor death (*mawet*) is deemed a part of divinity. The Song text continues with words such as "hell"/"grave" (*še'ôl*), "floods," and "drowning rivers," which are in good company with death. But then it shifts paradoxically to "fire" (*'eš*), an element of the theophany, and to a composite term with the theophoric *-yah* in "a flame of Yah[weh]."[35] The whole of the Canticle is encapsulated in this phrase. Again, it must be emphasized that everywhere

---

33. Reese, *The Book of Wisdom*, 251. Landy interprets "jealousy" negatively; he says, "Jealousy is in a sense the ghost, or shadow of love... only by being inseparable can [the lovers] never be jealous" (*Paradoxes of Paradise*, pp. 125–26).

34. It is noteworthy that the vocabulary of Cant 8.6–7 comes almost completely from Prov 30.15–16. In this connection, it is interesting that Bekkenkamp and van Dijk suggest that Proverbs provides a "countervoice of Song of Songs" ("Canon of the Old Testament," pp. 81–82); I would rather say that the Canticle takes exception to most of Proverbs.

35. The *TOB* translates, "un coup de foudre sacré" (a sacred clap of thunder/love at first sight).

else in the Bible sex and death are regarded as foreign to the realm of God, provoking impurity, belonging to the secular and not to the sacred (as they were in pagan cults to the dead or to fecundity/fertility). The Canticle integrates those foreign elements, snatching them from the profane and reclaiming them as intrinsic human elements in the dialogue with God, while avoiding to deify them. Not god Moth or goddess Anath but the "secular" becomes glorious, the all-too-human becomes a "flame of Yah"; for love, the human and carnal love is the supreme expression of humanity, by which and through which man and woman together are the image of God.

It is thus clear that the Canticle does not speak in general terms about human love. One of the best-known metaphors for divine action is here redirected to the human passion between genders. This is a parade example of the general trend in the Song of Songs: it regains for secular usage similes that had been expropriated by theologians for their exclusive semantic field. Such a trend is certainly not absent from the themes of death and Sheol. As Enrica Salvaneschi reminds us, both of them belong to God's domain in wisdom literature (Job 28.22; Prov 8.27–28), but they are also where the ways of the adulteress lead (Prov 7.27), for she holds an erotic sway over men. She is greedy for silver and gold, but wisdom cannot be bought with precious metal (Job 28.15; Prov 8.19).[36] In the Canticle, however, the development goes in the opposite direction. The Shulammite's erotic quest cannot be assimilated with the adulteress's in wisdom literature. What is not for sale is, not the aloof wisdom, but love, eros precisely. Love — like the "three things and even four" that never say, "Enough" — is insatiable like Sheol, like water, like fire (cf. Prov 30.15–16). These three are not negative when they are in reference to love.

It is perhaps not superfluous to recall that, in modern literature, Fyodor Dostoyevsky's heroes are experiencing the kinship of love with death. They know that love is strong as death. Akhmova realizes that Versilov's love for her would swallow her up like Sheol and destroy her. She flees for her life. On the contrary, Natasha Filippovna, because she wants to die, clings to Rogozhin! For Dostoyevsky, only humility saves from death the one in love. That is the

---

36. Salvaneschi, *Cantico dei cantici*, p. 110.

lesson taught to Raskolnikov by Sonia the prostitute. It is a love that is not self-feeding but is thrust toward its parousia. On the way, the interment of Iliusha, the young boy humiliated in the person of his father, is a station and an omen.[37]

Nothing in human experience comes closer to the infinite and the transcendent than love. But nothing, in way of consequence, is more of a provocation to Thanatos. Love is *the* provocation because, by contrast, it sheds a blinding light upon the mediocrity of our sentiments and achievements in general. Love evokes death; both are strangely allied and opposed, friends and foes. Love and death are thus the two sides of the same reality; they share the same ultimate finality. The early Christians had, of course, a large stake in this, seeing in the death of their Master the ultimate demonstration of his love of God and fellow humans. Once again, and in a manner that superseded all other examples before and after, death and love embraced. The dubious and indecisively brotherly and murderous hugging of love and death, acknowledged by the Canticle's equation of the two, had found its resolution, however. In Christ's love, indeed a love that proved *stronger* than death, the early Christians found truly the ultimate victory over death (see Rom 8.35–39; 1 Cor 15.54–55). For through self-oblation, love expects no requital and does embrace even hatred, which tries to kill it (see 1 Corinthians 13). This is not exclusively Christian. Jewish tradition reads Cant 8.6 in the sense of Israel's love of God unto death. The Targum here says, "[S]trong as death is our love for You, and powerful as Gehinnom is the jealousy which the nations bear against us." An echo of this is found in Jewish Middle Ages commentaries. Rashi writes, "To me the extent of my love for You is as strong as the deaths which I suffered for Your sake."[38] Pope says that the verse was finally applied to "the love which the generation of the destruction (the period of the Hadrianic Wars) exhibited in their martyrdom (Ps 44:23 [22E]) and the jealousy to God's zeal for Zion (Zech 1:14)."[39]

In parallel to the putting on a par death and love, the author continues with a similar metaphor regarding the insatiability of jealousy:

---

37. F. Dostoyevsky, *The Brothers Karamazov; Crime and Punishment;* see also Bakhtin, *Problems of Dostoevsky's Poetics.*

38. See Rashi, on Cant 8.6.

39. Pope, *Song of Songs,* p. 671.

"jealousy is hard as the grave" (*qašâ kiše'ôl qin'â*). Franz Delitzsch has written about "the jealousy of love asserting its possession and right of property; the reaction of love against any diminution of its possession, against any reserve in its response, the 'self-vindication of angry love.' "[40] Ralph Klein translates *qin'â* by "passion" in Ezek 5.13; he adds, "Passion is the kind of emotion displayed by an irate spouse who suspects unfaithfulness in his or her mate (cf. Num 5.14–31; Prov 6.34)."[41] Interestingly, Greeley translates this term by "panting desire."[42] There is something of what Greeley sees in *qin'â*, but the normal rendering by "jealousy" makes a lot of sense here, after the statement about love and the request to be like a seal on the heart and the arm of the lover. As an oath of fidelity is followed by curses on the one who is unfaithful to the terms of the partnership, so the declaration of love is accompanied by its claim to absoluteness. There is undoubtedly a note of threat in the proclamation that "jealousy is hard as Sheol."

Rešapîm, "flashes" (the *Hebrew-English Lexicon of the Bible* proposes for here the sense of "lust"),[43] is a cognate of the name for the Canaanite god *Rešeph,* who is depicted as brandishing a battle-ax and other weapons. Pope's translation here of "darts" takes into account the Canaanite background, although the English word rather evokes the darts of Cupid or Eros. The parallels of Ps 76.4 and Job 5.7 go in the direction of "burning arrows." Elsewhere Pope cites the Ugaritic text 1001:3, where Rešeph is called "Lord of the arrow" (*b'l ḥṣ ršph*).[44] Thus, the author continues to use a religious language, whether she borrows it from the genuinely Israelite tradition or from the ancient Near Eastern repertoire. The sages of old, as regards the relationship between the divine and the human, used the vocabulary of human feelings. They said that God was moved by the same "emotion" as "an irate spouse who suspects unfaithfulness in his or her mate." That is the background of the Canticle's development. It implies that the metaphoric language of theology is not random and disposable, albeit being contingent. As writes Harold

---

40. Delitzsch, *Commentary on the Song of Song*, pp. 127–29.
41. Klein, *Ezekiel*, p. 46.
42. In Greeley and Neusner, *The Bible and Us*, p. 33.
43. *Hebrew-English Lexicon*, s.v., *rešeph*, p. 251
44. Pope, *Job*, p. 42.

Fisch, the Bible uses multifarious images to describe the relationship between God and Israel, "but none of these images proves ultimately satisfactory.... There is, however, one image that seems to have a better chance than the others. It is the image of bride and bridegroom, man and wife."[45] As we said above, the Canticle reclaims this vocabulary and reassigns it to the realm of its origin. It is not sheer retrogression, however, for the discourse is now charged with the meaning it acquired by being used theologically. The poet's defiance does not consist in the snatching back of a terminology she would deem abusively applied to a sphere foreign to it. Her defiance is in her bold application of a now sublimated vocabulary to human love. In other words, love in the Song is reincarnated; one could anachronistically say that *agape* — the word used by the LXX in Cant 8.6! — is not allowed to detach itself from *eros*. But *eros* will never be the same again after having been transfigured by *agape*. One must carefully distinguish between the iconoclasm of the Song and a pagan deification of love. The Canticle is chastening theology, not dismissing it. Here exactly resides the truth in Rabbi Aqiba's reading of the Canticle. The latter is no paean to goddess Love; nor is it a secular ditty to be sung in taverns. The Song is a reformation piece, a reaction against a certain religious and societal ethos that promoted a bourgeois frame of mind as theological propriety. Single-handedly, it seems, the author of the Song of Songs accomplished a tour de force. She threw a pebble in the cogs of the religious and societal machine. In a short and deceivingly innocent poem, she took back possession of the cleric discourse and reapplied it to its original domain. Of particular interest for the moderns is the fact that the Song's revolution occurred in the realm of *language*.[46] The phenomenon is far from being unique in history, but it certainly deserves mention. Cant 8.6 says it all in a nutshell. Here more than ever, the medium is the tenor. For the Torah and the Prophets, God's love was to be described in terms of human love. The Canticle now models human love on God's love. Love between a man and a woman is "a flame of Yah."

All of the above development concurs with Harper's position

---

45. Fisch, *Poetry with a Purpose*, p. 101.
46. Another aspect of this revolution in language — or is it simply poetic license? — is seen in the astounding number here of *hapax legomena* (thirty-seven, says Murphy, *The Song of Songs*, p. 75; others count forty-seven of them!).

about the centrality of verses 6–7 in Song of Songs 8, rather than with the opinion that they were not part of the original text. For Harper, Song 8.6–7 represents the culmination and the whole purpose of the poem, "and everything else must be read in the light of it." He continues, "The praise of such love [in its exclusiveness] cannot but become a satire upon what passes usually for love in a world in which polygamy is practiced."[47] The latter is represented and personified in the Song by King Solomon. I fully agree with Harper's discernment of sarcasm in the poem. "Love is strong as death" is no aphorism; it is defiance. No authority, institution, custom, mores, coercion, dictate, or propriety can successfully oppose love. This is the whole message of the Song of Songs. If verses 1–6 of chapter 8 are to be seen as a later addition — and especially if they are of another hand than the poet's — then one must say that the editor did not lack the genius of condensation!

Canticle 8.7

In Cant 8.7, the expression *mayîm rabbîm* (many waters) represents one of the twenty-eight times it appears in the Hebrew Scripture ("surtout dans les écrits tardifs").[48] It is echoed in the Book of Revelation (1.15; 14.2; 17.1). The frequent biblical connection with the Canaanite and Babylonian myth of the conquest of the insurgent waters is well known. They are the waters of the great Deep, the waters of Death and the Netherworld (cf. Jonah 2.3, 5–6 [2.4, 6–7]). Incidentally, Jonah 2.3 [4] shows another instance in which *nahar*, also used in this verse of the Canticle, is set in connection with those deadly waters. Let us note that *neharôt*, with the same mythological content, is also present in Hab 3.8–9; Ps 24.2; but most especially in Ezek 31.4–5, 15 (the lofty cedar of Egypt, that "the waters nourished" and that withered miserably when God restrained them). Lys comments, "c'est plus qu'une simple mort, c'est l'engloutissement dans le Chaos originel."[49]

---

47. Harper, *Song of Solomon*, p. xxxi.
48. Tournay, *Le Cantique des Cantiques*, p. 153; RTF, *Le Cantique des Cantiques*, p. 303.
49. "It is more than just death, it is the immersion in primeval Chaos" (Lys, *Le plus beau chant*, p. 291).

Kabah means "to extinguish fire" but is also used figuratively, for example, in 2 Sam 21.17 and Amos 5.6. More than with those texts, however, the similarity of vocabulary with Isa 43.2 is striking,

> When you pass through the *waters*, I will be with you;
> and through the *rivers*, they shall not *overwhelm* you;
> when you walk through *fire* you shall not be *burned* [root
>   *kâwâh* in alliteration with the Canticle's *kâbâh*],
> and the *flame* [same word as in *šalᵉhêbêtyah* of Cant 8.6] shall
>   not consume you. (NRSV; emphasis added)

Robert, Tournay, and Feuillet are of the opinion that the Canticle here evokes the security of the eschatological era, as in Isaiah. But, if so, it must be added that the eschatological victory of God in Second Isaiah is daringly transferred to the ultimate victory of human love in the Song. It is a triumph over everything that would stymie it. Especially as, on the model of the contrasting terms in the expression "good and evil," "fire and water" represent the two antipodes that embrace everything else in between. In more theoretical language, Paul in the New Testament says that "nothing" can separate us from the love of God made manifest in Jesus Christ; then, reverting to a familiar biblical term-to-term contrast, he adds, "neither death nor life...nor [the forces of] heights or depths" (Rom 8.38–39). Clearly, Paul could have added, on the model of Isa 43.2 or Cant 8.7, "nor fire nor waters," for he is referring, he also, to the forces of chaos or death that threaten love and life. Paul saw in Christ the eschatological fulfillment of Isa 43.2; the Canticle foresaw such accomplishment in the love between man and woman. The hermeneutical trajectory thus spanning the texts of Isaiah, of the Canticle, and of Romans brings together terms that become, if not interchangeable, at least mutually illuminating. The Canticle is entitled to proclaim the invincibility of human love (that no fire of hell can consume and no waters of chaos can flood) because love, eros, is the presence of eternity.

Again at this point of our inquiry, let it be emphasized that, if indeed Canticle speaks not of divine but of human love, the latter remains absolutely unique; no substitute whatsoever could be set in its place within the Song's discourse. It is love's uniqueness that promotes it to the rank it occupies in the whole Bible, whether love refers to the vertical relationship between God and humans or to the horizontal human relations. It is no accident if, in the whole of Christian Scriptures, the sole definition of God we can find in terms of an equation is the one of John's, "God is love."

It is a similar conviction that gives to the poet the strength and the right to pursue the same idea in the second half of verse 7, "If a man would give all the wealth of his family in exchange for love, he would be utterly ridiculed!" Again here, the allegorizing school becomes very uncomfortable. Tournay feels compelled to see in this part of the verse "the marginal reflection of a scribe who misunderstood the whole section as dealing with love in general."[50] For Robert, who is of the same opinion, verse 7b "devient inexplicable."[51] Anticipating such an objection, though, Harper had written, "[I]n any case it [this verse] could not have been a commonplace at marriages such as have been described [by some]."[52]

By contrast with allegorizing scholars, Harper, as already said, sees in verses 6–7 the climax of the book. They show, he thinks, the unity of the Canticle's composition around this ethical conception of love. The Song is subversive among a people accustomed to marriage transactions on an economical plane. Here such practice is condemned "in an arrow-like phrase, which having first transfixed the gorgeous and voluptuous Solomon, goes straight to the heart of the ordinary practice of the time."[53] Lys supports such a view: the *mohar* (prenuptial dowry) cannot buy the maiden's heart; it cannot prevent her from loving another man. The *mohar*, to recall, mentioned in the Laws of Hammurabi (par. 159; see also Exod 22.15–16, *mohar habbetûlôt*), was paid by the fiancé to the father-in-law as an economical compensation for the loss of a member of the latter's family at the benefit of the new husband's clan. Of importance to us is the contrasted parallel found in Hos 3.2, where the prophet says that he "bought her [Gomer] for fifteen shekels of silver and a homer of barley and a measure of wine" (NRSV). Against that backdrop, in the Canticle, it is a question of someone who is so wrong about love that he thinks he can buy it if only he

50. Tournay, *Le Cantique des Cantiques*, p. 156.
51. RTF, *Le Cantique des Cantiques*, p. 306.
52. So, by Budde, e.g., see above. Harper, *The Song of Solomon*, p. 59.
53. Harper, *The Song of Solomon*, pp. 58–59.

comes with enough money. He thus accredits the folly that love is for sale.[54] Along the same line, the visionary Daniel refuses any reward for his wisdom (Dan 5.17; cf. Josephus, who comments that wisdom cannot be acquired with money, *JA* 10.239–41). One will also remember that Balak's money could not buy Balaam's curse on Israel (Num 23.12ff.). Thus, I for one fail to see why Pope calls our Canticle text "an anticlimax."[55] It is a matter of taste, perhaps. See what sapience has to say about wisdom in Prov 3.15 and 8.11: wisdom is more precious than pearls (cf. Prov 4.7, Wis 7.7–14). (By the way, "all the wealth of his house" is an expression also found in Prov 6.31.) Wilhelm Wittekindt has drawn a contrasted parallel with Lucian's *De Dea*, where it is said that women prostituted themselves and donated the proceeds to the goddess.[56]

Canticle 8.8–10

It is not easy to decide who is speaking in verses 8–10. One could imagine that the Shulammite is speaking about a younger sister of hers and expressing her concern about protecting the child against improper courtship. By using the pronoun *we* ("we have a little sister"), she would also involve her lover because they have united.[57] But why the intervention in extremis of a new personage in the Song? What complementary role would "a little sister" of the Shulammite play? As a foil for the heroine? As an alter ego? Failing to discern a rationale for such a hypothesis, my preference goes to an alternative solution: the brothers are speaking about the Shulammite, who reports their words.[58] I gave a more substantial argument in favor of

---

54. Reese envisages the possibility that we have here a question to which the expected answer is no (*The Book of Wisdom*, p. 252). There is something akin to this already in Philo of Carpasia, who understood that there is here a reference to Christ, who gave everything for love but was despised, scorned, spat on, scourged, and crucified! The mistake comes from the Vg, which understood that the man in the Canticle has only contempt for his own money (∥Matt 13.44–46, the expensive pearl), and earlier from the LXX, which read "give his [own] life." That we should not read as Vg here is shown by texts like 1 Kgs 13.8 and Prov 6.31.
55. Pope, *Song of Songs*, p. 676.
56. Wittekindt, *Das Hohelied*, p. 56.
57. So, Knight, *Esther, Song of Songs, Lamentations*.
58. She reminisces, says Harper (cf. 1.6).

this option when I advanced the idea that the Canticle is a ritornello. I shall elaborate on this further below (see p. 190). Suffice it here to suggest that the whole poem is an inclusio; the end recalls the beginning, thematically and even philologically. Thus, some of the initial themes of the poem are repeated in verses 8–10 of chapter 8; so are others, as we shall see, in verses 11–12 as well,[59] and perhaps even in a clearer way in verses 13–14. But, for now let us notice that one of these themes, present here as it was in 1.6, is the negative attitude of the belle's brothers, representing custom and propriety in the family and society at large. The "free love" of their sister runs counter to their social standards. In a first move, they start by expressing the view that their sister is too young for any love affair. And, indeed, they may be objectively right, although chances are that theirs is a *pro domo* argument. A Sumerian poem quoted by Murphy has god Dumuzi's elder sister exclaiming, "To my paternal eye [*sic*] you are verily still a small child, — yonder Baba [Inanna] may know you for a man. I shall let you go to her!"[60]

In a second move, the brothers swear that when the time for such an "affair" will come (that is, a suitable time after their standards), fool is the one who thinks that they will become more lax. They will be as strict as before, only in a different way. Comes the day when "she will be spoken for"[61] then they will even raise the stakes. *Dabbér be-* generally means "to speak against." But the expression also means "to ask in marriage," as is attested in 1 Sam 25.39. Within such a context, the girl's brothers anticipate for themselves a day of glory. They will act according to estimable and unexceptionable custom; they will play a major role in their sister's courtship and marriage (Gen 24.29, 50, 55, 60) and, before that, in the protection of her chastity (Gen 34.6–17; 2 Sam 13.20, 32). Little do they know that such a time is long past!

The tone in the Canticle continues, therefore, to be highly ironic. Presented at this point of the poem, the brothers' discourse is especially pompous and preposterous.[62] The "little sister" did not wait

---

59. Cf. Lys: Le vocabulaire de ce verset (v. 11) "va en faveur de l'unité d'auteur avec le reste du Cantique" (*Le plus beau chant*, p. 301).

60. Murphy, *The Song of Songs*, p. 49.

61. Ibid., p. 190.

62. For the allegorical school, this cannot be; on the contrary, the brothers are "animés d'excellentes intentions (*sic*)" (RTF, *Le Cantique des Cantiques*, p. 314).

for their permission to fall in love. Her breasts, which they refuse
to see and persist in considering as nonexistent, have already been
praised by someone else — who assuredly knows better — and compared to "two fawns" (4.5; 7.3). Besides, later on in the chapter, she
herself speaks of her chest in terms of twin towers (v. 10)! Yes, time
has elapsed since the "wall" and the "door" she was supposed to be
against her suitors have surrendered to her lover's "onslaught." In
her response to the brothers, verse 10, the irony becomes sarcasm:
The one who found me discovered — to his delight — that I am a
wall (to others only), but not because of my immaturity!

Before we leave this verse, let us note the parallel with Ezek 16.7,
which, incidentally, compares Jerusalem in the most unexpected way
to a "myriad," a cognate of the term *hamôn* in Cant 8.11. Another
parallel is with Hosea 2, where there is also a question of a hedge
within which YHWH intends to wall His people (vv. 8–9) so that
"she shall look for [her lovers], but she shall not find [them]." Interestingly enough, according to Henry McKeating, "The talk about
chasing lovers and being restrained by hedges and walls is more appropriate to an animal in heat than to a human being."[63] And as
to the quest (for lovers), in Hosea it was in vain, and it ended up
in hopelessness, a direction that the Canticle takes in reverse. The
Canticle takes exception also with the text of Isa 26.1–5, where several of the terms used by Cant 8.8–10 can be found, to the extent
that we may consider the Isaianic development as the source text for
the Canticle: "the wall" in 26.1; "the door" in 26.2 (or rather, here,
gates); the verb *ṣûr* in 26.3 (the noun in v. 4); and then the unexpected motif in both texts of *šalôm*, "peace" (Cant 8.10; Isa 26.3
[two times]).

A closer look at some details of verses 8–10 is worth our while.
First, we turn to the materials used by the brothers in the description of their little sister's natural and moral defenses (vv. 8–9). They
are as attractive as they are forbidding: "a turret of silver," "pan-
els of cedar." Clearly, the Shulammite's siblings want to protect the
virginity of the girl while stressing her richness and her attractiveness.[64] Besides, characteristically, those materials find their fitting

---

63. McKeating, *Amos, Hosea, and Micah*, p. 83.
64. RTF speak here of a "protection solide et coûteuse" (*Le Cantique des Cantiques*,
p. 311).

reference, once more, in the temple of Jerusalem. The term *tîrâ* is almost the same as *tûr* (*tûrîm*), which in 1 Kgs 6.36 (*tûrê-gazît*) and 7.12 (*tûrîm gâzît wetûr kerutot 'ᵃrazîm*) describes the limits of the temple's court.[65]

Verse 10, in addition to what we saw above regarding it, is crammed with difficulties. They can, however, be considerably alleviated or outright resolved in the light of our approach to the whole poem. First, it must be realized that the Shulammite assumes for herself the terminology of her brothers, but she transforms its meaning (as the poet has done all along with prophetic, narrative, and hymnic discourse). She says something like, "You want me to be a wall? I am that wall, but not one that is as smooth and even as you may think. My breasts are like towers!" Then, she continues with what Delitzsch rightly sees as a play of words on the name of Solomon; she is in the eyes of a specific somebody as one who brings peace (cf. 1 Chr 22.9). But Delitzsch is wrong when he thinks that the woman made peace with the great king.[66] Rather, we understand that the Shulammite, the anti-Solomon, is *in the eyes of her lover* as one who found [or produced] peace (cf. Deut 20.10). During the "war," the fortress proved invincible to all others. But it capitulated at the first assault of her true love. So, Harper says that peace is Solomon's ceasing to besiege the "city" he could not capture. Confirmation of Harper's reading can be found in the term *naṣûr* of verse 9, which does not come from the root *ṣûr* (cf. *leṣayyér*, "to draw") but from *ṣrr*, "to tighten" (hence, here, "to enclose," "to surround"). See especially Isa 29.3: *we-ṣarᵉtî 'alayik muṣab we-haqîmotî 'alayik meṣurot*. In 2 Sam 20.3, women are "closed in" (*ṣerurôt*) the harem. The word *šalôm* here is synonymous subjectively with "surrender" (as in Deut 20.11; Josh 11.19) and objectively with "appeasement (of desire)," as such a meaning fits the entire context of the Canticle. Lys understands correctly that instead of being a defense against the shepherd, all walls and towers proclaim *shalom*.

I have identified as the shepherd-lover the one the Shulammite is speaking about in verse 10. True, the text remains ambiguous and

---

65. The whole of Jewish tradition understands that it is here a question of the temple.
66. Dussaud (*Le Cantique des Cantiques*) goes even so far as to say that she entered his harem!

does not say specifically who is meant by "in his eyes I have been as one who found [or, produced] *shalom.*" The LXX has the pronoun in the plural, "in their eyes" (of the brothers). But the context, I think, demands that we understand "his eyes" as the shepherd's. It is especially true if we follow Jacques Winandy,[67] who translates "aussi suis-je à ses yeux comme ayant atteint l'âge adulte" (I am in his eyes as come of age), by contrast with the brothers' opinion to the contrary. *Môṣ'ét* is the qal mode of *mṣ'*, "the one who finds," or the hifil mode of *yṣ'*, "the one who produces." She herself found *shalom,* or she brought to someone else *shalom.* At any rate, there is here a wordplay on the name *Shulammite* (whose form is a passive participle qal like *yûlad* in Judg 13.8). *Haššûlammît* means "the pacified" (so Aquila and Quinta: *eirēneuousa* in Cant 7.1), and our invitation above to render *šalôm* by "appeasement" suggests that she herself is "appeased" after her encounter with the shepherd. But the range of meaning of the word *šalôm,* whether used as a noun or as an element in the composite name of the maiden, transcends any of its shades. She may be found as the one "appeased" as well as the one who provides "appeasement"; she also stands in opposition to *šelomoh* and as the one who cannot be paid for (*šullam,* see Jer 18.20; Prov 11.31) at any price (cf. Cant 8.7), for her love is an echo of the restoration of Israel in God's covenant of *šalôm* (see Isa 42.19; cf. 54.10: Israel is reinstated in God's covenant of peace).

Finally, I mention one more possibility contemplated by other critics who see in verse 10 an allusion to the popular etymology of "Jeru-salem."[68] Within our interpretation of the Canticle, this apparent identification of the Shulammite with the city of peace is no surprise. It is sheer misunderstanding when Robert, Tournay, and Feuillet say that the metaphor is impossible after the "stark distinction [from Jerusalem] in 3.2–3; 5.7."[69]

---

67. Winandy, "Le Cantique des Cantiques et le Nouveau Testament."

68. So Joüon, *Le Cantique des Cantiques.* In Ps 76.3, the city is called, in parallel with "Zion," simply "Shalem" (cf. Gen 14.18). For C. Bloch, Shulammite "probably means 'woman of Jerusalem'" (Bloch and Bloch, *The Song of Songs,* p. 8). A. Bloch adds that the article before Shulammite has the value of a vocative; cf. 2 Sam 14.4, "O king!" (p. 198).

69. RTF, *Le Cantique des Cantiques,* p. 314.

Canticle 8:11–12

Verses 8–10, it must be said, break the flow of the development between verse 7 and verse 11. Without that intrusion (perhaps composed by the author but misplaced by a later redactor), the whole context is clearly one of quantity versus quality. Verse 7 spoke of "many waters...and rivers" incapable of submerging love,[70] and verse 11 now brings about the familiar theme of Croesus-like King Solomon, possessor of everything in sight and thus figuratively sitting in a fictional place called Baal-Hamon, "owner of multitude." By contrast, the Shulammite has only one vineyard, but she shuns the hundreds and the thousands of the king. In this instance, the "donor field" is Isa 17.12–14. This prophetic oracle speaks of *hamôn*, even creating a derivative verb with the same root (v. 12). It also uses the expression "many waters" as a metaphor for "the nations," opposing such awesome quantity and volume to their ultimate fate: they vanish in one stroke. "Such is the portion of those who pillage us, such is the fate of those who plunder us" (v. 14).

In Canticle 8, the "many waters" are demythologized while keeping their power of adverting to chaotic and negative forces and drawing a parallel with "death" in verse 6. Strikingly, where Isaiah 17 saw the Warrior God overcoming a multitude of enemies, the Canticle substitutes *'ahabâ* to God's intervention! As to "Solomon," he finds himself here on the wrong side of the chasm, but this is congruent with the rest of the poem.

A parable follows to illustrate with a *leçon de chose* what has just been stated above regarding the incompatibility of love with trade, money, or, more generally, with numbers. For the sake of its demonstration, the parable starts (v. 11) with the monetary evaluation of a "vineyard." Later, verse 12, the Shulammite leaves no room for hesitation as to the meaning of the metaphor; the vineyard is her body. She says, "My vineyard is mine to watch" (see Gen 13.9; 20.15; 24.51; 34.10; 47.6; 1 Sam 16.16; 2 Chr 14.6).

Verses 11–12 are embarrassing for the allegorical school, for Solo-

---

70. "Waters" and "rivers" is a most natural association since at least the time of Ugaritic literature (fourteenth century B.C.E.), which lies in the background of that motif. *Nahar* (river) is another term for the sea, and *rabbîm* is, according to Cross, an epithet of *nahar* (cf. *Canaanite Myth and Hebrew Epic*, p. 119).

mon cannot possibly be identified here with God or the messiah, for example, as had been suggested in other places. This is part of the reason why verses 8 and following are considered by those scholars as a late addition by a scribe who mistook [*sic*] the whole Song of Songs for a hymn to human love. By contrast, the reader will note this additional textual witness to an early reading of the Canticle in its plain and "naturalist" sense. The importance of such ancient understandings of the Song cannot be overstated.

Another question need not detain us long. Who is telling the parable? Clearly it is the one who says in verse 12, "My vineyard is mine to watch over." Unfortunately, the Hebrew like the English is here gender-ambiguous. But three elements of the phrase are decisive. First, if we surmise that the male lover is speaking here, saying something like, "To Solomon his ownership...I have mine in the person of the Shulammite," then he claims her as his own, and she is not the independent female she proclaims in the rest of the Song. For this reason, as well as for the ones that follow, it is preferable to think that she is the speaker. For, secondly, the formula is repeating Cant 1.6, which is an utterance of the heroine. A third reason has been spelled out earlier — when I emphasized with Lys that *'anî* (I, me) is always in *her* mouth (1.5–6; 2.1, 5, 16; 5.2, 8; 6.3; 7.11; 8.10). The same situation obtains with *nap^ešî* ("my soul"; 1.7; 3.1–4; 5.6; 6.12), *libbî* ("my heart"; 5.2), and, as Cant 1.6 has shown, *kar^emî* (my vineyard).

The parable locates the vineyard in *ba'al-hamôn,* a term that literally means "possessor of a crowd" (cf. Aq; Sym; Jerome, Syro-Hexapl.). Hence, Robert understands "la populeuse." Not surprisingly, it is for him a designation of the land of Israel as the vineyard of YHWH (cf. Ps 80.9–12). In that regard, the text of 1 Kgs 4.20 is interesting. It brings the reader to the time of Solomon's reign and describes the nation under him as numerous like the sand by the sea. Whether we should see this text of Kings as having had a direct or indirect influence on Cant 8.11 is a moot question. But the fundamental point in invoking Solomon, here as elsewhere in the Canticle, is that one conjures up ideas of abundance, of plenty, of numbers. Solomon has everything in quantity, including bedmates. As says Lys — who understands also *ba'al hamôn* as the "populeuse" but rightly sees in it Solomon's harem — Solomon has the quantity, but he misses the true love as it exists between the Shulammite and her shepherd. Marcia Falk comments that women can be treated as sexual objects (Solomon's vineyard must be constantly guarded), but the Song here "rejects the debasement of sexuality."[71]

Quantity, vineyard, and "a thousand pieces of silver" are three elements again packed together in the text of Isa 7.23. There the prophet also showed abundance defeated by catastrophe. It shall be no more. The idea has been picked up by the Canticle, replacing historical cataclysm by existential contempt. The reader will be sensitive to the abrupt and scornful tone of verse 12's address. The phrase sounds like a slap in the face of the establishment.

Clearly, with this new development, we are following up the idea expressed earlier of the impossibility to buy love. "Solomon" envisages love in terms of thousands and hundreds and must have recourse to others to watch over his "vineyards," as over the rest of his properties. "Let him keep that kind of trade," says the Shulammite. "I shall keep my own 'vineyard' outside of such monetary estimation." The opposition is between many and one. Paradoxically, "Solomon," representing integration, is numerous (8.12), while differentiation or discrimination by preference restores unity (6.9). We almost have here a parable around the statement that the one who wins loses, and the one who loses wins!

The metaphor of the vineyard attracted the word *not^erîm* here; it is a qal participial plural form of *natar*, "to watch," and a clear echo of 1.6, where the brothers set the maiden as guardian of vineyards. She probably did a good job at it but had to confess, *kar^emî šelî lo' natar^etî* (my own vineyard I did not keep).[72] In general, the *not^erîm* are hired guardians sent to the fields about to be harvested to keep away marauders or the "small foxes," as Cant 2.15 calls the undesirable. Thus, the Shulammite's admission parallels the earlier statement about her surrender to the shepherd (v. 10).

At the end of our study of this small sketch, it is not superfluous to reflect upon the main term of the metaphor, namely, the vineyard. It obviously occupies a choice place in the Song. In this parable, however, as never before, the author has brought us in close con-

---

71. Falk, *Love Lyrics from the Bible*, p. 133. Let us note here that *ba'al hamôn* also means "husband of a multitude"!

72. A further development is found at 1.6 and its context; see p. 73.

tact with the model text of Isa 5.1, *kerem hayah lîdîdî,* "my beloved had a vineyard."[73] The Canticle's consistence is remarkable. As we repeatedly noticed in what precedes, the heroine has taken over the role that Israel (or respectively the sacred chariot, the temple, the courts thereof, etc.) used to fill in Scriptures. Love claims its rights — and they are exorbitant, if only because love has now acquired an extravagant importance after having been used figuratively for allegedly superior purposes. Mutatis mutandis we can draw a parallel with Psalm 8 claiming almost the honor of God for the human, after being made, so to speak, God's self-portrait! The canvas used by Rembrandt is ennobled for having served the artist!

Canticle 8:13–14

An ultimate vignette is given in these last two verses of the poem. The shepherd is speaking, "O you [fem. sing.] who sit in the garden." Again, according to the style of the ritornello (see above chap. 6, and below in this chapter), a theme initiated at the beginning of the poem (cf. 2.14, where also *he* is speaking) is here presented verbatim as an echo that, through sheer repetition, emphasizes the power of duplication: now as then, he is begging to hear her voice. All the "development" in between has apparently not brought any progression in the lovers' togetherness. Stressed is her distance from him; there is as a screen between them. On the model of the frustrating separation that irremediably follows communion between genders ("post coitum triste animal est"), at the end of the poem we find ourselves like at its beginning. It is characteristic of the ritornello to be attuned with that eternal return of the same. As befits a ritornello, the *haberîm,* also mentioned at the beginning of the poem in 1.7 (*'al 'ederey habereyka,* "by the flocks of your companions"), reappear. The attitude of the shepherd's colleagues has not changed either. They still are on the lookout to "catch" the seemingly vagrant

---

73. Also the text of 1 Kings 21 on Naboth's vineyard comes to mind, all the more so as the syntactic construction falls in parallel with the Canticle's and Isaiah's. A. Bloch writes (about Cant 8.11), "The style is narrative, and the word order, beginning with an indefinite noun (literally 'a vineyard was to Solomon'), is like that in two other stories involving vineyards, the parable in Isa 5:1..., and the story of Naboth's vineyard in 1 Kings 21:1" (Bloch and Bloch, *The Song of Songs,* p. 218).

woman. Here again, the companions — that is, the other boys, the peers of the shepherd — might well try to evict the lover and take his place, so attractive and so apparently remote from her lover is the belle.[74] Another understanding is offered by Landy, "The [woman's] voice," he says, "is of course associated with, and survives only in, the Song; the friends listening to her could then include the entire audience of the Song, all of whom participate sympathetically in the experience of the lovers."[75] At any rate, here the lover comes to her and waits for her to give the word — a staggering reversal of the biblical ethos in general!

The beloved maiden "sits in gardens," as was said already in 4.12; 5.1; and 6.2, and she is herself often represented as a garden. Thus, all the initial themes of the poem reappear at the end. "With minor changes, *berah*, 'be swift,' for *sob*, 'turn'; the addition of the conjunction *we-*, 'and,' before *demeh*, 'be like'; and the change of *beter*, 'cleavage,' to *besamîm*, 'spices,' this verse [14] is a doublet of 2.17," says Pope.[76] Well-known motifs played upon by the poet all along come up now again in a crescendo tempo and in tighter sequence as we come to a close. In the words of Fisch, "[W]e have the urgency, the sense of a compelling need, as of a task still to be fulfilled, a race still to be run."[77] The time is short, and the poem must conclude, but it concludes as it started; it says at the end what was said at the outset. Surely the authorial intention is to affirm the endlessness of amorous attraction, the insatiable desire that time and again brings together the male and the female, the separation that follows the union, and the reunion that redeems the separation. The last call in the poem echoes Cant 1.4, "Draw me after you, let us make haste" (NRSV). Nothing has been resolved; the lovers have not settled down. No wedding comes to soothe the burning passion; no ceremony occurs to give ultimate vindication to societal customs. The shepherd must again flee, faithful to his nature and vocation to

---

74. Gerleman also opines that they are the rivals who with her shepherd listen to her voice (*Rut — Das Hohelied*, p. 223). (Lys: In 1.7 these *haberîm* are clearly hostile [*Le plus beau chant de la creation*, p. 305]).

75. Landy, "The Song of Songs," p. 317. Note how much this reading of Landy's contributes to the attribution of the poem to a poet, something Landy does not do, however.

76. Pope, *Song of Songs*, p. 697.

77. Fisch, *Poetry with a Purpose*, p. 103.

be "like a gazelle or a young hart upon the mountains of spices." As those mounts refer to the woman herself (see 2.17; 4.6), his fleeing is no escape from her, but to her, and hence a looping of the Song's loop.[78] And thus the poem, lest it end up by being itself a flimsy story, with a resolution tailored to satisfy romantic seamstresses, has no other choice but to be a ritornello and to start all over again — like the love it sings.

Excursus: Ritornello

It is not surprising and unexpected that the Song of Songs is built as a cycle. Verses 13–14 of Canticle 8 build an end that is, at the same time, a rebound of the whole poem, a return to the beginning. And thus the Canticle is an endless song.[79] Granted, there is no plot in the Song of Songs, and therefore one expects no relief of tension that would characterize the conclusion to a narrative or to a play. Cant 8.13–14 simply repeats 2.17, almost verbatim. This and other factors that we shall review below lead me to conclude that the Song of Songs is indeed a *round,* the *rondeau* of the Middle Ages, that is, an endlessly repeated song. This feature is a strong argument in favor of the unity of composition and of authorship. It has passed unnoticed by commentators, although some close readers put us on the right track. Robert, Tournay, and Feuillet, for instance, quote Denis Buzy, who stated that the Canticle's poems are variations on the same theme without progression of thought: "D'un poème à l'autre, la progression est nulle, puisque chaque fois tout recommence, pour s'achever de nouveau et recommencer encore."[80] Others have shown

---

78. In the words of Salvaneschi, "[T]hus the escape afar from the beloved one leads to the garden, which represents her" (*Cantico dei cantici,* p. 115).

79. Interestingly enough, Landy also speaks of "a certain circularity in the Song; the second half reflects the first," he says. He adds, "Concentricity is not strict, not mechanical, but it is nevertheless pervasive." Landy tallies still other texts, such as 8.1–2 and 3.1–4 (and 5.2–7); 7.1–6 and 4.1–7; 6.1–12 and 4.12–5.1 ("Song of Songs," pp. 315–16). As to Salvaneschi, she speaks of the Canticle as "opera aperta...un meandre a spirale" (*Cantico dei cantici,* p. 115). The Blochs say it is "like a musical da capo" (*The Song of Songs,* p. 18).

80. Buzy, "La composition littéraire," p. 192: "From one poem to the other, there is no progression, as each time everything starts again and ends again, to start once more." See also Buzy, "Le Cantique des Cantiques," p. 290. Speaking about Egyptian erotic literature, Derchain writes, "Les ensembles ne sont pas évidents pour qui n'a pas découvert les liens

the perfect equilibrium between the diverse parts of the poem (see in particular Exum, Shea, and Dorsey).

In what follows, I am giving a synopsis of parallels, most of which have been already mentioned above:

- Cant 8.1–2 recalls 1.2 (the kiss of his mouth).

- In 8.6 the word *ahabâ* recalls 1.3–4.

- Cant 8.12 sends us back to 1.2 (her vineyard).

- In 8.13, *hayyôšebet bagganîm* sends us back to 4.12; 6.2. In the same verse, *habérîm* sends us back to *'al 'êd*ᵉ*rey habéreyka* in 1.7; *leqôlék hašmî'înî,* to 2.14 (*hašmî'înî 'et qôlék*; see the whole verse of Cant 8.13).

- In 8.14, *berah dôdî* reminds one of 1.4 (*mâš*ᵉ*kénî ah*ᵃ*rêka narûṣah*). In the same verse, *deméh leka liṣebî 'ô le'oper ha'*ᵃ*y-yalîm* parallels 2.9 (*dômeh dôdî liṣebî 'ô le'oper ha'yyalîm*) and 2.17 (*deméh leka dôdî liṣebî 'ô le'oper ha'yyalîm*). The end of 8.14, *'al harey besamîm,* is a repetition of 2.17 (*'al harey bater*) in combination with *la'*ᵃ*rûgôt habbosem lir*ᵉ*'ôt bagganîm* of 6.2.

- Keel sees in 8.5 a possible play on 2.1–3 as well as on 3.6–8.[81]

subtils qui unissent ce qu'on a trop facilement accepté comme des pièces indépendantes" ("Le lotus, la mandragore et le perséa," p. 86).

81. Keel, *The Song,* p. 268.

Chapter Nine

IMAGINARY DIALOGUE WITH OTHMAR KEEL

೦ಃ ೦ಃ ೦ಃ ೦ಃ ೦ಃ ೦ಃ ೦ಃ ೦ಃ ೦ಃ ೦ಃ ೦ಃ ೦ಃ ೦ಃ ೦ಃ

In what follows, I have chosen to converse with Othmar Keel's *The Song of Songs: A Continental Commentary* (abbreviated as *The Song* and cited in the text of this chapter by page number) because it is one of the latest published in English (translation) and because in more than one way Keel's commentary, drawing heavily as it does on textual and iconographic materials from the ancient Near East, would seem to offer a viable alternative to my "intra-Israelite" interpretation. It thus appears to me that if I can at times defeat his argumentation (when he uses the term *husband,* for instance) and at other times radicalize his own premises (when he shows awareness to the flagrant opposition between the Song and prophetic texts, for example), I may infer for my approach an a fortiori supersession as regards other modern theories about the Canticle.

Keel is so convinced of the parallelism between the Canticle and erotic Egyptian literature that he feels compelled to date the Canticle between the eighth and the sixth century B.C.E.: "[A]t that time ancient Egyptian love literature was still flourishing (a fact that has not been demonstrated for the Hellenistic era)" (p. 5). Such dating and his attributing the poem to a well-to-do author are consistent with Keel's general approach. He understands the Song as an apologue affirming societal mores and rules and turns to wisdom literature for confirmation. But Israel's sages glorify gender relations only when they occur within the bonds of legitimated unions (cf. Prov 5.15–20; 30.19). Furthermore they tend to be remarkably austere, as a look into Jesus ben Sirach (ca. 180 B.C.E.) will attest (see Sir 26.15–21;

cf. Proverbs 31). How does this fit with the unconventional loves described in the Canticle? Regarding social matters, it is true that there is in the Song a "context of art and luxury" (p. 27), but such context, I claim, belongs to sarcasm and turns into parody the language and world of the well-to-do.[1] Anyone subverting the established "world" must immerse herself into that world and deconstruct it from the inside.[2] Keel should have drawn the inescapable conclusions from his own statement,

> Astonishingly, just as the Song sovereignly ignores any tendency to deny the body, it also ignores the claims of society that often come into conflict with spontaneous expressions of love. In the OT world, society's interests are expressed primarily in the patriarchal family, the institution of marriage, and the production of offspring. But the Song simply has nothing to do with such things. (p. 32)

And again, "[b]oth little books [Song and Ecclesiastes] contain a measure of anarchy" (p. 37). Chana Bloch speaks of the Shulammite's "sweeping aside the biblical hierarchies."[3]

More gravely, Keel's early dating of the Canticle is an a posteriori and *pro domo* argumentation in support of his general thesis regarding the usefulness of ancient Near Eastern iconography for throwing light on biblical texts. I fully agree with Hans-Josef Heinevetter's critique that "[a]greement between individual images and motifs says little about where their sources are to be found."[4] Heinevetter then quotes Hans Müller who, about Qoh 9.7–10, says that although its wording may be closer to the Gilgamesh epic than to comparable Greek texts, this does not wrench Qoheleth from its Hellenistic milieu. Egyptian parallels to the Canticle can be explained by Hellenistic accommodation of Oriental motifs (see, e.g., Theocritus).

Heinevetter, after Heinrich Graetz, puts to rest Keel's speculations on a preexilic date of the Song of Songs, a dating that demands that we consider late philological elements in the book as later additions.[5]

---

1. See p. 44 and n. 106 there.
2. This is badly missed by Clines in his article "Why Is There a Song of Songs."
3. Bloch and Bloch, *The Song of Songs*, p. 9.
4. Heinevetter, *"Komm nun, mein Liebster,"* p. 219.
5. See Heinevetter, *"Komm nun, mein Liebster,"* p. 14.

There are in the Canticle a number of allusions to Greek customs; Heinevetter lists some of them:[6]

1.12   It is a question here of the round table about which one eats while reclining (see above, p. 79).

3.9–10   The palanquin is not Israelite; even Keel acknowledges that much (p. 130).

3.11   The crowning of the groom is again un-Israelite (instead of the crowning of the bride! See above, p. 101).

3.1–5   The guardians of the city are *peripoloi,* the city police in
and 5.7   a Hellenistic *polis.*

8.6   The arrows of love belong to Greek mythological poetry of Eros.

Furthermore, in contrast with the ancient world, country life in the Canticle is not part of the everyday experience; it is depicted as an ideal bucolic or pastoral life. This is a Greek discovery within a fast-growing city culture that spread over the Hellenized Near East as well. Heinevetter, therefore, thinks of a time before Antiochus the Great, a time of peace and luxury, when the Ptolemaic king could be called Pharaoh, that is, under Ptolemy III Euergetes (ca. 240 B.C.E.). So much for the Canticle's date.[7]

Turning to Keel's tallying, we start with what he says apropos Cant 7.8, which compares the woman with a palm tree. Keel insists that the metaphor is theomorphic. He asks,

But what is the origin of the metaphors used even in these late, often thoroughly profane poems? . . . [T]o deny any connections between [the Song] and mythic-cultic patterns would be to deprive oneself of an insight into the sources from which many of its metaphors receive the power and intensity that they retain down through the centuries. (p. 243)

---

6. Heinevetter, *"Komm nun, mein Liebster,"* p. 212.

7. The attribution of the Song to Solomon goes in the same direction. Hengel speculates that the attribution to Solomon of such diverse works as Proverbs, Qoheleth, the Canticle, *Psalms of Solomon,* Wisdom of Solomon, and the *Testament of Solomon* during the Hellenistic period was in order to demonstrate the antiquity and superiority of Jewish wisdom over the Greek one.

In this essay of mine, I take Keel's statement in all earnestness, something he himself, I believe, does not always do. But I grant much less trust to comparative ancient Near Eastern iconography and a great deal more to Israelite genuine traditions than does Keel. About the iconographic material, which deserves so much of the reader's appreciation, I would sound a caveat. Comparative iconography, like comparative religion or comparative linguistics and for the same reasons, is somewhat deceptive.[8] The same picture may mean vastly different things as its message varies in time and space. The highly erotic statues in India would stir a starkly different reaction if exported in neighboring Pakistan or Tibet. If we imagine for a moment that a Muslim artist imitates a Hindu carving, the modern interpreter's task would consist not only in spotting the Indian parallels but in being sensitive to the subversive character of the borrowing art.[9]

As far as the Song is concerned, an example amidst many is provided by Keel's dealing with Cant 1.13. The "bag of myrrh that lies between [the woman's] breasts" (NRSV) is, he says, a bag amulet (see p. 65). He then brings about Egyptian parallels (see p. 66 nn. 3, 4) where also the beloved is to her lover as an amulet. But Keel does not continue with the necessary warning that what in Egypt stirs no surprise becomes aberrant or outright offensive in an Israelite milieu. The prophetic ire against idolatry makes that point crystal clear.

Furthermore, in spite of the richness of ancient Near Eastern iconography, Keel's exegesis remains singularly one-sided. The Song of Songs becomes in the process one more "Egyptian" or "Sumerian" love song. Its belonging to biblical literature teaches very little that is new, and our wisdom (other than aesthetic) is not greatly enhanced. We remain puzzled by an obvious problem: What in the world did the early allegoretes see in this particular love song that was conducive to the understanding they proposed? If nothing distinguishes the Canticle from the rest of Near Eastern pictures and literatures, why single it out? Why speculate on its hidden meaning? Why eventually canonize it? If the Canticle is the most "unbiblical book of the Bible," not

---

8. A. Bloch writes, "The semantic range of a linguistic expression in one language does not guarantee the same range in another" (Bloch and Bloch, *The Song of Songs*, p. 151).

9. A nonfictional example is provided by the swastika as a symbol in India and in Nazi Germany.

only by what it does not say but also by what it does say, what is it doing in Hebrew sacred Scripture? I propose a solution; what is Keel's?

One of the main objections that will be made to my exegesis is that there might have been aristocratic milieus in Israel cultivating erotic poetry, even, for that matter, after the exilic failure of monarchy. Keel intimates, for instance, that there was some kind of frolic singing at the occasion of festivals, and he mentions (p. 6) a Talmudic text involving Rabbi Simeon b. Gamliel (140 C.E.!). What is remarkable in the cited text (*mTa'an* 4.8; *Ta'an* 31a), however, is the strong accent put on the uniformity of the *unmarried* girls' dress and on their charge to the young men, "Don't look for beauty, look for family" — a far cry from the Song of Songs! Of course, it would be unwarranted on my part to deny the existence of *waṣf*s celebrating "the pulchritude of a woman, or, rarely, of a man," as says Gustav Dalman (cited in Keel, p. 12). But two points must be highlighted. First, in conformity with the Canticle, such *waṣf*s were not specific to weddings; second, in contrast with the Canticle, their language was not necessarily allusive to "biblical" traditions.

Such judgment must, however, be tempered if we turn to the pseudepigraphic tale of Hellenistic times *Joseph and Aseneth*. Composed probably in Alexandria at the beginning of the second century C.E. at the latest,[10] it contains a *waṣf* in 18.9–10[11] (in the long version) in which biblical metaphors are used ("fields of the Most High . . . vine of the paradise of God . . . like the mountains of the Most High")! But what has been gained in terms of similitude with the Song of Songs' use of Israelite traditional formulas is lost in terms of the respective moods in the two documents. Far from being an erotic novel, the ethos in *Joseph and Aseneth* is Victorian, even prudish. The biblical metaphors carefully mention the Jewish God, and they are perfectly innocuous. Albeit largely dependent as well upon its Egyptian setting, the tale prudently remains afar from any libertinism, insisting, for example, upon the virginity of the lovers (1.6; 8.1). In short, if this pseudepigraph and the Song of Songs can at all be compared, it is in terms of contrast, not of identity. It is clear that a designation like "apples of Damascus" is not to be put on a par with "Lebanon,"

---

10. Dupont-Sommer and Philonenko, eds., *La Bible*, pp. 1559–1602.
11. Charlesworth, *The Old Testament Pseudepigrapha*, vol. 2, p. 232.

"Tirzah," or "Jerusalem" in Cant. Only the latter ones are susceptible to being used in such a way as to become ironic and irreverent and to shift the poetry character from the aesthetic to the subversive.

There is also an interesting *waṣf* in 1QGenApoc 20.1–8 — a document present in Qumran but not reflecting its ideology — but it is made of an exclamatory description of Sarai's beauty proceeding from top to bottom and back to the height of her hands. But the description is without metaphors or similes and is put in the mouths of *Pharaoh's ministers*.

As to the Canticle's parallels with Egyptian love songs and with the Near Eastern repertoire of poetry for sacred marriages, they are undeniable. That the Israelite poet was in no need to "reinvent the wheel" goes without saying. The whole issue for the reader of the Canticle is what is being done here with the wheel. For instance, from the premise that the Solomonic court was conceived on an Egyptian model, one would be adventurous to infer the "Egyptian-ization" of Israel in the tenth century B.C.E. As regards the kinship of the Canticle with Egyptian literature, it originates from the arresting fact that in ancient Egypt men and women enjoyed a legal and economical equality, a rare feature in the old world.[12] The lack of comparability in other cultures is emphasized by Keel when he acknowledges that "no collection of love songs comparable to the Song or to the Egyptian collections has been found in Phoenicia, Canaan, or Assyria" (p. 28). More decisive yet is what he says regarding the Song and biblical traditions: "[M]any situations that the Song views as expressions of heavenly bliss for the lovers are seen quite differently by the wisdom teachers and prophets; with just a slight shift in accent and nuance, they condemn the same situations" (p. 30).

Response to Keel's Exegesis

How Keel's general stance affects his exegesis will be evident, I think, from what follows. It will also be clear how close to each other and how far apart we stand. Regarding Cant 1.2, Keel speaks of the woman's "husband," an unwarranted title that makes the rest of the

---

12. See Quirke, *Ancient Egyptian Religion*.

verse ("the maidens love you") and verses 4b and 6b, for instance, very troubling! Verse 7 presents us with an unusual "husband" that conceals to his wife his whereabouts and relies on the members of his "fraternity" to bring her to him. In 5.2–8 the situation is still more improper, for if he is her husband, then he behaves as a drunkard, and she must look through the whole town for him.[13]

Regarding the tone of 1.5, I note with Keel the contrast when the prophets use the expression "daughter of Zion" for condemning her coquettishness and vanity. On that score, Keel is right on target when he writes,

> The constellation that is here found so praiseworthy — pride, outstretched neck, and jewelry — is precisely what arouses the indignation of the prophet in Isa 3.16–17. This phenomenon recurs: what the Song celebrates, the prophets criticize. (pp. 58–59)

Noting another such contrast, he adds, "Verse 9 is one of the few passages in the OT that mention horses positively" (p. 59). In the same vein, Keel rightly states that if Cant 1.16b–17 is understood as alluding to sacred fornication, which was denounced by the prophets (e.g., Hos 4.13; cf. Deut 12.2), as seems to be indicated by the term *ra'anan* in the majority of its occurrences, then the conclusion is unmistakable. In Keel's words,

> As in 1.10–11, the Song and the prophetic critique speak again of the same thing from different perspectives. The prophets combat love-making under every leafy tree because they see it as a continuation of and concession to the cult of Baal. (p. 75)

By contrast, I cannot concur with Keel's statement that the oath by the gazelles and hinds in 2.7; 3.5 just substitutes God's creatures for the deity himself (pp. 93–94). I have discussed this theme above (see p. 63) and shown its deliberate insolence.

Keel sees in Cant 2.14, as I also do (see above, p. 89), the parallel with Exod 33.18, but he limits the comparison to the request expressed in both texts to see the face (of the woman in Cant 2.14 and the glory of God in Exod 33.18). This is insufficient, for the

---

13. Besides, Keel says that the term *re'ah* (in 1.9, 15; 2.10, 13; 4.1, 7; 5.2; 6.4) means "girlfriend" (p. 58).

similarities between the two texts are more striking than that. The form of the verb *let me see* is common to both; *panîm* in Exodus is replaced in the Canticle by its synonym *mar'eh* to insist on the desire to see the whole of her; *sela'* appears in Canticle 2 for *ṣûr* and clearly with the same meaning here and there. In Exodus 33, like in Cant 2.14, the issue of seeing is central. The people "watch/see" when Moses comes out of the tent (v. 8), and they "watch/see" the pillar of cloud (v. 10). Moses says to God, "See!" (vv. 12–13) and "Let me see" (v. 18). To which God answers, "you cannot see," for no one "will see" (v. 20); "you will see," but... "my face is not to be seen" (v. 23). There are thus nine occurrences of the verb, to which must be added five references to the "eyes." As also in Cant 2.14, to the seeing in Exodus 33 is added the hearing. Exodus 33 starts with a discourse of God, and the nation hears "these harsh words, [and] they mourned" (v. 4). But, as usual in such cases of borrowing, the Canticle takes the opposite course to the statement of doom that served as a model!

On the shocking text of Cant 3.1–5, Keel wavers between contradictory conclusions. He attempts to minimize the impropriety of the scene describing a woman alone, roaming by night the city streets in search of her lover. But, even if we suppose with Keel that the moral codes before the exile were more lax than after it ([?] cf. Sir 42.11; 2 Macc 3.19) and even if we grant that "poetry does not merely reflect reality," a comparison with Cant 8.1–2 shows that such a scene as sketched in 3.1–5 was socially and ethically "unacceptable," as is attested by Prov 7.11–13 (cf. p. 120). The woman's question to the guards is "impudent," as Keel himself admits (p. 124). But then, at this point, he turns to mythology and invokes licenses taken by Anath or Isis, not realizing that Cant 5.7 becomes obscure, for if under some circumstances (poetic, mythological) the woman's behavior is mimetic, hence considered permissible, why should she be beaten up by the guards? Does the text abruptly cease to be mythological or poetic at that point?

In 3.4, Keel is acutely aware of the striking linguistic formation *lo' 'arpennu* (*rph* with the negation). He mentions (p. 124) the parallels of Deut 31.6, 8 and Job 7.19. But he bypasses the most important text of *Deut 4.31*, where the verb *rph* is not only also in the hifil mode and with the negation but as well in close relation with other terms present in Cant 3.1–5. Thus, regarding the verbs, "to seek" is found in Deut 4.29 twice and in 4.32 twice; "to find" is in verses 29, 30; "to hear," in verses 30, 32, 33 (twice), 36 (twice); "to come," in verse 34 and in the hifil (to let come) in verse 37 (see below); "to see," in verses 34, 35, 36; "to love," in verse 37. Regarding the nouns of Cant 3.1–5, "soul" is found in Deut 4.29; "voice," in verses 30, 33, 36; "oath," in verse 31. The preposition "unto" is found in Deut 4.30, 32. As recalled in verse 37, Deuteronomy 4's historical context is the divine miraculous taking of Israel out of Egypt, something they could see and hear. In Canticle 3, to our surprise, the woman is substituted, at times for the people (seeking, finding, hearing, seeing), sometimes for God (taking, showing, voicing). The search is now erotic, and the finding occurs in spite of the sentinels/prophets (cf. Ezekiel 33). The decision not to let go has become an amorous embrace, and the bringing to the Promised Land is replaced by a bringing to the mother's house!

Cant 4.4 "describes the beloved as a proud, unconquered city," says Keel, who connects this verse with Isa 3.16b and rightly concludes, "This attitude [of 'proud reticence and provocative liveliness'] is clearly evaluated differently in the prophetic context than in the Song" (p. 147). But when he passes to the following verse, his consistency is at fault. For if Keel is correct that the similes in Cant 4.5 ("Your two breasts are like two fawns, twins of a gazelle"; NRSV) are chosen to emphasize life conquering death/chaos/desert, then the shift from prophetic ideology should have been stressed. The woman is substituted for the divine Giver of life; the one who planted the tree of life (Gen 2.9); the Rock, which begot Israel (Deut 32.18) and provided them with water (Num 20.8; Isa 48.21; cf. Cant 4.15!) and which, according to 1 Cor 10.4, was following them in the desert to suckle them with its breasts.[14] Eros is set in competition with divine care or, at least, in concurrence with it.

Noticeably, Keel contrasts Cant 4.12–15 with Psalm 148 and the *Prayer of Azariah* 26–68 and concludes, "Here, an inventory of spice plants is transformed into praise not of God but of the 'sister bride' " (p. 168). Similarly about 5.2–6, Keel notes the obvious:

---

14. According to Jewish tradition, the Rock was called "the well of Miriam" (*Ta'an* 9a). It stopped "nursing" at her death (Num 20.2) but only for a time (*Mek Exod* 16.35 [600]; *Shabb* 35a).

"[T]he notion that a girl or woman would sleep in a room with a door opening onto the street is improbable" (p. 186), a judgment that should apply to 3.1–5 above.

In regards to Cant 5.6, Keel mentions, as I do, Jer 31.22, where the rare word *ḥmq* (turn aside, vacillate) is used. He does not miss either the parallel between the quest without finding or the call without answer in this verse of the Canticle, on the one hand, and the prophetic statements with the same elements in Hos 2.7 [9]; 5.6; Jer 7.27; 29.13; and Isa 65.1, 12, on the other. Where we differ, however, is on the conclusion to draw from the tally.

On Cant 6.10, another chord is struck by Keel. He notes that the verb *šqp* "is used especially of God, looking down from heaven (Deut 26.15; Ps 14.2; 85.11 [12]; 102.19 [20]; Lam 3.50)." The dawn is a Canaanite divinity, he continues. That is true but not particularly useful here, as the poem once again demythicizes the notion and eroticizes it. At any rate, the Canticle proceeds "despite all the prophetic instruction," in the words of Keel (p. 220).

Cant 6.11 is understood by Keel as a discrete song without connection with the context; while verse 12 is in the woman's mouth, verses 8–11 are allegedly in the man's mouth, even verse 11 in spite of the clear male symbolism of the nut orchard. The point might be unimportant were it not for the astute remark of Keel's that the "institutional basis" of the vignette might be the custom that "young girls were often promised in marriage and engaged to an older cousin" (p. 224). If he is correct, the motif is definitely indicative of the direction that has been mine all along. The Canticle is reacting negatively to societal mores that religionists of her time attempted to justify on spiritual grounds.

After noticing that violet-dyed textiles "were used almost exclusively for cultic...and royal purposes," Keel writes of Cant 7.5, "The description of the hair as 'dangling,' 'free-hanging,' or 'flowing'" is unusual since women would wear their hair bound and/or veiled (p. 238). The Swiss scholar finds numerous parallels, however, in pictures showing Egyptian women with free-hanging hair (fig. 78, 79, 131, and 132 in his book). But, those graphic representations exclusively designate dancers or servants, mostly in the nude, belonging to the lower ranks of society. From that perspective, "to be caught in her tresses" takes on an economic and moral dimension and provides in hindsight an explicit rationale on the part of the woman for letting her hair dangle. The scene, in other words, is a great deal more *osé* in the Canticle than admitted by Keel. Tikva Frymer-Kensky reminds us that the wanton Ishtar and Lamashtu, the female demon who kills newborn children, keep their hair loose!

As already mentioned, Keel says of the palm tree in Cant 7.7 [8] that it is "a manifestation of divinity...connected with important goddesses.... Portraying the woman in the Song as a palm is one of those theomorphisms" (pp. 242–43). He also says of the grapes in 7.9 that they have a "theomorphic background" (p. 246). This only underscores the religious atmosphere of the Song. If not obvious to the modern reader, it was evident to the original audience.

On 7.10 [11], Keel contrasts this verse, as I do, with Gen 3.16 and adds, "Love is experienced [here] as a return to paradise" (p. 252). Granted, but what does the reversal of the Genesis terms by Canticle hermeneutically mean?

"The speaker of Cant 8.1," Keel writes judiciously, "wants to be able to kiss her lover in public without altering her social status and without being lumped together with prostitutes and adulteresses (cf. Prov 7.13). The verb in Cant 8.1e means more than disdaining people or blaming them for something; it means holding them in contempt, ruining them socially (cf., e.g., Prov 14.21; Ps 107.40), in the way that prostitutes and adulteresses were socially contemptible" (p. 261). He adds (p. 262) that such an erotic episode between siblings is "forbidden in the real world (Lev 18.9; 2 Sam 13.1–9)." Poetic license then? Or protest against societal obstacles to erotic love?

It is also with approval that I flag Keel's reaction to the daring wording of Cant 8.5. Apart from the unexpected active feminine role in arousing the male, such an awakening is said to repeat his mother's arousing of her lover and becoming pregnant by the latter,

> Against this background, the awakening of love has something faithful and heroic about it. It brings the woman into the same camp as Lot's daughters (Gen 19.30–38) or Tamar (Gen 38), who used the boldest means to insure the continuity of generations. (pp. 268–69)

Of course, beside "faithful and heroic," I would stress the irreverence bordering on outrage and bawdiness of the expression.

Beyond Exegesis

There is between Keel's commentary and my reading at least a difference of accent. For Keel, the Song of Songs is another love song amidst ancient Near Eastern, particularly Egyptian, compositions belonging to the same genre. The religious background is not denied, as everything in the ancient world was permeated anyway by religion and mythology. Thus, it is without surprise and wonder that he sees the biblical poem using expressions and terms drawn from that Near Eastern repertoire. But in fact, the very comparability of Canticle's scenes and allusions with the rich iconography from that region of the world definitely goes in the direction of trivializing the Song. It becomes far from being unique or original, for there exist parallels for close to all the Song's components. This way, the Canticle closes the ranks with other compositions of the same kind. Surrounded by so many love songs and such diverse pictures on the theme of sexual attraction, the Canticle's contours become blurred. One is allowed to wonder, What are the Song's beloved ones more than any other beloved that they thus adjure us? If I may be permitted an example of another order, numerous have been the "demonstrations" that all the words and actions attributed to Jesus in the Gospels find their parallels in rabbinic texts. But, although this comparative endeavor deserves our greatest respect and appreciation, it is, needless to say, only scratching the surface of things. Comparison is no demonstration.

In my opinion, there is in the Song of Songs much more than Keel delivers. I for one am persuaded that Rabbi Aqiba was right in seeing in this (somewhat deceptive) booklet a/the peak in Scripture because of its subject — love. The numerous parallels with concepts and idioms of the ancient Near East are at the service of a message that is not exhausted by the correspondences. The message is no witty flirt, but a subversive reaction against what had become societal propriety in a patriarchal worldview from which, of course, theological reflection was not absent. That is why there is so much harmony between the material provided by the ambient world, on the one hand, and its reuse in the Song, on the other, and so much disharmony between the socioreligious Israelite traditions and their radical reshaping by the Song. As regards the vehicle of her composition, it was quite natural that the poet utilize a diction readily existing in Egypt, where women and men were legally and religiously equal. As regards the tenor, however, the poet took exception with the prevalently conservative and patriarchal conceptions of her time. Love, she wrote, transfigures reality; it is strong as death, even stronger; it moves mountains and is a "flame of Yah." All the rest is commentary.

Conclusion

THE "HOLY OF HOLIES"
IN SCRIPTURE

$\mathfrak{O} \mathfrak{G}$ $\mathfrak{O} \mathfrak{G}$ $\mathfrak{O} \mathfrak{G}$ $\mathfrak{O} \mathfrak{G}$ $\mathfrak{O} \mathfrak{G}$ $\mathfrak{O} \mathfrak{G}$ $\mathfrak{O} \mathfrak{G}$ $\mathfrak{O} \mathfrak{G}$ $\mathfrak{O} \mathfrak{G}$ $\mathfrak{O} \mathfrak{G}$ $\mathfrak{O} \mathfrak{G}$ $\mathfrak{O} \mathfrak{G}$ $\mathfrak{O} \mathfrak{G}$ $\mathfrak{O} \mathfrak{G}$

The discrete conclusions drawn at the end of each section of this essay on the Canticle are also applicable to the Song in its entirety. We have been led repeatedly by this uncanny poem into total irreverence regarding religious and social propriety. The author has used ironically expressions become "sacred" in Israel of the second temple period. She has deftly manipulated such vocabulary, sometimes submitting it to transparent allusive deformations, so that no one in her audience could entertain the smallest doubt as to her sources of inspiration, and sometimes reversing its meaning into its opposite, but always substituting erotic referents for the religious ones in Israel's traditions. Prophetic discourse in particular — more specifically, samples of prophecies of doom — became fair game. This she demetaphorized, as it were, and reapplied to the domain from which the images had been in part borrowed: the area of love, of Eros. And, as the original trope or shift of language from the literal to the figurative had occasioned surprise and shock (see Hosea 1–3, for example), so the return in the Song to the nonfigurative inaugurates a veritable revolution. Proofs of this are the twisted interpretations that were imposed on the Canticle almost from the outset. The defigurativation of the language of love has been felt so offensive, so subversive, so "impossible" — as say repeatedly those of the allegorizing school — that the plain sense of the booklet has been repeatedly ignored, dismissed, despised. But, as the Song is no booklet for a pagan hierogamy, neither is it an allegory for the straight-laced, harping on the intimate relations between God and Israel (even less, of course,

205

between Christ and the church). It is openly and unabashedly an exaltation of Eros; it speaks of free love, untamed, unofficial, between a man and a woman (cf. Cant 3.1–4; 5.2–7; 8.1–3, 14). The language of the author is at times naturalistic, and thus exposed to censorship by men of the cloth, and at times parody-like as it imitates mockingly the jargon of the "fundamentalists" of its time. On that score, the Canticle belongs with other pieces of literature — including the Gospels — to a literary genre whose purpose is to subvert the world.

Now, there are two ways to submit the world to irony or to subversion. Either one demonstrates that the world is in its essence but a fraud — this stance in the Bible is found in the apocalyptic genre — or else one protests against what some have *made* of the world, fundamentally beautiful yet presently disfigured — this stance is present in prophetic books. In the former case, the world must be destroyed, and room must be made for an antiworld, that is, a new world (*neos*). In the latter case, the world must be chastened and reformed; the world must be made new, that is, renewed (*kainos*). The Canticle is no apocalyptic work. It finds a large part of its inspiration in prophetic oracles, which it transforms to fit its own purposes, but without rejecting their subversive sharpness. Like the prophets, the poet wants to subvert the world. To do so, she claims for love absolute rights, using prophetic discourse that claimed God's absolute ownership over the human. There is thereby a promiscuity of sorts established by the Canticle between claims that might be construed as conflicting. Evidently, one way open before love's advocate was to deify Love and thus oppose this sweet goddess to the stern God of the prophets of doom. This is not, though, the path trodden by the author of the Song of Songs. On the contrary, if the Song takes exception with prophetic oracles of doom in particular, in the name of a fundamental optimism based on faith in the transformative power of Eros, it does, however, follow suit to the ultimate valorization of love among the prophets of Israel. Suffice it to look in a Bible concordance s.v. 'ahab and 'agap- (in the LXX, all occurrences in the Prophets or in the Canticle of 'ahab and derivatives are translated by using the root 'agap-) to be convinced of its importance. That is why the Song of Songs is an Israelite writing, and in spite of its negative reaction to a certain conception of propriety perpetuated in societal customs in the Israel of the second temple period, it also legitimately belongs to its legacy (like Ruth, Esther, or Judith). Without that background or backbone, the poem would look drastically different. It would probably deify Love or reduce it to the proportions of a biological need. It possibly would not advocate exclusivity in human mating, and it would surely be oriented toward fecundity. What distinguishes, on the contrary, the singing of love in the Canticle is its extensive use of "biblical" language embedded here in a discourse that is the least religious in Hebrew Scripture. All the same, the borrowing is of utmost importance, for, if I am permitted to repeat a point already emphasized above, that language had definitively acquired a transcendent dimension by being found worthy of conveying the message that God so much cared for the world that he allowed that love of his to be incarnated in human love.[1] Thereby and forever, love had ceased to be profane (if it ever was). It can be demystified in the Canticle, but it can never return(?) to pure secularity. Love, in Israel, is the choice paradigm of the relationship between God and the human. This is exactly the background that has made the composition of the Song of Songs possible in Israel's literature.

Sensitive to this very point of no return in the sublimation of love, the Alexandrian Jews responsible for the Greek version of the Bible had recourse to the Greek poetic and rather uncommon word of *agape* to render that notion. They never used *eros* in the Song (see LXX of 2.4, 5, 7; 3.5, 10; 5.8; 7.6; 8.4, 6, 7a, 7b). *Eros* translates *'ahabâ* only in Prov 7.18–19, which is in the mouth of the promiscuous woman, and in Prov 24.51 (MT 30.16), where "the love of a woman" is interpreted by the LXX as adverting to a prostitute.[2] But this LXX touchiness proved to be a double-edged sword. It played in the hands of those who looked at human love as unworthy and at sexuality as the prime source of sin. In hindsight it would have

---

1. Incidentally, in my opinion the Song of Songs could be an important document in the Jewish-Christian dialogue (see also Urbach, "The Homiletical Interpretations"). While the Christian allegorical school tried to show that the loving relations between God and people allegedly depicted in the Canticle can be transposed to the loving relations between Christ and the church, the need for allegory is unwarranted and unnecessary for our purpose. *Analogy* does a better job. For the Canticle, human love is in the analogy of God's love, of which it is the incarnation. Using another analogy, provided by Cant 8.12, one can easily imagine how the latter text could be used (by Rosenzweig, e.g.) against the rabbinic computation of 613 commandments and prohibitions in the name of the uniqueness of love!

2. *Erōtaō* occurs often in the LXX to render the Hebrew *ša'al* (to ask, to request), not *'ahab* (to love).

been less damageable — and also less foreign to the authorial intention in the Song — to use the regular term *eros*. For, if anything, the
Canticle protests against the substitution by "religionists" of a kind
of misunderstood *agape* for *eros* and the ensuing contempt for the
woman's attractiveness, considered as a snare, and her wiles, seen as
expressions of feminine congenital evil.

To diffuse such a fundamental (and cruel) misunderstanding, the
poet found it appropriate to celebrate — "with all her strength," like
David in 2 Samuel 6 — "the love of a woman" and to transform
that "symbolism of evil" into the symbolism of redemption. In the
process, she showed that there is an opposite face to prophetic condemnation, namely, the lyric expression of love, for "love is strong
as death"! This is why, in this least "biblical" book of the Bible,
the message hidden behind poetic aesthetics is decidedly *theological*.
Love "pure and simple," love faithful and wholly integrated, love
that is *eros* as much as it is *agape*, is a reflection of the covenant
between the divine and the human.[3]

Among all biblical literary pieces, the Canticle presents the greatest challenge possible to modern hermeneutics. The gap between the
authorial purpose, on the one hand, and the Song's allegorical interpretation, on the other, is such that they seem to be poles apart, thus
forcing the reader to opt either for one or for the other. And, however, I have suggested all throughout this essay that this need not be
the final conclusion. In the case presented by the Song of Songs, it is
more than ever verified that,

Any text interpretation implies by necessity a break from the
text. But in the very break happens the encounter. Hermeneu-

---

3. One finds a logic akin to mine here in Landy's rhetorical question, "the Song in
which every song partakes. Can we . . . say that every song is holy?" Then Landy quotes
Octavio Paz, "When two kiss, the world changes" (Landy, *Paradoxes of Paradise*, pp. 17,
67). Alter (afterword to *The Song of Songs*, by Bloch and Bloch, p. 131) writes, "Under-
lying the physicality of love in the Song is an implicit metaphysics of love." More pointed
still, 1 John 4.7–8 reads, "Beloved, let us love one another, because love is from God;
everyone who loves is born of God and knows God. Whoever does not love does not
know God, for God is love" (NRSV). In the same line of thought, Jesus declares that the
"sinful woman" saw all her many sins forgiven because she loved much (NRSV understands, like several modern interpreters of the text of Luke 7.47, that the forgiveness of
her sins comes before the woman's demonstration of love, but [1] this does not fit the
context that shows the woman weeping and silently asking for forgiveness; and [2] the
preposition *hoti* in v. 47 does not mean *dioti* [hence], but "because," "since").

tical dialogue aims at filling the difference which gives birth to it.... Fidelity to the spirit always seems a treason of the letter.[4]

True, the break between our text and its centuries-long interpretation is particularly serious, but break there is always. Because the interpretative community of readers becomes actually the owner of the text,[5] there is no justification in divorcing the text from its readers. But text ownership is a dialectical reality. The readers become the true possessors of text only on the condition that their interpretation *enriches* the meaning given by the author of the text. No one, for instance, has the right to force into anti-Semitic molds discrete texts of the Gospels and declare such interpretation (although hoary and recurrent) authoritative. The disregard for the intention of the text destroys the meaning of the text.

The question, therefore, as regards the traditional-allegorical interpretation of the Song of Songs is *which* allegorical/mystical reading enhances its true meaning; it is not whether such reading is permissible. The latter would be a legitimate issue if the poem were univocal, unileveled, that is, without depth, without memory (see above p. 167), but such is not the case. For, as we just saw, the Canticle stands in a relation of intertextuality with Israel's narrative and prophecy; it sings the same power of love as proclaimed and praised by prophets and psalmists, even if applied by the ones and the other to objects differently understood than in the Canticle. Chana Bloch writes that "the prophets look forward to a peaceable kingdom at the End of Days. The Song of Songs locates that kingdom in human love, in the habitable present, and for the space of our attention, allows us to enter it."[6] It is *that* love that the Song of Songs magnifies in terms of erotic love between a man and a woman, in substitution for an agape-like vertical relationship sung by its traditional predecessors. It is that fondness and fidelity that the poet elevates to the point that it becomes paradigmatic for all authentic love and, more particularly, for the love of God for his people. That is why nothing precludes the "mystic" reading of the Song. It is, however, prohibited that one come with a dualistic opposition between Eros

---

4. Resweber, *La Pensée de M. Heidegger,* pp. 71–72.
5. See the introduction above p. 4.
6. Bloch and Bloch, *The Song of Songs,* p. 35.

and Agape. And that is exactly what happened — either overtly or covertly — time and again in the Christian church's reading of the Song of Songs. In order to keep away from that forbidden fruit of an interpretation gone awry, the modern exegete must by necessity return to the original intent of the text before its distortions.

When we consider the tormented history of the Canticle's "foreground" in both the synagogue and church, it is nothing short of a miracle that the Song of Songs' authentic message reaches us still today and with such power of relevance and urgency in a world without love (Agape or Eros) addicted to violence and hatred. When Rabbi Aqiba came to the striking conclusion that "all the Scriptures are holy, but the Song of Songs is the Holy of holies" (*Tos Sanh* 12.10), he definitely had a heaven of a point!

BIBLIOGRAPHY

Aichele, George, and Gary A. Phillips, eds. *Intertextuality and the Bible*. Semeia 69/70. Atlanta: Scholars Press, 1995.

Albright, William F. "Archaic Survivals in the Text of Canticles." In *Hebrew and Semitic Studies*, edited by D. Winton Thomas and W. D. McHardy. Oxford: Clarendon, 1963, pp. 1–7.

———. *Yhwh and the Gods of Canaan*. Garden City, N.Y.: Doubleday, 1968.

Alter, Robert. Afterword to *The Song of Songs*, by Ariel Bloch and Chana Bloch. New York: Random House, 1995.

———. *The Art of Biblical Poetry*. New York: Basic Books, 1985.

Alter, Robert, and Frank Kermode, eds. *The Literary Guide to the Bible*. Cambridge: Harvard University Press, 1987.

Angénieux, Joseph. "Structure du Cantique des Cantiques en chants encadrés par des refrains alternants." *ETL* 41 (1965): 96–142.

Arendt, Hannah. Introduction to Walter Benjamin, *Illuminations*. Translated by E. T. H. Zohn. New York: Schocken, 1969 (1955).

Audet, Jean-Paul. "Le sens du Cantique des Cantiques." *RB* 62 (1955): 197–221.

Auld, A. Graeme, ed. *Understanding Poets and Prophets: Essays in Honour of George Wishart Anderson*. JSOTSup 152. Sheffield: JSOT, 1993.

Bakhtin, Mikhail. *Problems of Dostoevsky's Poetics*. Translated and edited by C. Emerson. Minneapolis: University of Minnesota Press, 1984.

Banon, David. *La lecture infinie*. Paris: Seuil, 1987.

Barth, Karl. *Church Dogmatics*. Vol. 3, pt. 2. Edinburgh: T. & T. Clark, 1956–62.

Barthélemy, Dominique. "Comment le Cantique des Cantiques est-il devenu canonique?" In *Mélanges M. Delcor*. AOAT 215. Neukirchen-Vluyn: Neukirchener Verlag, 1985, pp. 13–22.

Bekkenkamp, J., and Fokkelien van Dijk. "The Canon of the Old Testament and Women's Cultural Traditions." In *A Feminist Companion to the Song of Songs*, edited by Athalya Brenner. Sheffield: JSOT, 1993, pp. 67–85.

Bentzen, Aage. "Remarks on the Canonization of the Song of Solomon." In *Studia Orientalia Ioanni Pedersen*. Hauniac: Einar Munksgaard, 1953, pp. 41–47.

Bernard of Clairvaux. *Sermones in Canticum*. PL 183.

Bloch, Ariel, and Chana Bloch. *The Song of Songs: A New Translation with an Introduction and Commentary*. New York: Random House, 1995.

211

Boyarin, Daniel. *Intertextuality and the Reading of Midrash.* Bloomington: Indiana University Press, 1990.

Brawley, Robert. "Resistance to the Carnivalization of Jesus." In *Intertextuality and the Bible,* edited by George Aichele and Gary A. Phillips. Semeia 69/70. Atlanta: Scholars Press, 1995, pp. 33–60.

Brenner, Athalya, " 'Come back, come back the Shulammite' (Song of Songs 7.11): A Parody of the *waṣf* Genre." In Athalya Brenner, ed., *A Feminist Companion to the Song of Songs.* Sheffield: JSOT, 1993, pp. 234–57.

⸻, ed. *A Feminist Companion to the Song of Songs.* Sheffield: JSOT, 1993.

Bruns, Gerald L. "Midrash and Allegory: The Beginnings of Scriptural Interpretation." In *The Literary Guide to the Bible,* edited by Robert Alter and Frank Kermode, 625–46. Cambridge: Harvard University Press, 1987.

Budde, Karl. *Das Hohelied erklärt.* KHCAT 17. Freiburg im Breisgau, 1898.

Bultmann, Rudolf. *History of the Synoptic Traditions.* New York: Harper and Row, 1963.

Buzy, Denis. "Le Cantique des Cantiques." In *La Sainte Bible,* edited by L. Pirot and A. Clamer. Vol. 6. Paris: Letouzey et Ané, 1946, pp. 283–363

⸻. "La composition littéraire du Cantique des Cantiques." *RB* 49 (1940): 169–94.

Carr, G. Lloyd. *Song of Solomon.* Tyndale O.T. Commentaries. Wheaton: InterVarsity, 1984.

Charlesworth, James H., ed. *The Old Testament Pseudepigrapha,* vol. 2. Garden City, N.Y.: Doubleday, 1985.

Childs, Brevard. *Introduction to the Old Testament as Scripture.* Philadelphia: Fortress, 1979.

Clines, David. "Why Is There a Song of Songs and What Does It Do to You If You Read It?" *Jian Dao* 1 (1994): 3–27.

Cook, Albert S. *The Root of the Thing: A Study of Job and the Song of Songs.* Bloomington: Indiana University Press, 1968.

Crenshaw, James L. *Ecclesiastes.* OTL. Philadelphia: Westminster, 1987.

Crim, Keith R. " 'Your Neck Is Like the Tower of David' (The Meaning of a Simile in the Song of Solomon 4.4)." *BT* 22 (1971): 70–74.

Cross, Frank M. *Canaanite Myth and Hebrew Epic.* Cambridge: Harvard University Press, 1973.

⸻. "The Cave Inscriptions from Khirbet Beit Lei." In *Near Eastern Archaeology in the 20th Century: Festschrift N. Glueck.* Edited by J. A. Sanders. Garden City, N.Y.: Doubleday, 1970.

Dalman, Gustav. *Arbeit und Sitte in Palästina.* Vol. 1. Gütersloh: G. Bertelsmann, 1928.

⸻. *Palästinischer Diwan.* Leipzig: J. C. Hinrichs, 1901.

Daniélou, Jean. *Origène,* "Le génie du Christianisme." Paris: La Table Ronde, 1948. English translation by W. Mitchell (New York: Sheed and Ward, 1955).

Danthine, Hélène. *Le palmier-dattier et les arbres sacrés dans l'iconographie de l'Asie occidentale ancienne.* Paris, 1937.

Davies, Philip R. "Reading Daniel Sociologically." In *The Book of Daniel in the Light of New Findings,* edited by A. S. van der Woude. Louvain: LUP, 1993, pp. 345–61.

Deckers, Mimi. "The Structure of the Song of Songs and the Centrality of nepeš." In *A Feminist Companion to the Song of Songs,* edited by Athalya Brenner. Sheffield: JSOT, 1993, pp. 172–96.

Delitzsch, Franz. *Commentary on the Song of Song and Ecclesiastes.* Grand Rapids: Eerdmans, 1885.

Derchain, Philippe. "Le lotus, la mandragore et le perséa." *Chronique d'Egypte* 50 (1975): 65–86.

de Vaux, Roland. *Ancient Israel: Its Life and Institutions.* Translated by John McHugh. New York: McGraw-Hill, 1961 (1958–60).

Dijk, Fokkelien van. "The Imagination of Power and the Power of Imagination." In *A Feminist Companion to the Song of Songs,* edited by Athalya Brenner. Sheffield: JSOT, 1993, pp. 156–71.

Dirksen, Peter B. "Song of Songs III 6–7." *VT* 39/2 (1989): 219–25.

Dorsey, David A. "Literary Structuring in the Song of Songs." *JSOT* 46 (1990): 81–96.

Driver, G. R. "Lice in the Old Testament." *PEQ* 106 (1974): 159–60.

Dubarle, André-Marie. "L'amour humain dans le Cantique des Cantiques." *RB* 61 (1954): 67–86.

———. "Le Cantique des Cantiques dans l'exégèse récente." In Charles Hauret, ed., *Aux grands carrefours de la révélation et de l'exégèse de l'Ancien Testament.* RechBib 8. Paris: Desclée de Brouwer, 1967, pp. 139–52.

Dupont-Sommer, André, and Marc Philonenko, eds. *La Bible: Ecrits intertestamentaires.* Paris: Gallimard (Pléiade), 1987.

Dussaud, René. *Le Cantique des Cantiques: Essai de reconstitution des sources du poème attribué à Salomon.* Paris: Ernest Leroux, 1919.

Edgerton, Dow. *The Passion of Interpretation.* LCBI. Louisville: Westminster/John Knox Press, 1992.

Eissfeldt, Otto. *The Old Testament: An Introduction.* Translated by Peter Ackroyd. New York: Harper and Row, 1965.

Emerton, John A. "Lice or a Veil in the Song of Songs 1.7?" In *Understanding Poets and Prophets: Essays in Honour of George Wishart Anderson,* edited by A. G. Auld. JSOTSup 152. Sheffield: JSOT, 1993, 127–40.

Exum, J. Cheryl. "A Literary and Structural Analysis of the Song of Songs." *ZAW* 85 (1973): 47–79.

Falk, Marcia. *Love Lyrics from the Bible: A Translation and Literary Study of the Song of Songs.* Sheffield: Almond, 1982.

Feuillet, André. *Le Cantique des Cantiques.* LD 10. Paris: Cerf, 1953.

Fisch, Harold. *Poetry with a Purpose.* Bloomington: Indiana University Press, 1988.

———. "Ruth and the Structure of Covenant History." *VT* 32/4 (1982): 425–37.

Fishbane, Michael. "The Book of Job and the Inner-biblical Discourse." In *The Voice from the Whirlwind: Interpreting the Book of Job,* edited by Leo G. Perdue and W. Clark Gilpin. Nashville: Abingdon, 1992, pp. 86–98.

Fox, Michael V. "Scholia to Canticles." *VT* 33 (1983): 199–206.

———. *The Song of Songs and Ancient Egyptian Love Songs.* Madison: University of Wisconsin Press, 1985.

Freedman, H., and Maurice Simon, eds. "Song of Songs," *Midrash Rabbah,* vol. 9. London: Soncino, 1951.

Freud, Sigmund. *Five Lectures on Psychoanalysis*. Standard ed. New York: Norton, 1989 (1910).

———. *Moses and Monotheism*. Standard ed. New York: Norton, 1989 (1939).

———. *New Introductory Lectures on Psychoanalysis*. Standard ed. New York: Norton, 1989 (1933).

Frye, Northrop. *The Great Code: The Bible and Literature*. New York: Harcourt Brace Jovanovich, 1982.

Frymer-Kensky, Tikva. *In the Wake of the Goddesses*. New York: Free Press, 1992.

Fuerst, Wesley J. *The Books of Ruth, Esther, Ecclesiastes, the Song of Songs, Lamentations*. CBC. Cambridge: Cambridge University Press, 1975, pp. 159–200.

Gall, August von. "Jeremias 43,12 und das Zeitwort '*th.*" ZAW 24 (1904): 105–21.

Galling, Karl. *Die Bücher der Chronick, Esra, Nehemia*. Göttingen: Vandenhoeck & Ruprecht, 1954.

Gardner, John, and John Maier. *Gilgamesh Translated from the Sîn-Leqi-Unninni Version*. New York: Vintage, 1984.

Gaster, Theodor H. "Canticles i.4." *ExpTim* 72 (1961): 195.

———. "The Song of Songs." In *Myth, Legend, and Custom in the Old Testament*. New York: Harper and Row, 1969, pp. 808–14.

———. *Thespis: Ritual, Myth and Drama in the ANE*. Rev. ed. New York: Gordian, 1975.

Gerleman, Gillis. *Rut — Das Hohelied*. BKAT 18. Neukirchen-Vluyn: Neukirchener Verlag, 1960, 1981.

Ginsburg, Christian. *The Song of Songs, Translated from the Original Hebrew with a Commentary, Historical and Critical*. Reprinted in *The Song of Songs and Qoheleth*. New York: Ktav, 1970.

Ginzberg. Louis. *The Legends of the Jews*. Vol. 1. Philadelphia: Jewish Publication Society, 1954.

Goitein, Shlomo Dov. "The Song of Songs: A Female Composition." In *A Feminist Companion to the Song of Songs*, edited by Athalya Brenner. Sheffield: JSOT, 1993.

———. "Women as Creators of Biblical Genres." *Prooftexts* 8 (1988): 1–33.

Gollwitzer, Helmut. *Song of Love: A Biblical Understanding of Sex*. Translated by Keith Crim. Philadelphia: Fortress, 1979.

Gordis, Robert. *The Song of Songs and Lamentations: A Study, Modern Translation, and Commentary*. New York: Ktav, 1974.

———. "A Wedding Song for Solomon." *JBL* 63 (1944): 263–70.

Gottwald, Norman. "Song of Songs." In *IDB* 4:420–26.

Goulder, Michael. *The Song of Fourteen Songs*. JSOTSup. Sheffield: JSOT, 1986.

Graetz, Heinrich. *Schir Ha-Schirim oder das salomonische Hohelied*. Vienna, 1871; Breslau: W. Jacobsohn, 1885.

Greeley, Andrew M., and Jacob Neusner. *The Bible and Us: A Priest and a Rabbi Read Scripture Together*. New York: Warner Books, 1990.

Greenberg, Moshe. *Ezekiel 1–20*. AB 22. Garden City, N.Y.: Doubleday, 1983.

Greer, Rowan A. *Origen: An Exhortation to Martyrdom . . . Prologue to the Commentary on the Song of Songs*. Classics of Western Spirituality. New York: Paulist Press, 1979.

Grossfeld, Bernard, ed. *The Targum of the Five Megilloth*. New York: Hermon, 1973.

Haller, Max. *Das Hohe Lied*. HAT 18. Tübingen: J. C. B. Mohr, 1940.

Hamp, Vincenz. "Zur Textkritik am Hohenlied." *BZ* 1 (1957): 197–214.

Harper, Andrew. *The Song of Solomon, with Introduction and Notes*. Cambridge Bible for Schools and Colleges. Cambridge: Cambridge University Press, 1902.

Hartman, Geoffrey, and S. Budick, eds. *Midrash and Literature*. New Haven: Yale University Press, 1986.

Haupt, Paul. *Biblische Liebeslieder: Das sogenannte Hohelied Salomos*. Leipzig: J. C. Hinrichs, 1907.

———. "The Book of Canticles." *AJSL* 18 (1902): 193–241.

———. "The Book of Canticles." *AJSL* 19 (1903): 1–32.

———. *The Book of Canticles, A New Rhythmical Translation with Restoration of the Hebrew Text*. Chicago: University of Chicago Press, 1902.

Hebrew-English Lexicon of the Bible. New York: Schocken, 1975.

Heinemann, Joseph. "The Nature of the Aggadah." In *Midrash and Literature*, edited by Geoffrey Hartman and S. Budick. New Haven: Yale University Press, 1986.

Heinevetter, Hans-Josef. *"Komm nun, mein Liebster, Dein Garten ruft Dich!" Das Hohelied as programmatische Komposition*. BBB 69. Frankfurt am Main: Athenaeum Monografien, 1988.

Held, Moshe. "A Faithful Lover in an Old Babylonian Dialogue," *JCS* 15 (1961): 1–26.

Hengel, Martin. *Judaism and Hellenism: Studies in Their Encounter in Palestine during the Early Hellenistic Period*. Translated by J. Bowden. 2 vols. Philadelphia: Fortress, 1974.

Herbert, A. S. "The Song of Songs." In *Peake's Commentary on the Bible*, 468–74. London: Thomas Nelson, 1962.

Herford, Travers. *Pirke Aboth: The Ethics of the Talmud: Sayings of the Fathers*. New York: Schocken, 1945.

Hertzberg, Hans W. *Beiträge zur Traditionsgeschichte und Theologie des Alten Testaments*. Göttingen: Vandenhoeck & Ruprecht, 1962.

Heschel, Abraham. *The Prophets*. New York: Harper and Row, 1962.

Hitzig, Ferdinand. *Das Holelied erklärt*. Kurzgefasste exegetische Handbuch zum Alten Testament 16. Leipzig, 1855.

Holman, Jan. "A Fresh Attempt at Understanding the Imagery of Canticles 3:6–11." Paper presented at the IOSOT Conference, Cambridge, 1995.

Ibn Ezra. *Commentary on the Canticles after the First Recension*. London: H. J. Matthews, 1874 (English translation of the twelfth-century text).

Jakobson, Roman. "Linguistics and Poetics." In *Selected Writings* 3. New York: Mouton, 1981.

Jastrow, Morris. *The Song of Songs: Being a Collection of Love Lyrics of Ancient Palestine*. Philadelphia: Lippincott, 1921.

Jirku, Anton. *Die Welt der Bibel*. Stuttgart: Gustav Kilppert, 1958.

Joüon, Paul. *Le Cantique des Cantiques: Commentaire philologique et exégétique*. Paris: Gabriel Beauchesne, 1909.

Keel, Othmar. *Deine Blicke sind Tauben: Zur Metaphorik des Hohen Liedes*. Stuttgart: Katholisches Bibelwerk, 1984.

————. *Das Hohelied.* ZBK 18. Zurich: Theologischer Verlag, 1986. English translation published as *The Song of Songs: A Continental Commentary,* translated by F. J. Gaiser (Minneapolis: Fortress, 1994). (Cited as *The Song.*)

Kierkegaard, Søren. *Fear and Trembling.* Translated by Walter Lowrie. Princeton: Princeton University Press, 1968.

Kittay, Eva, and Adrienne Lehrer. "Semantic Fields and the Structure of Metaphor." *Studies in Language* 5/1 (1981): 31–63.

Klein, Ralph. *Ezekiel: The Prophet and His Message.* Columbia: University of South Carolina Press, 1988.

Knight, George A. F. *Esther, Song of Songs, Lamentations.* Torch Bible Commentaries. London: SCM, 1955.

Koch, Klaus. *The Growth of the Biblical Tradition: The Form-Critical Method.* New York. Scribner, 1969.

Koehler, Ludwig, and Walter Baumgartner. *Lexicon in Veteris Testamenti libros.* Leiden: Brill, 1953.

Kramer, Samuel N. *The Sacred Marriage Rite: Aspects of Faith, Myth, and Ritual in Ancient Sumer.* Bloomington: Indiana University Press, 1969.

————. "Sumerian Sacred Marriage Songs and the Biblical Song of Songs." *MIOF* 15 (1969): 262–74.

Krinetzki, Leo (=Günter). "Die erotische Psychologie des Hoheliedes." *TQ* 150 (1970): 404–16.

————. *Das Hohe Lied: Kommentar zu Gestalt und Kerygma eines Alten Testamenten Liebesliedes.* Düsseldorf: Patmos, 1964.

————. *Kommentar zum Hohenlied: Bildsprache und theologische Botschaft.* BBET 16. Frankfurt: Peter Lang, 1981.

Kristeva, Julia. *Desire in Language: A Semiotic Approach to Literature and Art.* Edited by L. S. Roudiez; translated by T. Gora, A. Jardine, L. S. Roudiez. New York: Columbia University Press, 1980.

————. *New Maladies of the Soul.* Translated by R. Guberman. European Perspectives. New York: Columbia University Press, 1995.

————. *La révolution du langage poétique.* Tel Quel. Paris: Seuil, 1974.

Kuhl, Curt. "Das Hohelied und seine Deutung." *TRu* NF 9 (1937): 137–67.

Kuhn, Karl G. *Erklärung des Hohenliedes.* Leipzig: A. Deichert, 1926.

LaCocque, André. *The Feminine Unconventional: Four Subversive Figures in Israel's Tradition.* OBT. Minneapolis. Fortress, 1990.

————. "God after Auschwitz: A Contribution to Contemporary Theology." *JES* 33/2 (spring 1996): 157–72.

————. "L'insertion du Cantique des Cantiques dans le Canon." *RHPR* 42 (1962): 38–44.

————. "The Land in D and P." In *"Dort Ziehen Schiffe dahin."* Beiträge zur Erforschung des Alten Testaments und des Antiken Judentums. M. Augustin and K.-D. Schunck, eds. Frankfurt: Peter Lang, 1996.

————. *Subversives.* LD 148. Paris: Cerf, 1992.

————. "Une Terre qui découle de lait et de miel." *Vav: Revue de Dialogue* 2 (1966): 28–36.

LaCocque, André, and Paul Ricoeur. *Thinking Biblically.* Chicago: University of Chicago Press, 1998.

Landy, Francis. *Paradoxes of Paradise: Identity and Difference in the Song of Songs.* Sheffield: Almond, 1983.

———. "The Song of Songs." In *The Literary Guide to the Bible,* edited by Robert Alter and Frank Kermode, 305–19. Cambridge: Harvard University Press, 1987.

Lauha, Aarre. *Kohelet.* BKAT 19. Neukirchen: Neukirchener Verlag, 1978.

Lawson, R. P., trans. *Origen: The Song of Songs: Commentary and Homilies.* Westminster, Md.: Newman, 1957.

Loretz, Oswald. "Die theologische Bedeutung des Hohenliedes." *BZ* NF 10 (1966): 29–43.

———. "Zum Probleme des Eros im Hohenlied." *BZ* NF 8 (1964): 191–216.

Lys, Daniel. "Notes sur le Cantique." In *Congress Volume: Rome 1968.* VTSup 17. Leiden: Brill, 1969, pp. 170–78.

———. *Le plus beau chant de la création: Commentaire du Cantique des Cantiques.* LD 51. Paris: Cerf, 1968.

Lys, Daniel, and Raymond Tournay. "Le Cantique des Cantiques" In *TOB.*

Martin, Hugh. *On Loving God and Selections from Sermons by Bernard of Clairvaux.* London: SCM, 1959.

Martindale, Colin. *Romantic Progression: The Psychology of Literary History.* New York: Hemisphere, 1975.

McKeating, Henry. *The Books of Amos, Hosea, and Micah.* CBC. Cambridge: Cambridge University Press, 1971.

Meek, Theophile J. "Canticles and the Tammuz Cult." *AJSL* 39 (1922–23): 1–14.

———. "The Song of Songs." In *IB* 5 (1953): 98–148.

Meyers, Carol. *Discovering Eve: Ancient Israelite Women in Context.* New York: Oxford University Press, 1988.

———. "Gender Imagery in the Song of Songs." HAR 10 (1986): 209–23.

Müller, Hans-Peter. "Die lyrische Reproduktion des Mythischen im Hohenlied." *ZTK* 73 (1976): 23–41.

———. "Poesie und Magie in Cant 4.12–5.1" *ZDMGSup* 3/1 (1977): 157–64.

Murphy, Roland. "Form-Critical Studies of the Song of Songs." *Int* 27 (1973): 413–22.

———. "Interpreting the Song of Songs." *BTB* 9 (1979): 99–105.

———. "Patristic and Medieval Exegesis — Help or Hindrance?" *CBQ* 43 (1981): 505–16.

———. "Song of Songs." In *IDBSup:* 836–38.

———. *The Song of Songs.* Hermeneia. Minneapolis: Fortress, 1990.

———. "The Unity of the Song of Songs." *VT* 29 (1979): 436–43.

———. *Wisdom Literature.* Forms of the OT Literature 13. Grand Rapids: Eerdmans, 1981.

———. *Wisdom Literature and Psalms.* Nashville: Abingdon, 1983.

Neusner, Jacob. *Israel's Love Affair with God: Song of Songs.* The Bible of Judaism Library. Valley Forge, Pa.: Trinity Press International, 1993.

North, Christopher. *The Second Isaiah: Introduction, Translation, and Commentary to Chapters XL–LV.* London: Oxford University Press, 1964.

Paul, Shalom. "Shir ha-shirim." In *Encyclopedia Mikraït* 7:645–55. Jerusalem: Bialik, 1981.

————. "An Unrecognized Medical Idiom in Ct 6.12 and Job 9.21." *Biblica* 59 (1978): 545–47.

Pelletier, Anne-Marie. *Lectures du Cantique des Cantiques: De l'énigme du sens aux figures du lecteur.* Rome: Editrice Pontifico Istituto Biblico, 1989.

Perdue, Leo G., and W. Clark Gilpin, eds. *The Voice from the Whirlwind: Interpreting the Book of Job.* Nashville: Abingdon, 1992.

Pfeiffer, Robert H. *Introduction to the Old Testament.* New York: Harper, 1941.

Phillips, George A. " 'What Is Written? How Are You Reading?' Gospel, Intertextuality." In *Intertextuality and the Bible,* edited by George Aichele and Gary A. Phillips. Semeia 69/70. Atlanta: Scholars Press, 1995, pp. 111–48.

Pope, Marvin. *Job.* AB 15. 3d ed. Garden City, N.Y.: Doubleday, 1973.

————. *Song of Songs.* AB 7C. Garden City, N.Y.: Doubleday, 1977.

Prat, Ferdinand. *Origène, le théologien et l'exégète.* Paris: Bloud, 1907.

Pritchard, James B., ed. *Ancient Near Eastern Texts Relating to the Old Testament.* Princeton: Princeton University Press, 1950. (Cited as *ANET.*)

Quirke, Stephen. *Ancient Egyptian Religion.* London: British Museum Press, 1992.

Rabin, Chaim. "The Indian Connections of the Song of Songs." In *B. Kurzweil Memorial Volume.* Edited by A. Saltman, M. Z. Kaddari, M. Schwarcz, and M. Adler. Jerusalem: Schocken, 1975, pp. 264–74.

————. "The Song of Songs and Tamil Poetry." *SR* 3 (1973): 205–19.

Reese, James M. *The Book of Wisdom, The Song of Songs.* Wilmington, Del.: Glazier, 1983.

Rendtorff, Rolph. *The Old Testament: An Introduction.* Translated by J. Bowden. Philadelphia: Fortress, 1986 (1983).

Resweber, Jean P. *La Pensée de Martin Heidegger.* Toulouse: Privat, 1971.

Ricciotti, Giuseppe. *Il Cantico dei Cantici: Versione critica dal testo ebraico con introduzione e commento.* Turin: Società editrice internazionale, 1928.

Ricoeur, Paul. "La Bible et l'imagination." *RHPR* 62/4 (1982): 339-60. (English: "The Bible and the Imagination," in H. D. Betz, ed. *The Bible as a Document of the University.* Chico, Calif.: Scholars Press, 1981, pp. 49–75.)

————. "Biblical Hermeneutics." In *Paul Ricoeur on Biblical Hermeneutics.* Edited by D. Crossan. Semeia 4. Missoula, Mont.: Scholars Press, 1975, pp. 27–148.

————. *Interpretation Theory: Discourse and the Surplus of Meaning.* Fort Worth: Texas Christian University Press, 1976.

————. *Le Juste.* Paris: Editions Esprit, 1995.

————. *The Rule of Metaphor.* Toronto: University of Toronto Press, 1977 (1975).

————. "Sexualité: la merveille, l'errance, l'énigme." In P. Ricoeur, *Histoire et Vérité.* Paris: Seuil, 1955, pp. 198–209.

————. "Théonomie et/ou autonomie." *Archivio di Filosophia* 62/1–3 (1994): 19–36.

Ringgren, Helmer. *Das Hohelied.* ATD 16/2. Göttingen: Vandenhoeck & Ruprecht, 1958.

Robert, André. "Cantique des Cantiques." In *Bible de Jérusalem.*

Robert, André, Raymond Tournay, and André Feuillet. *Le Cantiques des Cantiques: Traduction et commentaire.* Et. Bib. Paris: Gabalda, 1963. (Authors cited in notes as RTF.)

Rosenzweig, Franz. *The Star of Redemption.* Translated by W. W. Hallo. Boston: Beacon Press, 1972.

Rowley, Harold H. "The Meaning of the Shulammite." *AJSL* 56 (1939): 84–91.

———. *The Servant of the Lord and Other Essays on the Old Testament.* Oxford: Basil Blackwell, 1965.

Rudolph, Wilhelm. *Das Buch Ruth. Das Hohe Lied. Die Klagelieder.* KAT 16/2. Gütersloh: Gerd Mohn, 1962.

Salvaneschi, Enrica. *Cantico dei cantici: Interpretatio ludica.* Genoa: Il Melangolo, 1982.

Sasson, Jack. "The Worship of the Golden Calf." In H. A. Hoffner, ed. *Orient and Occident: Essays Presented to Cyrus H. Gordon.* AOAT 22. Neukirchen-Vluyn: Neukirchener Verlag, 1973, 151–59.

Scherman, Nosson, and Meir Zlotowitz. *Shir haShirim.* New York: Mesorah Publications, 1969.

Schmökel, Hartmut. *Heilige Hochzeit und Hoheslied.* AKM 32/1. Wiesbaden: F. Steiner (Deutsche Morgenländische Gesellschaft), 1956.

Scholem, Gershom G. *Major Trends in Jewish Mysticism.* Rev. ed. New York: Schocken, 1946.

———. *On the Kabbalah and Its Symbolism.* New York: Schocken, 1965.

Scott, R. B. Y. *Proverbs; Ecclesiastes.* AB 18. Garden City, N.Y.: Doubleday, 1982.

Segal, Moses H. "The Song of Songs." *VT* 12/4 (1962): 470–90.

Selms, Adrianus van. "Hosea and Canticles." *Die Oud Testamentise Werkgemeenskap in Suid-Afrika* (Potchefstroom) 7–8 (1966): 85–89.

Shea, William H. "The Chiastic Structure of the Song of Songs." *ZAW* 92 (1980): 378–96.

Siegfried, Carl. "Hoheslied." In W. Frankenberg and Carl Siegfried, *Die Sprüche, Prediger und Hoheslied, übersetzt und erklärt.* HKAT. Göttingen: Vandenhoeck & Ruprecht, 1898, pp. 78–126.

Soulem, Richard N. "The Waṣfs of the Song of Songs and Hermeneutic." *JBL* 86 (1967): 183–90.

Speiser, E. A. *Genesis.* AB 1. New York: Doubleday, n.d.

Stadelman, Luis. *Love and Politics.* Mahwah, N.J.: Paulist Press, 1982.

Stienstra, Nelly. *Yhwh Is the Husband of His People.* Kampen: Kok Pharos, 1993.

Tournay, Raymond. *Le Cantique des Cantiques.* Lire la Bible 9. Paris: Cerf, 1967.

———. "Les chariots d'Aminadab (Cant 6.12): Israël, peuple théophore." *VT* 9 (1959): 288–309.

———. *Quand Dieu parle aux hommes le langage de l'amour.* Cahiers de la Revue Biblique 21. Paris: Gabalda, 1982.

Trible, Phyllis. "Depatriarchalizing in Biblical Interpretation." *JAAR* 41 (1973): 30–48.

———. *God and the Rhetoric of Sexuality.* Philadelphia: Fortress, 1978.

———. "Woman." In *IDBSup*, pp. 963–66.

Tur-Sinai, Naftali H. *Hallašôn we-hasséper.* Vol. 2. Jerusalem: Bialik, 1950.

Urbach, Ephraim E. "The Homiletical Interpretations of the Sages and the Exposition of Origen on Canticles, and the Jewish-Christian Disputation." In Joseph Heinemann and Dov Noy, eds. *Studies on Aggadah and Folk Literature,* Scripta Hierosolymitana 22. Jerusalem: Magnes, 1971, 247–75.

Volz, Paul. *Jüdische Eschatologie von Daniel bis Akiba.* Tübingen: Mohr, 1903.

von Rad, Gerhard. *Wisdom in Israel.* Nashville: Abingdon, 1973 (1970).

Weems, Renita, J. *Battered Love: Marriage, Sex, and Violence in the Hebrew Prophets.* OBT. Minneapolis: Fortress, 1995.

Westermann, Claus. *Genesis 1–11: A Commentary.* Translated by J. J. Scullion. Minneapolis: Augsburg, 1984 (1974).

———. *Isaiah 40–66: A Commentary.* Translated by D. M. G. Stalker. OTL. Philadelphia: Westminster, 1969.

———. *The Living Psalms.* Translated by J. R. Porter. Grand Rapids: Eerdmans, 1989 (1984).

Wetzstein, J.-G. "Die syrische Dreschtafel." *Zeitschrift für Ethnologie* 5 (1873): 270–302.

Whedbee, J. William. "Paradox and Parody in the Song of Solomon: Towards a Comic Reading of the Most Sublime Song." In *A Feminist Companion to the Song of Songs,* edited by Athalya Brenner. Sheffield: JSOT, 1993, pp. 266–78.

White, John B. *A Study of the Language of Love in the Song of Songs and Ancient Egyptian Poetry.* SBLDS 38. Missoula, Mont.: Scholars Press, 1978.

Winandy, Jacques. "Le Cantique des Cantiques et le Nouveau Testament." *RB* 71 (1964): 161–90.

———. *Le Cantique des Cantiques: Poème d'amour mué en écrit de sagesse.* Tournai: Castermann, 1960.

———. "La litière de Salomon (Ct 3.9–10)." *VT* 15 (1965): 103–10.

Winckler, Hugo. *Altorientalische Forschungen.* Vol 1. Leipzig: Pfeiffer, 1893.

Wittekindt, Wilhelm. *Das Hohelied und seine Beziehungen zum Ishtarkult.* Hanover: H. Lafaire, 1926.

Würthwein, Ernst. *Die fünf Megilloth: Ruth, das Hohelied, Esther.* HAT 18. Tübingen: Mohr, 1969.

———. *Der Text des Alten Testaments: Eine Einführung in die Biblia Hebraica von Rudolf Kittel.* Stuttgart, 1973. English translation published as *The Text of the Old Testament: An Introduction to Kittel-Kahle's Biblia Hebraica.* Translated by Peter Ackroyd. Ann Arbor: University of Michigan Press, 1979.

———. "Zum Verständnis des Hohenliedes." *TRu* NF 32 (1967): 177–212.

Zimmerli, Walther. *Ezekiel.* Vol. 1. Translated by R. E. Clements. Hermeneia. Philadelphia: Fortress, 1979.

INDEX OF
SCRIPTURAL REFERENCES

Proverbs

INDEX OF SUBJECTS

INDEX OF
MODERN AUTHORS